Belgian Fence

Shade Garden

Smoke House

Rose Garden

Apples

Herb Garden

Old Chicken Coop

Original Orchard

Old Perennial Garden

Studio Kitchen

West Orchard

Perennial Borders

Pool

Quince

Yew Hedge

Croquet Lawn

Saucer Magnolias

Antique Brick Path

Apples

Pachysandra

House Entrance

BLACK HAMBURG GRAPE.

From a cluster grown by F. Smith. Esqr. Lambeth.

Drawn by F.W. Smith.

MARTHA STEWART'S GARDENING

MARTHA STEWART'S
GARDENING

MONTH
by
MONTH

photographs by ELIZABETH ZESCHIN

CLARKSON POTTER PUBLISHERS
NEW YORK

Pour l'avenir

TO THE CHILDREN
WHO DEPEND ON US TO GARDEN
FOR THEIR FUTURE

Published by Clarkson N. Potter, Inc.,
201 East 50th Street, New York, New York 10022.
Member of the Crown Publishing Group.
CLARKSON N. POTTER, POTTER,
and colophon are trademarks of Clarkson N. Potter, Inc.

Manufactured in Japan
Text set in MonoType Bembo with Poliphilis Titling

DESIGN BY GAEL TOWEY WITH WAYNE WOLF

LIBRARY OF CONGRESS CATALOGING-IN-PUBLICATION DATA
Stewart, Martha
Martha Stewart's gardening, month by month; by Martha Stewart.
Photographs by Elizabeth Zeschin.
Includes index.
1. Gardening—Connecticut.   2. Cookery.   I. Title
SB453.2.CBS74   1991   91-14726635—dc20   CIP

ISBN 0-517-57413-6

10 9 8 7 6 5 4 3 2 1

First Edition

ACKNOWLEDGMENTS

THIS BOOK HAS TAKEN MORE THAN four years to photograph and write; many more years were spent in the garden, accumulating knowledge. My thanks go to all those who worked on the book itself, and to others who inspired me, instructed me, and physically helped to create my garden. ～ My gratitude to Elizabeth Zeschin, whose superb photographs reveal the garden to the reader. Oftentimes, upon viewing a new group of slides, I could not believe that Elizabeth could so capture the essence of the place. ～ My plaudits to my editor, Isolde Motley, for her patience and intense dedication in organizing the work of four years into an understandable, useful, and clear text. ～ My admiration to Gael Towey, whose graceful, serene design so perfectly reflects the spirit of the garden itself. ～ My appreciation to Betsy Kissam and Christine Douglas, whose botanical expertise gave validity to my text; to my long-time supporter, Alan Mirken; to everyone at Clarkson Potter, champions of this long project: Carol Southern, Michelle Sidrane, Susan Magrino, Chip Gibson, Howard Klein, Alexandra Enders, Ed Otto, Teresa Nicholas, and Mark McCauslin; and to Amy Schuler, Wayne Wolf, Rodica Prato, and the master craftsmen of Toppan Printing. ～ My homage to Fred Specht, for his inspiring

education, and to the growers and plantsmen who helped me with information and materials: J. Liddon Pennock, Jr., Allen C. Haskell, Sal Gilbertie, Carl Askenback of The Flower Farm, John Ellsley of Wayside Gardens, and the staffs of Sunny Border, Roses of Yesterday and Today, Van Engelen, Van Bourgondien, and White Flower Farm. ～ My thanks to all those who gardened with me, harvested the fruits of our labors, and cooked with me: Laura Herbert Plimpton, the late Kim Herbert, Necy Fernandes, Lisa Wagner, Renato Abreu, Renaldo Abreu, Celso Lima, Ademir Oliveira, Victor Perkowski, John Henske, George McCormack, the two Bulpitt brothers, my mother Martha Kostyra, and my young friends Sophie Martha Herbert and Monica Pasternak.

～ My love and my thanks to my daughter, Alexis, who spent many, many hours of her childhood with me in the garden while I cultivated, weeded, planted,

and picked. Alexis has grown up loving flowers—especially roses—unusual fruits, and vegetables (to this day, she asks me to plant certain kinds of carrots just for her), and remembers still some of the botanical nomenclature we learned together as we gardened side by side. ～ Most of all, my thanks to my father, for being my first teacher of gardening. His love of growing things was transferred to me though our gardening together; I will remember what he taught me forever. ～

5

CONTENTS

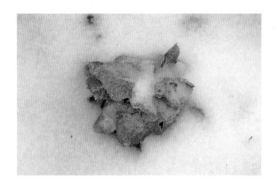

WINTER

SPRING

INTRODUCTION 9

JANUARY 15
Rooting Slips 19   Forcing Flowering Branches 22   MENU: Osso Buco Gremolata
Saffron Couscous   Blood Orange and Arugula Salad   Pears with Gorgonzola 24

FEBRUARY 27
Pruning Fruit Trees 30   Gardening Tools 32   Antiquing Urns 36   MENU: Broiled
Saffron Chicken   Shoestring Potatoes   Sautéed Winter Greens   Steamed Cherry
Pudding 38

MARCH 41
Understanding the Soil 43   Feeding and Fertilizing 44   Growing Media 45   Seed
Starting 46   Making Raised Beds 48   MENU: Chicken Soup   Broiled Herb Bread
Tomato-Red Pepper Rouille   Pink Applesauce 50

APRIL 55
Narcissi 59   Planting a Tree 63   Tulips 65   Fritillaria 73   Bleeding Hearts 74   MENU:
Fresh Orange Juice   Soft-Boiled Eggs on Breakfast Bread   Breakfast Gravlax   Orange
Pound Cake 80

MAY 83
Poppies 87   Clematis 90   Perennial Borders 92   Irises 94   Peonies 103   MENU: Campfire
Skillet Trout   Sautéed Vegetables   Rhubarb Tartlets 117

JUNE 119
Pest and Disease Prevention and Control 121   Garden Diseases 121   Common
Garden Pests 126   Companion Planting 130   Salad Greens (and Reds) 134   Shade
Garden 140   Drying Flowers 147   MENU: Dill Fettucine with Poached Salmon
Herb-Zucchini Sauté   Spiced Peach Ice Cream   Spiced Peaches in White Wine
Syrup 150

ROSES 152
How to Plant a Rosebush 156   The Name of the Rose 166   Caring for Roses 182

6

SUMMER

AUTUMN

INTROD

U C T I O N

IT WAS A MOST EXCITING DAY, THAT FEBRUARY SUNDAY twenty years ago, when we first saw the old property. My husband, five-year-old daughter, and I had outgrown our New York City apartment and craved a "place in the country." While we looked around Fairfield County, friends told us about The Haunted House of Turkey Hill. ∾ Built in 1805 by Captain Thorpe, an onion farmer and barge owner of some repute, the house sat on the highest hill in the Greens Farms neighborhood, with spectacular views to the south, east, and west. It was a Federal farmhouse, with a center hall and floorplan of four rooms over four. The proportions were lovely, but rented out for fifty years by the widowed Bulkeley sisters, it had fallen into great disrepair. All the barns and outbuildings were gone; there was no heat, little electricity, and primitive plumbing. The fields around it had been sold off by the sisters in two-acre building lots; suburbia encroached. But there remained two fertile acres, with unimpeded views of Long Island Sound. ∾ We loved it from the very first. Here was the "place" where we could realize our dreams of a home, and a garden. Before we took title, we planted an orchard

9

(with permission from the Misses Bulkeley) on the southern part of the property. I knew little about European varieties of apples, pears, or cherries, but I was quite determined to grow those fruits I had read about: the tender, snowy white Fameuse apple, the Atlantic Queen pear with its fine melting flesh, the yellow mirabelle plums so prized in France for tarts and jams.

Once the house was ours, we began in earnest to clear the tangled masses of brambles and blackberries. The huge bushes we were convinced were ancient lilacs turned out to be miserable, overgrown privets, and had to be torn out at the roots. We staked out the vegetable garden and the two large perennial, herb, and cutting borders that still exist in somewhat their original shape and size. While the restoration proceeded slowly—more layers of paint to be removed than expected, the chimneys weaker and roof older than anticipated—the gardening projects provided more immediate enjoyment. A new border cost a fraction of new plumbing and was quickly visible.

Our ambitions enlarged daily. Soon there were plans for a barn-garage, a swimming pool, a chicken coop, a tool shed. We built a six-foot-high fieldstone

The Clematis montana I planted round the base of the newly constructed pergola will bloom with pale pink star-shaped flowers, making the kitchen terrace an extremely pleasant place to dine. Planting the clematis in the shade of a homegrown yew hedge is just one example of how we can make the garden grow.

wall to protect us from the road, and added four adjoining acres. After a visit to the great English gardens, two giant perennial borders were dug and planted. A trellis was built to surround the vegetable gardens. Almost everything we planted took hold and thrived: the ground was rich, the rainfall almost adequate, and the bad weather minimal.

After two decades, the place has assumed a character all its own, an indefinable aura. The influences of my mentors, the ideas garnered from travels and readings have become part of the whole. And still, I will always have plans: I just added a herb garden; I crave two more acres directly south of the barn. A true garden grows forever: there are always new trees to place, new seeds to sow.

But for me, the garden is not just a place to grow things. It is wonderful, of course, to have a piece of land on which one can propagate trees, berries, flowers, and vegetables for one's own use and the enjoyment of others. But a garden is also a place where one can walk and think, sit and contemplate. A garden should have surprises, and should offer solace.

My own garden has its secrets: I love to share them with friends who come to enjoy the beauty and quiet of the place. The swamp maple tree that grows by the road in front of the house has a peculiar branch that has somehow grown into another, creating a kind of natural tie. The 'Lavender Lassie' rose has reverted in part to its red 'Blaze' root stock, resulting in a climber that is half red, half purple. The steps up to the raised rose bed behind the barn are really rocks jutting out from the stone wall, copied from an old staircase I

saw in Tuscany. The 'Veilchenblau' rose bush is climbing up the giant shagbark hickory and will soon cover over a glaring scar.

A garden is also a place for children. I encourage my nieces and nephews and their friends of all ages to play here: little Kristina runs with abandon down the gently sloping orchard grass to visit the chickens. When she was just two, Sophie would spend hours alone in the chicken coop making friends with the hens, observing and learning. (There is nothing to compare with watching a shy child build up the courage to reach under a big, fat Araucana hen and pull out a pale blue egg—and then to hear that child, who won't even consider eating a store-bought egg, say he wants to take *this* egg home for supper.) I have given each of the young children I know my favorite garden stories, hoping that at least one or two will grow up with the love of the land that I have, derived in part, I think, from reading *The Secret Garden, Freckles,* and *Green Mansions.*

I entertain in the garden. I keep a mental calendar of what happens when and where so that I can set a table in the pumpkin patch when the potirons are huge and bright orange, or near the white 'Belle of Georgia' peaches so that we can pick our dessert right off the trees. I like to walk my friends through the tomatoes so we can pluck off the bright red cherries and yellow plums and pop the warm fruits into our mouths as hors d'oeuvres. Even the most jaded guest cannot resist commenting on the freshness of the fruits and vegetables, the bright golden yellow of the egg yolks, or

the variety of raspberries atop the tarts. I haven't missed an Easter egg hunt in the garden since we moved to Turkey Hill; every Halloween there is a Harvest Moon party with scores of luminarias lighting the way to the barn. At holiday time, the trees around the house are strung with hundreds of tiny lights, and the garden offers materials for the wreaths that hang in every window. Friends and family who come for the yearly Christmas buffet leave with baskets full of jams and jellies from the berry patch and great bags of potpourri made with petals from the rose borders.

Most of all, the garden is a place where I learn. Gardening is a humbling experience. Mistakes are often made, but they can be corrected with few or no lasting effects. I was always a very impatient person. I thought that by force of will I could get things done immediately; gardening has taught me patience. Nature, with her timetables, cannot be rushed. There is always work to be done, too. And yet, I never begrudge the effort, because gardening teaches a sense of optimism and hope for the future.

I think I may be a better person for having given serious time and thought and effort to gardening. I am proud of having learned to work with nature to encourage beauty in my backyard. The hours I have spent cultivating the soil, weeding and planting, and just looking at what has come to be have given me boundless pleasure. I no longer say, as I once did, "I have to work in the garden today." I say, with deep contentment, "I'm gardening today." I have truly reaped the bounty of the garden. ❧

W   I   N

THE MARIE LOUISE PEAR.

Drawn by J.T.Hart. at
Mʳ Lee's Hammersmith.

T E R

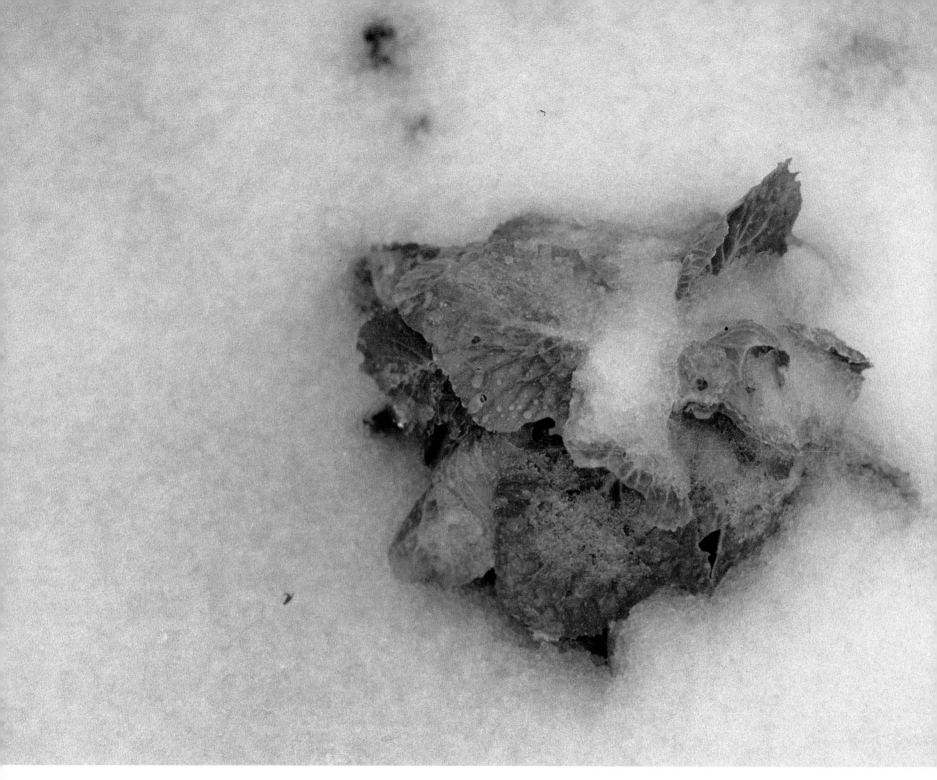

JANUA

THE GARDEN ON TURKEY HILL ROAD is in repose, frozen solid, its growth halted. But I, the gardener, am not at rest. All during the Christmas holidays the mailbox was filled to brimming every day with catalogues of all descriptions, each presaging the newest, the biggest, the best, and the most unusual in seeds, nursery stock, and summer bulbs. My mind races; whatever modest plans I had formulated after the last year's blooming season are now expanded beyond all reason. ❧ I force myself to stop, take a deep breath, and reexamine every aspect of my overall garden plan. Then order forms are greedily filled in. Gardening, in all its diversity, is

ABOVE AND LEFT:
Here in Westport, which is Zone 6, we have, theoretically, 225 days of growing season. A couple of inches of snow during the coldest spells of winter act as protection, insulating the roots and tender shoots of all the garden plants.

America's most popular outdoor activity, so there is some foundation to my belief that if I don't get my order in to Roses of Yesterday and Today in a timely fashion, someone else will receive the 'Heinrich Munch' pink cabbage roses that I so much need in the perennial border. I send off the orders for the long-season annuals—the snapdragons, impatiens, and the ruffled petunias (pink, white,

R Y

15

and magenta this time) so that I will be able to sow them in the greenhouse before it is too late. I forgo the latest movies to start the lobelias and slip the ivies for the urns, and put off dinners with friends to putter for hours, mixing potting soils, washing down the greenhouse, and attending to the topiaries. In the house, the luscious flowers of narcissus, amaryllis, and hyacinth forced in November and December begin to fade. Toward the end of the month, I cut the first forsythia for early blossoms in the house, choosing very long, bushy branches so that there will be lots of yellow bells to grace the halls and porch with a promise of coming spring.

JOURNAL

Added new books to garden library.

Reviewed garden plans.

Visited gardens to study landscaping.

Gathered catalogues.

Began seed orders.

Ordered roses and trees to replace those dead or damaged.

Picked Brussels sprouts.

Thoroughly cleaned greenhouse.

Started herb seeds in greenhouse.

Rooted slips for edgings and urns.

LEFT AND RIGHT: *The trellised vegetable garden is still productive, even in January, covered with snow. There are stalks laden with Brussels sprouts, rich in vitamins A, B, C, calcium, iron, and potassium, superb when not overcooked. For making hearty winter soups, there are still collards, carrots, parsnips, and salsify.*

ABOVE AND LEFT: *A lone iris and 'Giallo de Milano' onions poke their green tops through the snow cover. Even after freezing, onions can add flavor to stocks.* RIGHT: *Some herbs are amazingly hardy in the snow.* Salvia officinalis *is the most common sage, but there are others that are good for companion planting with cabbages and carrots, or for edging herb and vegetable gardens.*

Rooting Slips

MOST OF MY POTTED HERBS AND decorative plants for edgings and outdoor urns are rooted indoors from slips and transplanted later when the weather permits. I take cuttings of strong, new growth from woody-stemmed plants like rosemary, ivy, oregano, thyme, scented geraniums, and santolinas. Make the cutting about 3 inches long, strip the lower half of leaves, moisten in water, dip in root hormone compound (available in plant centers), and insert the lower half of the cutting in a shallow flat of sandy loam potting soil. Once a good root is established, the slip is potted and allowed to branch out. In summer and fall, I use the same technique to root cuttings from teucrium, euonymus, and myrtle. A great deal of money can be saved by this simple process; a home-rooted teucrium edge for one of my rose gardens costs a fraction of the charge for nursery plants.

RIGHT: *While I picked lady apples in the fall for the house, this cluster was forgotten.* OVERLEAF: *The "bones" of a garden are what ultimately give it character and shape at all times of the year. Before beginning to garden, it is important to take an overview; a season or so spent developing a good garden layout, providing for present and future development, is worth years of time and energy. Here, the brick-lined paths of grass or gravel give access and definition to the large perennial borders accented by semidwarf fruit trees and unshaped boxwoods. Stone walls were built over the years in old New England fashion, with local stones and dry-wall methods to blend in with the landscape.*

Forcing Flowering Branches

HERE IN CONNECTICUT, WE BEGIN "forcing" forsythia for indoor bloom as early as January, after we have had about six weeks of very cold weather.

Cut forsythia branches on a sunny day when the mercury rises above freezing. Choose young branches loaded with flower buds—fatter and larger than leaf buds. Use sharp pruners to cut sprays flush with a major branch, and think about shaping your shrub while you work. Once indoors, recut branches on a slant just above the original cut and peel back about an inch of bark; or mash the ends lightly with a hammer (this aids water intake). Remove foliage from lower third of branch, and place stripped stems into a pail of tepid water. Change the water often and mist the branches daily. Remember, you are mimicking the cool rainy days when spring-flowering shrubs bloom; indoor temperatures of 60°F. to 70°F. are best. Higher temperatures speed forcing but diminish flower size and color (as well as the life of your arrangement).

When the buds begin to swell, arrange the branches in a vase and move to a well-lit room, never in direct sun. They will blossom two to three weeks after cutting—or sooner, if it's close to

As I become more involved with gardening, I find my collecting habits changing. I now accumulate porcelains, needlepoint, and fabrics that reiterate botanical themes: these are nineteenth-century Spode plates, made for Tiffany's.

their natural outdoor flowering time—and will keep for about a week.

You may find roots growing on your branches after they have finished blossoming. If you want new plants, continue to change the water and add a pinch of 10-10-10 soluble plant food, until the roots show ¼ inch in length. Prune the branches to roughly 6 inches and bury each rooted portion in a small pot filled with a good potting soil mix. Keep moist for several weeks; take the pot outdoors when the weather warms. It is a good idea to protect your new plants for the first two winters (I bring mine into a little greenhouse). Once sturdy, these can be planted in the ground.

Many varieties of spring-flowering plants respond well to forcing. The earliest candidates are forsythia, witch-hazel (*Hamamelis mollis* and *H. japonica*), and pussy willows (*Salix* sp.). Some forsythia varieties flower more dramatically than others; try gold charm (*Forsythia* 'Goldzauber') and Lynwood gold (*Forsythia* 'Lynwood'). Other woody plants such as magnolias, flowering fruit trees, and flowering quince (*Chaenomeles* sp.) can be forced later, about six weeks before outdoor flowering time. Japanese maple (*Acer palmatum*) and birches (*Betula* sp.) can be forced for unusual displays; for fragrance, try honeysuckle (*Lonicera* sp.) and witch-hazel.

As catalogues arrive, I file them alphabetically in baskets; orders are sent early to make sure the desired varieties are available. The spiky, towering plants by my side—extra inspiration—are potted delphiniums and foxgloves.

Menu

Osso Buco Gremolata

SERVES 4

Osso Buco, or braised veal knuckle, is a real treat and a superb dish for a party.

$\frac{1}{3}$ cup all-purpose flour
1 tablespoon salt
1½ teaspoons freshly ground pepper
4 pieces veal shank, 3 inches thick (choose large-diameter pieces with broad marrow bones)
3 tablespoons unsalted butter
3 tablespoons olive oil
1 cup finely diced carrots
1 cup minced onions
1 cup finely diced celery
1 cup plum tomatoes, peeled, seeded, and chopped
1 cup chicken stock, preferably homemade
1 cup dry white wine
5-6 garlic cloves, peeled
4 fresh bay leaves
8 sprigs flat-leaf parsley
8 fresh basil leaves
1 tablespoon minced lemon zest
1 tablespoon minced orange zest
1 tablespoon minced garlic
Fresh sage leaves, for garnish

1. Preheat oven to 350°.
2. Mix together the flour, salt, and pepper. Dredge the shanks in the mixture.
3. In a large, heavy-bottomed sauté pan, melt the butter with the olive oil over medium heat. Brown the shanks all over. Remove them from the pan and set aside.
4. Add carrots, onions, and celery to pan. Sauté for 8 to 10 minutes. Add tomatoes, stock, and wine; simmer for 8 minutes.
5. Transfer vegetable mixture into a large, heavy casserole. Add meat, garlic, bay leaves, parsley, and basil. Cover and bake for 1½ hours, or until meat is tender.
6. Remove veal and set on a warm platter. Cover with foil to keep it warm.
7. Strain the cooking liquid and reduce to 2 cups. Remove herbs from the vegetables and discard. Puree vegetables in a food processor and add to the liquid.
8. To make the gremolata, mix together zests and garlic. To serve, place 1 shank on a warm plate and spoon sauce over the meat. Garnish with gremolata and a sage leaf. Serve with Saffron Couscous.

Saffron Couscous

SERVES 4

I first had couscous on a trip to Morocco, and now serve it frequently in place of rice or pasta. Don't overcook the grains.

2 tablespoons olive oil
2 cups quick-cooking couscous
2 cups rich chicken stock
4 tablespoons (½ stick) unsalted butter
1 generous pinch of saffron
Salt and freshly ground pepper

1. In a heavy saucepan over medium heat, heat the oil and add the couscous. Sauté for 1 to 2 minutes.
2. In a separate saucepan, bring the chicken stock and butter to a boil until butter melts. Immediately pour over the couscous. Stir in saffron. Cover and let stand until liquid has been absorbed, about 10 to 15 minutes.
3. Season to taste with salt and pepper, and fluff with a fork before serving.

LEFT: *Osso Buco is rich and hearty. Here, I serve it in scalloped, gold-rimmed bowls for a special presentation. A full-bodied red Bordeaux wine, such as Cordier St. Julien, is a good accompaniment.*

Blood Orange and Arugula Salad

SERVES 4

Blood oranges are available only for a very short time in midwinter. Delicious and colorful in salads, they are also magnificent in sorbet or custard.

4 handfuls fresh arugula
2 large (or 4 small) blood oranges
1 tablespoon balsamic vinegar
2½ tablespoons avocado or
  grapeseed oil
  Salt and freshly ground pepper

1. With a sharp knife, trim the skin and white pith from the oranges, being careful to save any juice that runs off. With the tip of the knife, cut the meat of the orange from the membrane of each section. Set the sections aside, and save the juice that accumulates.

2. Whisk together 1 tablespoon orange juice with the remaining ingredients. Just before serving, mix the orange sections and arugula and gently toss with dressing.

Pears with Gorgonzola

SERVES 4

This simple dessert of fruit and cheese is a perfect finale for the rich Osso Buco.

4 ripe, firm pears
½ pound Gorgonzola cheese

Serve the pears on individual plates, with freshly cut wedges of cheese.

RIGHT: *Winter pears such as Forelle, Bartlett, Comice, or Packham are all delicious with cheese. This is a classic dessert combination, and is very elegant served with pearl-handled flatware.*

FEBRUA

OUTDOOR CHORES BEGIN IN EARNEST in February. I am a very early riser, and am often outside at 5:30 A.M.; I welcome the longer days and the weak rays of sunlight that begin to appear as the month enters its second and third weeks. I use these early hours to walk the dogs around the property and take note of the tasks that need to be accomplished. I am never without my secateurs on these dim-lit excursions, for it is then that I remove broken branches from the dwarf and semidwarf fruit trees that I've planted everywhere, and begin the pruning of trees, berry bushes, and even roses. ❧ As I walk, too, I examine the garden urns, trellises, and furniture for winter damage. In Connecticut, the winters are too harsh to leave ceramic or terra-cotta pots outdoors, so I try to buy only iron or cement containers, which can be emptied, covered, and left exposed all winter. Every year, I collect a few more secondhand ones, lugging them home to be sandblasted

LEFT: *Most of my fruit trees are of the semidwarf variety, growing 1o to 12 feet tall at maturity. I chose this type because I could conceivably prune them myself.*
BELOW: *This arched trellis is a perfect example of good garden architecture, practical—supporting climbing plants like sweet peas, roses, and clematis—and beautiful, forming garden "rooms" in the summertime.*

R Y

clean; I also purchase new but well-shaped examples, which can look very beautiful if I spend some time finishing them with my special mixtures of paint. I take the same approach with garden furniture: rekindled interest in garden design has made antiques very costly and rare, but I find some of the better catalogues now offer very good reproductions, which can be made more individual with a little paint. (Experience—and much wasted time and paint—has taught me to have furniture spray-painted by a professional, outdoors on tarpaulins in a sheltered spot.)

I also use these fallow days to review and repair my garden tools. I try to buy only the highest quality equipment, and good maintenance prolongs their life and usefulness. I take care of my garden tools as I take care of my kitchen and household utensils; most of them can last years if well serviced and well cared for.

ABOVE AND RIGHT: *Parts of the garden are sheltered from chilling winds by the stone walls surrounding the property; less protected areas—the perennial and rose gardens—are screened with burlap, stapled and wired to upright posts that we painted my favorite green.*

JOURNAL

Branches, leaves, and other garden debris picked up and disposed of.

Fruit trees pruned.

All garden machinery (tractor, mower, etc.) sent out for servicing and cleaning.

Tools cleaned and repainted.

New gloves and tools ordered.

Garden furniture cleaned, repaired, or replaced.

Garden ornaments purchased and painted.

Seed packages organized as January orders begin to arrive.

Pruning Fruit Trees

ONE FEBRUARY SIX OR SEVEN YEARS ago, I went on a book tour, leaving instructions for pruning the fruit trees with a young man who helped us care for the garden. The job was done: every tree on the property was pruned to within inches of its fruit-bearing life. Every lateral, every fruiting spur, was cut off—as well as water sprouts and terminals. Our trees were as naked as could be—and so were those of our neighbor, who had sent her gardener to my orchard to observe, firmly believing that "if that's how Martha does it, it must be right."

Ever since, I have tried to do most of the pruning myself, calling in a professional to help only with the largest trees. It is a very time-consuming task, but essential: pruning fruit trees increases fruit productivity and size. By providing good air circulation and maximum exposure to sunlight within trees, regular pruning diminishes insect and disease problems.

It is best to prune in early spring when trees are dormant; I prune heavily at that time, and again lightly in fall. The two principal types of cuts are called heading, when a branch is shortened to an outward-facing bud, and thinning or cutting

I cannot stress enough the importance of having the right tools for each garden job. For pruning my fruit trees, I use several different shears: secateurs for small shoots and thin branches; loppers (I have three sizes) for branches over ¾-inch thick; and a pole-saw-cum-trimmer, to avoid strain on arms and neck when reaching overhead.

out the entire branch at its base. Always prune damaged, dead, or diseased limbs first. Take out the weakest of crossed or crowded limbs and remove all suckers and straight vertical shoots, except the central leader. If disease is present, disinfect pruners with alcohol after each cut.

How one proceeds depends on the type of tree and how it bears its fruit. Many varieties of pears, apples, and apricots produce on spurs—6-inch or less contorted twigs growing from older branches and recognized by swollen, round buds that will become the fruit blossoms. Peaches, on the other hand, bear on year-old wood; once fruit is harvested from a section of branch, that portion of wood will not bear again. Trees can be pruned into many different configurations. Choose the method best for you—fruit production or ornamentation requires different methods.

CENTRAL LEADER METHOD (I prune pear trees in this manner). The central or main branch is allowed to grow vertically without pruning. Trees maintained this way are well-shaped, less susceptible to winter injury. Most young fruit trees are pruned at the nursery; however, if you are starting with a year-old whip, cut to 24 to 30 inches at planting. The first few years are critical for developing a balanced, strong framework. Too-heavy pruning in these years can result in small trees and delayed fruit production. As new shoots grow, select 5 or 6 strong lateral ones for scaffold limbs: the main branches radiating from the trunk and relatively evenly spaced around it. Choose strong, large-angled branches—at 45 to 90 degrees from the trunk—and

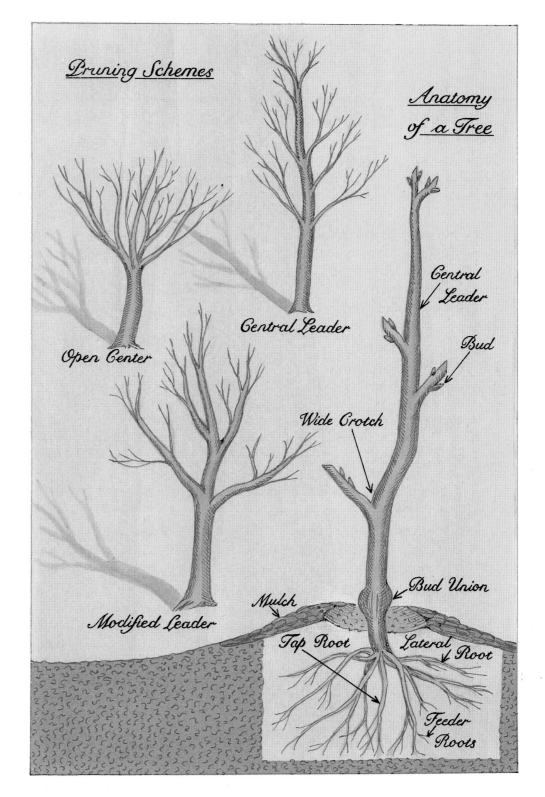

Pruning Schemes

Anatomy of a Tree

Open Center

Central Leader

Central Leader

Bud

Wide Crotch

Modified Leader

Mulch

Bud Union

Tap Root

Lateral Root

Feeder Roots

prune other weaker ones. Eliminate any that compete with the central leader.

MODIFIED LEADER METHOD (my apples get this treatment). Young trees are treated in the same manner as those pruned to the central leader method. In the third season, during dormancy, prune the central leader to the level of the top scaffold branches—about 4 to 6 feet high for dwarf and semidwarf varieties, 6 to 8 feet for standards.

OPEN CENTER METHOD (best for peaches). At planting, prune year-old whips to 24 to 30 inches. In the first dormant season, select three to four strong, wide-angled scaffold branches that are evenly spaced around the trunk, 6 to 8 inches apart (vertically), the lowest at least 15 inches from the ground. Thin the others at their bases. The following season, choose about a third of the strongest side branches from the scaffolds. Thin all others. In the third dormant season, keep about a third of the strongest new shoots; those nearest the branch tips will be better placed for air and sunlight. Keep the tree balanced in an open vase shape with branches leading outward. Direct branches by selecting a bud pointing in the chosen direction and then prune just above it, making a diagonal cut.

When peach trees begin to bear, prune heavily. Fruit is produced on year-old wood that has grown at least a foot the previous summer. Thin one-third to half of the weakest twigs each spring. In general, older peach trees require more pruning than younger bearing ones.

For trees with upright growth habits, especially peaches, you may need to use wooden spreaders to force open angles. Wider angles ensure a stronger branch, better able to withstand the weight of heavy fruit production and winter snow and ice. To make spreaders, use short pieces of 1-by-4s; cut a "V" into both ends and wedge into the crotch where the branch meets the trunk. Longer spreaders may be used the following season. Remove all upright shoots (water spouts) that develop from spread limbs; they are an indication that the branch has been spread too far.

After three years, a well-trained fruit tree will have an established framework of about six strong scaffold branches. Prune new shoots at their base, except those designated to replace scaffold branches that may have died, been damaged, or become diseased. In the third year, dwarf fruit trees usually begin bearing fruit, semidwarfs in the fourth or fifth year; standards take longer. Take care not to remove fruit-bearing spurs.

Gardening Tools

GARDENERS, LIKE ALL ARTISTS, will find themselves acquiring more and more tools for their craft. If gardening is your passion, consider buying only the best—with care your tools can outlast you. The best-quality tools are crafted from steel—in one-piece construction. Ash handles are the most durable. Buy from reputable stores or mail-order establishments. Always compare prices.

TOOL CARE. The best way to ensure the longevity of your tools is to clean them after each use. A quick once-over with a stiff bristle brush will clean shovels, spades, forks, and hoes. If soil is caked on, scrape with a putty knife before brushing. On rainy days, be sure to dry metal tool surfaces before storing. I use a piece of old towel.

Choose a dry place to store tools. A 5-gallon bucket filled with oily sand is an excellent receptacle to keep shovels, forks, and spades. If this is not possible, coat them with a thin film of oil—using an oily rag—before putting away. Keep a file handy to maintain a relatively sharp blade on shovels and hoes.

Blades on cutting tools need sharpening at least once a year. If you use dull pruners, you risk twisting the blades. Dismantle shears and loppers; scrub with kerosene to remove sap, and sharpen the beveled side of blades with a Carborundum stone. If blades are very dull or nicked, it is best to have a professional sharpen them for you (often a service of hardware stores). Sharpening saws (teeth must be properly calibrated) is also best left to professionals—most saw blades are replaceable.

Oil frequently used cutting tools weekly. For occasional pruning, put a few drops of machine oil on the bolt and spring before each use. Wrap pruning blades in an oily rag when not in use.

Power tools require their own maintenance. Read instructions carefully, and always ascertain convenient available service before purchasing.

CULTIVATING TOOLS
Hand trowel. Excellent for container and small-space gardening; to mix soil media; plant seedlings; or dig out weeds. Wooden shank; broad and narrow blades; I most often use a broad, 3- to 4-inch-

wide blade, about 6 to 8 inches long.

Hand cultivator. Three-pronged fork with short wooden handle; sharp points make digging easier. To dislodge weeds, and to cultivate in narrow spaces between plants.

Hand weeder. Hardwood handle and angled triangular steel blade with knifelike sharpness and pointed tips. To break soil, weed, and cultivate. My favorite and most indispensable tool—I buy these in Japan.

Long-handled, round-point shovel. To dig up garden plots; move soil, compost; transplant; pry up rocks. (A turned step keeps soil from sliding off the top of the blade.)

Long-handled spade (with flatter blade than a shovel). To dig planting holes; move compost, soil; sever invasive roots. The narrow blade is excellent for double digging.

Garden fork. Four flat tines about a foot across. Short handle. To break up hard soil; work in soil conditioners.

Spading fork. Lighter and smaller than the garden fork. To turn over loose soil; dig out perennials with few severed roots; harvest root vegetables; turn compost.

Border spade. 8- to 12-inch flat-edged blade, ideal for edging. Important to keep edges sharp.

Round blade edger. Long handle and half-moon blade with sharp edge for neat demarcation of garden beds and walks. Also good for weeding in difficult places.

Flathead rake. Metal rake with straight head, teeth a few inches long and about an inch apart; best with bowed steel brace. To level planting beds (after cultivation); to remove thatch from lawns.

Hoe. Long-handled; my favorite is small and heart-shaped—similar to the larger warren hoe. To dig out weeds; make planting rows and transplanting holes.

Bulb planter. A metal cylinder (with depth markings in inches) to make bulb-sized holes. I find a long handle is easier to work with. Look for very sturdy cast-steel construction.

Tiller. Gas-powered with rotary blades. Wheel-driven tillers are more expensive but easier to control than blade-driven. To mix soil amendments into the garden beds; break up dense soils. (Consider renting.)

Seed and fertilizer spreaders. Hopper for grass seeds can be canvas or plastic. Rust-proof. Metal types usually supported on two wheels with a handle for spreading 20 to 30 feet (good for fertilizers and lime).

Soil testing kit. Testing kits for acidity are simpler and less expensive than those for both nutrients (NPK) and acidity. Inexpensive probe tests are not considered generally reliable.

CLEAN-UP TOOLS

Bamboo rake. Bamboo tines, fan up to 30 inches—24 most versatile. To rake leaves,

RIGHT, ABOVE AND BELOW:
With the correct equipment, I can prune most of the orchards myself; hard work, but I remind myself that it is excellent upper-body exercise. With standard fruit trees, which grow to 20 feet or more, I could not possibly manage the task. Dwarf fruit trees, which mature at just 8 to 10 feet, could be pruned with ease, but would look unnatural in this landscape. I have had great luck with the semidwarf apple trees; these seem to thrive in our erratic climate.

FEBRUARY

3 3

grass clippings. (A 6-inch fan is ideal for small spaces.) Metal rakes excellent also.

Corn-fiber broom. To sweep paths, patios and driveways. I keep in these in a handy place.

Leaf blower. Hand-held gasoline-powered for small jobs, wheel-motivated electric or gas best for large clean-up jobs. Electric is quieter (gasoline-driven blowers are banned in some areas). Goggles and earplugs are essential when operating.

Leaf and twig shredder. Gasoline or electric powered. Safety extremely important when operating. A big investment: long-term payoff. To make mulch from leaves and small woody pruning; shred garden debris to hasten decomposition in the compost bin.

Garden cart. Sturdy platformed cart with two large wheels; easy to push or pull with ample carrying space. Wheelbase should not exceed width of garden paths; choose nonrusting material. A wire cage more than doubles capacity of cart for leaves and branches.

Wheelbarrow. A mason's wheelbarrow is durable with a deep tray; pneumatic tires for easier pushing. More maneuverable than a cart, but less stable.

WATERING EQUIPMENT

Hose. Range up to 75 feet; can be connected for longer length; rubber is long-lasting, but vinyl is lighter and easier to work with; look for pounds per square inch rating of around 500; ⅝-inch diameter. Good-quality couplings important; a nozzle attachment for fine spray good for seedlings.

Hose hanger. Inexpensive rounded metal plate (wall mounted) will prevent hose from crimping and cracking.

Soaker hose. Rubber or vinyl; lay above ground or bury in a trench; round with small holes or flat with holes on one side (face holes down); removeable ends for easy cleaning.

Watering cans. At least two—one conventional spout and one long-necked for hard-to-reach areas. I prefer galvanized metal; choose the largest you can comfortably carry. Attachments: fine spray nozzles for watering seedlings.

Sprayer. Backpack sprayers provide freedom for hand and arm movement; sprayers on wheels allow you to move heavier loads. Always wear gloves and a mask designed to screen out poisons; clean equipment after each use; wash clothes and shower immediately.

CUTTING TOOLS

Secateurs (hand pruners). Bypass or scissor-type pruners are best (anvil pruning shears, with only one sharp blade, crush branches). Straight bypass shears for multistemmed shrubs and hard-to-get-to places; curved bypass with wider blades cut up to one a ½-inch diameter hardwood. Ratchet-type shears require less strength. Choose handles that feel comfortable and an easy-open lock. Replaceable blades are a feature of top-quality shears. (I prefer Felco pruners because of their convex grips.)

Thinning shears. Small, pointed narrow scissor bypass blades—about 7 inches overall length. To deadhead flowers, cut flowers; harvest fruit, vegetables.

Ikebana shears. Japanese-style shears used by bonsai gardeners and flower arrangers. Large butterfly handles; two-inch blades for precision cutting. To cut flowers, small branches.

Loppers. Branches over a ½ inch require the leverage of long-handled loppers. Choose bypass cutting blades.

Bow saw. Prunes large-diameter branches—up to 20 inches. Thin blade, like a hack saw, speeds cutting. Good for making firewood.

Pole saw. A combination pole saw/trimmer efficient for overhead pruning. Trimmer snips smaller branches, the saw cuts larger ones.

Hedge shears. Scissor-type, 9-inch serrated blades with long straight handles. Try out shears for ease of handling.

Electric hedge trimmer. Only for branches ¼- inch in diameter or less; use hand-held hedge shears for larger branches. Electric trimmers are lighter than gasoline-powered—but take care not to cut cord. Find a comfortable weight.

Lawn shears. To trim grass along sidewalks, flower beds, and tree trunks. Scissor-type blades are moved by squeezing handles arranged one on top of the other.

String trimmer. Electric- or gasoline-driven long-handled tool; nylon cord with circular motion cuts weeds and grass. Heavy boots and socks and goggles suggested protection. Take care that wanted plants aren't accidentally cut off at base.

Lawn mower. Reel mowers cut cleaner than rotary. Hand-powered for small spaces and paths, gasoline- or electric-powered for lawns, and sit-down model for large acreage. Adjustable cutting height. Look for lightweight but all-steel mower. Keep blades sharp and adjusted.

MY GARDEN ESSENTIALS

Gloves. Well-stitched heavy-duty leather, such as cowhide, good when using tools or collecting garden debris. Lighter goatskin gloves are good for pruning and weeding.

Shoes. I keep a pair of sturdy cotton-lined rubber clogs at my back door; excellent when watering or for dewy mornings and rainy days. To clean, hose them down. Plastic shoes are more readily available, but are stiffer.

Baskets. I keep wicker and wooden baskets with handles for collecting vegetables and fruits. Good for carrying hand tools into the garden. Spiked baskets for flowers.

Plant rings or guards. Metal rings for supporting peonies, delphiniums, asters, lilies, etc. Green or galvanized is least visible—use nothing that rusts. Put in place when plants are small.

Vine supports. To train young vines or support old ones. Masonry nails with pliable hooks; attach to walls or concrete.

Metal markers. Outdoor labels; usually come with black carbon pencil. Good for names of new plantings or unusual varieties. Various sizes available.

Bamboo stakes. Natural or green. To support leggy or top-heavy plants. About 4 to 6 feet are good heights.

Raffia, sisal, or jute. To tie plants to supports outdoors and in. Natural and biodegradable.

Tree wrap. Dark brown kraft-type paper with a crinkled waterproof finish. Protects young trees against insect, pet and other animal damage; also against early frost and weather stress. Tie with jute.

Burlap. 100-yard rolls of untreated burlap, 36 inches wide. Handy for winter protection of evergreens, roses, and perennial borders.

Staple gun. For attaching burlap or wire fencing to posts for winter plant protec-

tion or trellising. Staples come in a variety of lengths and widths.

Rabbit fencing. 16-gauge galvanized steel fencing; 24 to 50 inches wide. Sold at garden supply or hardware stores in 50-foot rolls or by the foot. (I use for training topiary, outdoor trellising; hog wire is also very useful.)

OPTIONAL EQUIPMENT

Lawn roller. Drum, made of plastic or steel, designed to be filled with water (for weight). Usually 2 or 3 feet wide with handle for pushing or pulling. To smooth lawn surface. Consider renting.

Pick mattock. Pointed pick on one side, wide blade on the other; generally 3-foot handle; weight from 2 to 7 pounds. To break up hard-packed soil; dig trenches; cut through roots.

Post-hole digger. Two hinged scoops attached to long handles. To make holes for posts for sweet pea trellis, compost bin, and all garden fencing.

Sledge hammer. Long hardwood handle with double-faced head. Choose a comfortable weight. To sink posts, break large stones.

ABOVE: *I like to visit garden supply stores as I travel, picking up different kinds of tools. Here is an assortment of English, Japanese, and American scissors and hand clippers; I keep all of my cutting tools in a basket, dried, oiled, and sharpened. Once a pair of shears is bent or chipped, I discard it, since cuts will not be sharp and clean—a must in all trimming and pruning.*

1. My goal was to find a way to paint cement containers so as to simulate old copper or lead. I chose five colors of semigloss oil-base paint: black, dark green, chrome green, light green, and olive green. Inexpensive foam brushes are excellent for applying the paint.

2. The raw cement is first sprayed with metallic copper undercoating, on the exterior only. The spray fills in most of the indentations, but a brush-applied metallic paint would work as well. Apply in a well-ventilated, wind-free area.

3. Once the copper paint dries (almost immediately on the porous cement), I paint over it with layers of black, taking care not to cover the undercoat completely.

4. Little by little, the simulation takes effect. It is all the more effective on these urns with their well-shaped "antique" forms.

5. *Before the black paint is quite dry, I add a coat of thinned, dark green paint, then dabbings of olive green and chrome green.*

6. *The last color to be applied is the light "verdigris" green, a shade that highlights the raised designs and gives a true antiqued finish to the planter.*

7. *When I embark on this type of project, I try to do several objects at a time so as to work assembly-line fashion. In one afternoon I was able to paint eight large urns, which completed the ornamentation of the wall around the swimming pool.*

8. *I have successfully painted other garden ornaments to simulate terra-cotta and blackened iron. It is very important to choose well-mixed colors, and to layer them on the objects for the correct look of material, texture, and age.*

Menu

BROILED SAFFRON CHICKEN

SHOESTRING POTATOES

SAUTÉED WINTER GREENS

STEAMED CHERRY PUDDING

Broiled Saffron Chicken

SERVES 4

My mother always made broiled chicken on Wednesdays. I think I've improved on her recipe by sprinkling the chicken with lemon juice and saffron.

 1 3-pound chicken, cut into 8 pieces (backbone removed)
 2 lemons
 ¼ ounce container of saffron threads
   Salt and freshly ground pepper

1. Preheat the broiler. Line a shallow roasting pan with aluminum foil.
2. Arrange chicken skin side up on a wire rack in the pan. Place under the broiler until skin is lightly browned, about 5 to 7 minutes. Turn the chicken over and broil on the other side for about 7 to 8 minutes.
3. Turn the chicken skin side up again. Squeeze lemon juice over each piece, and sprinkle with saffron, salt, and pepper to taste. Return to the broiler until crisp and brown, about 3 to 4 minutes.

Shoestring Potatoes

SERVES 4

When I fry potatoes I like to use virgin olive oil. I find the taste unique, and I never can make too many.

 4 large Idaho potatoes
 2 quarts olive, peanut, or corn oil
   Salt and freshly ground pepper

1. Peel the potatoes and place in cold water to prevent browning.
2. Using a mandoline, cut the potatoes into thin, long strips. Keep in cold water until ready to fry.
3. In a deep fryer or large heavy pot,

heat the oil to 395°. Dry the potato strips by gently patting them between 2 clean kitchen towels.

4. Fry the potatoes, 2 handfuls at a time, until they are golden brown. Remove with a slotted spoon and drain on paper towels. Season with salt and pepper and serve immediately.

Sautéed Winter Greens

SERVES 4

Winter greens are rich in iron and potassium, and very easy to prepare when you use the quick sauté method described here.

1 pound broccoli raab
1 pound kale
6 stalks Swiss chard
⅓ cup olive oil
4 garlic cloves, peeled and sliced
  Salt and freshly ground pepper
  Lemon wedges

1. Wash and dry the greens. Trim off the tough stems of the broccoli raab and kale. Leave the broccoli raab whole, but cut the chard into a wide chiffonade.
2. In a large sauté pan, heat the oil over low heat. Add the garlic and cook until slightly brown, about 3 minutes. Raise heat to medium and add greens. Gently toss greens until they are wilted, about 6 minutes. Season with salt and pepper.
3. Serve hot with lemon wedges.

Steamed Cherry Pudding

SERVES 4

My brother George shares Washington's birthday, and traditionally, sour cherry pie was his "cake." Lately, this pudding has become a favorite alternative.

1¼ cups sugar
3 large eggs
1 cup scalded milk
1 tablespoon brandy
1 1-pound loaf white bread, crusts removed, cut in ¾-inch cubes
2½ cups whole pitted sour Montmorency cherries, fresh or frozen
  Fresh mint sprigs
1 cup heavy cream, whipped

1. Thoroughly butter a 1-quart decorative pudding or cake mold. (Butter the top as well.) Sprinkle with ¼ cup sugar.
2. Whisk together the eggs and 1 cup sugar until thick and pale yellow. Add the scalded milk and brandy and continue whisking until thoroughly mixed.
3. Layer the bread and cherries in the mold, starting and finishing with bread.
4. Pour the custard over the bread and cherries. Cover the mold with its top. If using a cake mold, cover tightly with foil and secure with a rubber band or string.
5. Place the mold on a rack inside a large pot. Fill the pot with enough boiling water to come halfway up the side of the mold. Cover the pot, place over medium heat, and steam the pudding for 1 hour.
6. Remove the mold from the pot and allow to cool. Turn out the pudding onto a decorative platter or cake pedestal. Garnish with fresh mint sprigs.
7. Serve with softly whipped cream.

OPPOSITE: *The winter sun streams in, brightening a cold day. The deep red rose centerpiece and green-edged dishes repeat the pattern and color on the placemats. Green glassware completes the table setting.*
ABOVE RIGHT: *For the pudding, I used frozen sour cherries from the garden, and served it on a green Jadeite cake stand.*

SOME OF MY MOST VIVID MEMORIES OF CHILDHOOD come from those early March days when my father and I would plant seeds indoors. Our preparation was meticulous: I spent the winter months collecting hundreds of half-pint milk cartons

from the school cafeteria. With their tops cut off and bottoms pierced, they made perfect "pots" for starting the larger seedlings—tomatoes, peppers, eggplants, pumpkins, cucumbers, and the like. For smaller seeds, Dad constructed flats of wood salvaged from packing crates.

ABOVE: *Outdoors, the cherry trees are among the first to bloom; spring is almost here.*

During Christmas vacation, we spent hours poring over seed catalogues, debating the merits of one choice over another, and carefully filling out the order forms. ❧ In February and March, our seeds would arrive, to be methodically sown and placed in the only sunny spot, the kitchen. By mid-May, the room was a jungle of plants, each straining to reach the sunlit windows. Our hard work would have proved itself with stocky, sturdy seedlings. ❧ Seed starting nowadays is a much more sophisticated endeavor, with all types of special kits and mixes and plant foods available. But some things are constant; meticulous preparation is still essential, and it's still one of the most satisfying ways to spend one's time.

OPPOSITE: *As the seeds arrive, I make notes in my garden calendar. First, I enter the planting-out date (derived from instructions on the seed package, together with diaries from previous years). Then I work backward, allowing time for germination and seedling growth, to find the best date for sowing each variety.*

MARCH

JOURNAL

Seeds sown in pots and flats every day for flowers, vegetables, and herbs.

Pruning completed.

Awnings ordered for barn and upper porch.

Pool washed with acid; filter reinstalled.

Cold frames dug and built.

New sweet pea fencing built.

Burlap removed from all gardens.

Roses unwrapped; dead wood pruned; mulch removed from crown.

Manures and compost ordered.

All gardens fertilized with super phosphate; flowers served additional 10-20-10.

New ivies for urn planting purchased.

Fruit trees sprayed with dormant oil to control scale.

All evergreens fed.

Leaf mulch picked up.

Lawns blown of dead leaves, aerated, and bare patches seeded; then rolled smooth.

Sweet peas planted.

Phosphate promotes vigorous root, tuber, and seed development, and gives the perennials in my garden a superb boost. I use superphosphate (0-20-0) and triple phosphate (0-46-0) generously (I count on 50 pounds per 700 square feet of garden), sprinkling it over the flower borders in early spring and again in the autumn.

Understanding the Soil

THE SOIL IN MY GARDEN IS RICH AND fruitful, in part a legacy of old Captain Thorpe, who took such good care of his onion fields, in part the result of very hard work over the past twenty years.

To work with soil, the gardener must first understand it. Soil is made up of organic matter (animal and plant products) and mineral particles. Knowing how much of each one's soil contains is essential to good gardening.

SOIL TESTS. A pH analysis will tell if soil is acid, alkaline, or neutral (7.0 on the pH scale). Extremes in pH can render nutrients unavailable to plants. Knowing a soil's pH allows one to raise it (make it less acidic) by adding agricultural lime, or lower it (make it more acidic) with sulfur, depending on the needs of the plants.

Nutrients important for plant growth can be supplied with organic and inorganic fertilizers. Soil analysis tests indicate levels of nitrogen, phosphorus, and potassium (NPK) and trace elements.

HOW TO TEST. Do-it-yourself soil testing kits for pH and NPK nutrients are available from local garden centers or mail-order suppliers. For a precise nutrient test, contact the local County Cooperative Extension office (part of the U.S. Department of Agriculture); most will test soil free or for a nominal fee. If not, ask for a referral to a private soil laboratory (or check the Yellow Pages). Take several samples of soil, at least 5 inches deep, from one bed, and mix together. Areas with different types of plants require separate samples. Alert the laboratory as to the intended plantings so they can make recommendations for soil amendments. After the initial soil test, follow-ups every 3 or 4 years make good gardening sense.

Structure. An ideal soil for growing healthy plants is crumbly, rich in organic matter, drains well, and holds nutrients. Soils with too much clay in them are hard to work and drain poorly. Sandy soils are easier to work and provide good drainage, but they dry out quickly and do not hold nutrients well.

The fruit trees must also be fed each year for good growth and productivity: I make a series of holes with a crowbar, 8 to 12 inches deep, every 2 feet or so in a circle under the outermost branches, and fill each hole with a ½ cup of 8-6-4 fertilizer.

SOIL AMENDMENTS. Organic and mineral substances can correct soil structure and alter pH.

Compost. Decayed plant materials that improve soil structure—and enrich soil nutrient content if bonemeal, manure, or other fertilizer is added during the compost's decomposition.

Peat. Lightweight and moisture retentive, peat is partially decomposed plant residues harvested from wetlands. Sphagnum peat moss, most commonly avail-able, will lighten clay soil and improve moisture retention in sandy soils. Wet peat thoroughly before adding to the soil. Peat can lower the pH in soil a bit.

Sand. Builder's sand, from hardware or masonry supply stores, aerates dense, clay soil and improves drainage in containers. Sand should be coarse, not fine; beach sand is inappropriate because of the salt content.

Lime. All limes raise pH, making soil more sweet or alkaline. Ground limestone (calcium carbonate) is a slow-acting, fine white powder. Dolomitic or crushed limestone also adds a trace element, magnesium. Other lime sources: ground oyster shells and hardwood ashes.

Sulfur. Lowers pH, making soil more acidic. Sold in powder and granules; read directions carefully as sulfur is caustic.

IMPROVING THE SOIL. Choose a day when soil is neither too wet nor too dry. Squeeze a handful. If the soil stays in a loose ball, it is ready to dig. If water is pushed out of it or if it flakes apart, wait for a better day. It is advisable to at least add compost and manure to garden beds each spring. Layer these and other amendments on top of the garden in the amounts suggested by the soil-test report. With a garden fork or a spade, turn over soil to a depth of about 1 foot. Large areas can be turned over with a power cultivator.

DOUBLE DIGGING requires an inordinate amount of time and energy, but the thoroughly aerated, nutrient-rich soil is worth the effort. Double digging means turning the soil over twice in two separate layers—never mixing the topsoil with the denser clay subsoil under it. Only the resulting top layer needs to be supplemented with organic matter.

My version of double digging is a little different from the standard method. First divide the area of the bed into manageable sections, roughly 2 feet by 6 feet. Dig out 1 foot (roughly the depth of a spade) of topsoil from the first section and place it nearby on a tarpaulin. Next, dig out 1 foot of subsoil and set it aside, keeping it separate from the topsoil. Place the topsoil in the bottom of the trench, aerating it as you work; this "new" subsoil will be a rich source of nutrition for plant roots. The next step is to add fertilizers and soil conditioners to the original pile of subsoil, and to use this enriched soil to refill the trench to ground level. Proceed to the next section and continue in the same manner across the whole bed until all the soil has been removed, aerated, and enriched.

Feeding and Fertilizing

IT IS IN MARCH THAT THE GARDEN truly comes to life, taking on an altogether new vivacity. And so do I, rushing to feed the existing flowers, berries, and shrubs before there is any real top growth on the perennials and bulbs. My program is simple, devised after some trial and error and much studying to understand the underlying principles.

The elements nitrogen (N), phosphorus (P), and potassium (K) are so vital to plant growth that their percentages are listed on bags of chemical and sometimes organic fertilizers. Three numbers, always in the same order (NPK), identify the ratio of these elements; 5-10-5, for example. Plants respond differently to

My small lean-to greenhouse was built in 1974 from a Lord and Burnham kit. Just 16 feet long and 7 feet wide, it contains three planting benches. The interior wall is lined with glass shelves for more efficient use of this small space. Once seeds have germinated, the seedlings are placed on the shelves, where they can get plenty of light.

larger or smaller amounts of each one. *Nitrogen* aids strong leaf and stem growth. Promotes dark green leaf color. Too much causes an abundance of soft foliage and delays flowering and fruiting. Insufficient amounts cause leaves to yellow and stunted growth.

Phosphorus or phosphate encourages root growth. Aids development of flowers and fruit. Phosphorus is also excellent for transplants. Insufficient amounts cause stunted growth and delayed bearing of fruit trees.

Potassium or potash improves general plant hardiness. Helps seed production, size, and quality of flowers and fruit. A deficiency reduces flower and fruit size and causes leaves to yellow and brown at edges.

Other Nutrients. Amounts of magnesium, calcium, and sulfur and traces of iron, zinc, copper, manganese, boron, and molybdenum are essential for growth and are found in organic matter, compost, and manure. For iron deficiency (yellowing young leaves, especially at veins), burying rusty nails or tin cans a foot from the base of trees and shrubs will usually solve the problem.

Fertilizers are either naturally derived or inorganic (chemical). The natural fertilizers release elements more slowly than chemical fertilizers—hence they are less likely to "burn" a plant and will last longer in the soil. Chemical fertilizers act faster but need repeat application. All fertilizers should be used with care; wear gloves and never inhale fine particles. Never allow fertilizer to come in direct contact with plant foliage or roots. Perhaps the mistake gardeners most often make is to overfertilize. Test the soil to know its needs. Too much of a good thing is simply too much.

ORGANIC FERTILIZERS. These are made from plant and animal wastes. Natural mineral fertilizers are also often classed as organic.

Manure. Garden centers carry well-rotted or dehydrated packaged forms. Bagged, often odorless, manure can come with an NPK ratio as high as 5-5-5, but usually much less—as low as .5-.2-.5. Cow manure is best worked into the soil; in addition to replacing valuable nutrients, it also amends soil structure. The manure from my poultry is richer in NPK than that from horses and cows. Because it is fresh and raw, I put it in my compost bin to age, and all those nutrients augment my soil through the compost. Manures also carry trace amounts of copper, manganese, zinc, chlorine, sulfur, and boron.

Bonemeal. Mostly available as steamed, but sometimes raw, a much slower-acting form. The NPK ratio is roughly 3-12-0, a high phosphorus content good for root growth. (I use bonemeal to feed my roses every three weeks throughout the entire spring and summer growing season.)

Dried Blood. NPK ratio of about 12-1-0. Its extremely high nitrogen content makes it ideal for stimulating healthy bacterial growth in compost.

Potash. NPK ratio of 0-0-10. High potassium aids general plant hardiness. Potash combined with bonemeal and dried blood makes a complete organic fertilizer.

CHEMICAL FERTILIZERS. Most gardeners purchase granular fertilizer, excellent for working into the soil and as a fall and spring topdressing. Pellets are slower-releasing; they should be sprinkled on the soil in early spring. Bags come in all weights—bulk purchases reduce the price per pound. Store unused portions in a dry location.

I have found that an NPK ratio of 10-10-10 makes an excellent general fertilizer for my gardens. I often add superphosphate (0-20-0) and sometimes even try triple phosphate (0-46-0), which is good for transplanted young seedlings and for encouraging fruits and flowers.

Fast-acting fertilizers, liquid or water-soluble, are good for container-grown plants

The small plastic flats, marked with name and planting date, hold new seedlings until transplanting time. Large seeds should be well spaced when planting; the seedlings can be transplanted directly into the ground. Smaller seeds must be planted more closely, and are often transplanted once before being planted out.

and a quick fix for plants suffering nutrient deficiency. They are rapidly leached from the soil. Never apply to dry soil, or you will risk "burning" the plants.

Lawn fertilizers, high nitrogen and lower phosphorus (10-6-4 is typical), promote stem and leaf growth and healthy color.

Growing Media

WHEN MY FATHER AND I WERE STARTING seedlings, we made our own propagating medium, a combination of freshly dug

sandy loam (which I sterilized by baking in the oven), finely strained peat moss, and vermiculite. The resulting mixture had the essential properties of a good growing medium: it was moisture retentive, porous enough to provide adequate aeration, and sufficiently dense to hold the seeds in place for germination and root development. The laborious baking process destroyed disease and weed seeds, but kept the valuable nutrients intact.

Garden centers and nurseries all sell premixed sterile propagating media, well balanced combinations which generally include peat moss, vermiculite (heat-expanded mica rock), perlite (volcanic material), and small amounts of fertilizer.

To mix your own medium is time-consuming and generally messy, but is cost efficient. Perhaps the simplest mix to make is equal parts of sterile potting soil, peat moss, and clean sand, or substitute perlite for sand. Sprinkle in a small amount of vermiculite. Mix well with a hand trowel. With soil in the mix there is a chance of damping off—when young seedlings simply wilt and die. To combat this problem, spread a thin layer of perlite across the top of newly sown seeds. Moisture dissipates from perlite quickly, keeping the surface drier and helping to retard fungal activity. To create a mix without soil, combine equal parts of clean sand, peat moss, and vermiculite or perlite.

Whether you use a commercial medium or mix your own, remember to scrub plant containers and tools thoroughly to prevent contamination, wear cotton gloves, and never inhale fine particles when working with soil and soilless mixes, especially vermiculite and perlite.

1. Within my small greenhouse I have everything I need to propagate most of the seedlings for the garden: a water supply, a work bench, shades for controlling light, a space heater for controlling the temperature, big containers for mixing soils, and grow-lights to simulate sunlight.

2. I use a professional germinating mix, a sterile combination of peat moss, perlite, fine grade bark, and nutrients. It is very dry from the bag; I mix it with water in large bowls (or a plastic garbage pail) until damp but not soggy.

3. These compressed peat discs are good for one-step planting of annuals and large vegetables. The discs are soaked in water, and pop up to 4 or 5 times their height; their little net bags allow roots to grow freely.

4. The full, fat discs are arranged tightly to retain moisture. Like my father, I prefer to use wooden flats; this one came ready to assemble from a catalogue.

5. In addition to the peat discs, I use several different starter kits and pots. The white-sectioned tray is part of an English kit called APS (Accelerated Propagation System). Like a mini-greenhouse with built-in capillary watering system, it is expensive but can be reused year after year. The green plastic boxes are excellent for starting small seeds of annuals (snapdragons, pansies, petunias) and lettuces, which will be transplanted to larger pots when they are about 3 inches tall. Peat Jiffy Pots (lower left) are used for larger seedlings.

6. These reusable plastic plug trays are my favorite germinating method. At transplanting, seedlings pop easily out of the plugs with no damage to the tender roots.

7. Small containers, like the APS, discs, and "plugs" are planted with one seed apiece; the boxes are sown in tiny rows.

8. Empty seed packets should be marked with the planting date and filed away for future reference: many have pictures and useful planting instructions. Leftover seeds should be stored in small airtight containers; I do sometimes use seeds from a previous year, but with varying success.

9. Wooden markers can be bought in bulk and are perfect for the greenhouse; metal or plastic markers are better outdoors.

10. Cover seeds lightly with moist soil. Follow planting instructions for each variety: a good rule of thumb is to cover to a depth three times the diameter of the seed. Pat the soil lightly with the back of your hand and water with a fine mist or spray. The APS boxes have clear plastic tops to keep moisture in the newly planted trays; the other trays and pots will be covered with black plastic and kept at an even temperature of about 60 degrees until the seeds germinate.

11. Flowers that germinate in the boxes can be transplanted to large-size plug trays. Handle the seedlings gently.

12. Once the seedlings begin to grow and to establish leaf and root systems, they should be exposed to bright light for at least eight hours a day. The soil must be checked daily (it should be moist, but not waterlogged). I feed seedlings liquid nutrients every five days or so until they are strong and sturdy and ready to be transplanted outdoors. I find that good housekeeping in the greenhouse is key to the percentage of germination: sterile soil, clean trays and pots, and care in keeping unhealthy plants out of the greenhouse will help produce excellent seedlings.

Making Raised Beds

MY RAISED BEDS ARE EASY TO WEED, to cultivate, and to harvest. In addition, the patterns created by the beds are infinitely more interesting than straight rows. Intersecting the paths between the squares are established swaths of strong grass. These are permanent, and give the landscape architectural definition even when the garden is not planted. They are kept edged and mown throughout the summer; I have further outlined the main paths with edgings of chives, which in May and June are in full bloom with purple-blue flowers.

French intensive gardening maximizes time and space. Raised beds and well-prepared, nutrient-rich soil allow roots to grow rapidly and deeply. Planting en masse creates dense, lush patchwork greenery with little unshaded soil (for less evaporation and fewer weeds).

My vegetable garden is a variation of this practical method. To achieve a well-tilled and aerated soil, plow your vegetable garden in fall after harvest and again in spring. Supplement the fall

ABOVE AND RIGHT: *I outline the sections with wooden stakes and string, then pull the soil up above garden level.*

plowing with manure, compost, fertilizer, and amend soil so that the pH ranges between 6.0 and 6.8.

Plan the intensive garden during the winter. Draw to scale a pattern of squares, roughly 4 feet by 4 feet, separated by 12-inch paths. For vegetables that require staking or trellising (tomatoes, okra, cucumbers, and peas), add a few narrow rectangular beds for easier access. A good rule is to plant one crop per square, although sometimes I underplant a vegetable with a herb such as eggplant with chervil. I also companion plant vegetables and herbs, such as tomatoes and blue salvia for natural pest control.

After the spring plowing, use string and stakes (1-by-1-inch wooden sticks work well) to outline a pattern in the garden site. With a metal garden rake, pull the soil from the paths up into the beds, elevating them 6 inches. A mulch of grass clippings on paths will decrease weed growth and keep them from getting too muddy during rain or watering.

Early April to late May is the best time to sow seeds outdoors in Connecticut. Broadcast seeds of lettuce, spinach, mâche, and other fine-seeded crops thickly over the prepared, raised soil; cover lightly. Water deeply but use only a fine spray or seeds will be washed away. Thin seedlings as they grow and become too crowded. Early April is the time I transplant beets, cabbages, and peas from the greenhouse.

During the growing season, water when dry, about two hours before sunset. With more than twelve hours before the harshest rays of sun return, there will be less chance of water evaporation.

ABOVE: *Each raised-bed square is small enough to be accessible from all sides for easy weeding, watering, and harvesting.*

ABOVE: *In early spring, seedlings are taken from greenhouse to cold frame to harden off until ready for the raised beds.*

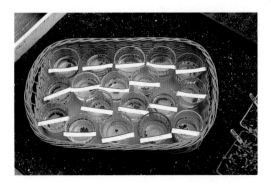

ABOVE: *Every St. Patrick's Day, I plant sweet peas around the vegetable garden. A water soaking gives the seeds a head start.*

ABOVE AND BELOW: *I start scallions, or "green onions," in the greenhouse, sowing their tiny seeds in boxes. When the seedlings are 6 inches tall, I transplant them to the raised beds. I use the stake-and-string method to make a straight line, then form a trench (about 2 inches deep) by drawing a heart hoe along the string. I make straight rows in my vegetable gardens not for aesthetic effect (though an orderly formation is attractive), but to ensure correct spacing of the plants. Scallions should be 2 inches apart, in rows 6 to 8 inches apart.*

Menu

Chicken Soup

SERVES 4 TO 6

White meat of chicken, simmered in rich stock until just tender, is served with a tasty mélange of flavorful vegetables.

1½ quarts chicken stock, preferably homemade
2 whole boneless, skinless chicken breasts
2 small leeks, washed, halved, and cut crosswise into ¼-inch pieces
1 large garlic clove, finely minced
½ butternut squash, peeled, seeded, cut into 1-inch cubes
5 carrots, peeled, and cut diagonally into 2-inch pieces
2 stalks celery, cut crosswise into ¼-inch pieces
1 small fennel bulb, halved, cored, cut crosswise into thin pieces
1 medium parsnip, peeled and cut into 2-inch diagonal pieces
2 cups coarsely julienned spinach leaves
1 small handful whole flat-leaf parsley leaves
Salt and freshly ground pepper

1. In a large pot, bring stock to a simmer. Add the chicken, cover, and poach until just done, about 10 minutes. Remove from the stock with a slotted spoon, and tear into large strips. Cover with plastic wrap and set aside.

2. Add the leeks and garlic to the stock and simmer for 10 minutes, stirring.

3. Add the remaining vegetables; simmer for 10 to 15 minutes more. When all vegetables are tender, stir in the chicken, spinach, and parsley. Once heated through, season with salt and pepper. Serve with a large spoonful of Rouille.

Tomato–Red Pepper Rouille

MAKES ABOUT 2 CUPS

Rouille is traditionally served in Brittany as the "spice" for fish soup. I serve it as a spread for the broiled bread.

12 garlic cloves, peeled
1 red pepper, cut into strips
3 large egg yolks
3 tablespoons tomato paste
1½ cups olive oil
Salt and freshly ground pepper

1. In a small pot of boiling water, blanch the garlic cloves for 4 to 5 minutes. Remove from the pot with a slotted spoon. Blanch the pepper in the same pot of boiling water for 3 to 4 minutes. Drain.
2. Place the egg yolks in the bowl of a food processor and blend until thick, about 2 to 3 minutes.
3. Add the garlic, red pepper, and tomato paste and blend for an additional 2 to 3 minutes, or until very smooth.
4. With the food processor running, pour the oil through the feed tube in a slow, steady stream. Continue to blend until the sauce resembles a thick cream. Season with salt and pepper to taste.

Broiled Herb Bread

SERVES 6

Herb toasts can be made easily in quantity in the broiler. I use whatever fresh herbs I have on hand.

¼ cup olive oil
2 tablespoons finely chopped mixed herbs (parsley, mint, thyme, chives, tarragon, etc.)
6 ½-inch-thick slices crusty bread

1. Preheat the broiler.
2. Mix together the oil and chopped herbs in a bowl. Brush the bread on both sides with the oil-and-herb mixture.
3. Broil or grill the slices on each side until golden brown, being careful not to burn them.

Pink Applesauce

MAKES 1 QUART

Bright-skinned red apples make applesauce pink if you follow these instructions. Choose tart, white-fleshed apples like Romes, Macouns, or Ida Reds. The applesauce is excellent by itself, or with soft gingerbread, spice cake, or a dollop of crème fraîche.

8 very red-skinned apples
⅔ cup freshly squeezed lemon juice (about 4 lemons)
1½ cups water
¼ cup sugar

1. Quarter the apples and remove the seeds and cores. (Do not peel.) Place them in a bowl, add the lemon juice, and toss thoroughly to coat.
2. Place the apples, water, and sugar in a heavy saucepan. Cover pot and simmer over low heat for about 30 minutes, or until the apples break down to a sauce-like consistency.
3. Remove from heat, uncover pot, and allow apples to cool slightly. Gently push the apples through a wire sieve using a rubber scraper. Discard the skins. Refrigerate the sauce until ready to use.

ABOVE: *The delicately shaded pink applesauce, served in two-handled pressed glass bowls, complements a vintage blue, yellow, and white woven tablecloth.*
OPPOSITE: *I like to serve chunky main-course soups in large, shallow soup plates. One of my Christmas rosemary topiaries is still going strong.*

S P R

GROOM'S REMBRANT.

I N G

THE OFFICIAL OPENING OF SPRING is always announced by a 6 A.M. phone call from the postmaster: the baby chicks have arrived, all ninety-seven of them, and disaster looms if we don't get right down to the post office to pick up the little things. Their arrival has been marked in bold letters on the calendar, but we are never quite prepared, and there is a bit of a panic before the babies are safely installed in a newsprint-lined, heat-lamp-warmed, starter-feed-strewn growing box. ❧ When I first moved to Connecticut, I joined the Fairfield Organic Gardeners, a group devoted to healthful and safe methods of gardening and raising livestock. It was then that we had all kinds of poultry, a pig or two, goats, and even sheep (one, Plantagenet Palliser, was served to a most discouraged Alexis, who promptly became a confirmed vegetarian). ❧ I learned a great deal about creating a small self-contained ecosystem, where plants and animals can grow and produce to their full potential. My birds ate vegetable scraps from the garden and table and produced fabulous eggs for the table and manure for the gardens. The bees pollinated the flowers, creating more prolific fruit-bearing plants and trees while donating delicately scented honey to the larder. The sheep, goats, and rabbits clipped the grass, ate the vines, made excellent manure, and fed the family. And we all garnered pleasure, knowledge, and an understanding of how nature works.

ABOVE: *The baby chicks must be taught to drink by having their beaks dunked in water (children love to help with this task).* OPPOSITE: *Spring's first mild day is perfect for tree planting.*

A P R I L

JOURNAL

Seedlings removed from greenhouse to cold frames.

Fruit trees sprayed.

Roses fed a second time.

Tea roses pruned and shaped.

Strawberry patch weeded and thinned.

Awnings replaced.

Garden furniture placed outdoors.

Garden urns refilled and planted.

Lawns top-dressed.

Hardy vegetables planted.

Lettuces and herbs planted.

More sweet peas soaked and planted.

All borders weeded for onion grass and chickweed.

Pool drained, cleaned and refilled.

Beets, cabbages, and all peas transplanted outdoors.

Tomatoes, peppers, eggplants planted in greenhouse.

Clapboard siding of house washed.

House paint retouched; stairs repainted.

Onions and leek seedlings planted out.

LEFT AND OPPOSITE BELOW: *I keep turkeys, guinea hens, and 20 to 30 breeds of chickens. The chicks are chosen for their productivity: I visit county fairs and peruse catalogues to find the best egg layers. Araucana hens, a South American breed, give 275 to 300 turquoise-shelled eggs apiece to the kitchens each year.*

ABOVE: *Bee keeping requires an initial investment of about $250 (for a complete standard hive and equipment). One well-tended hive will produce 70 pounds of honey each year—and the "side effect" of healthy bees in the garden is extraordinary. My garden was good without my bees, wonderful with the addition of these industrious creatures.*

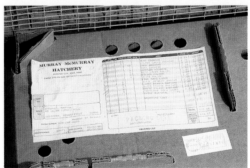

Narcissi

APRIL IN WESTPORT CAN STILL BE decidedly chilly. One day will be 70 degrees and I'll happily plant out the lettuces; on the next day a frigid wind forces me to worry for their safety. Snowdrops, crocuses, and fruit blossoms have been out for a while, but it's not until the first of the yellow trumpet daffodils opens that I know the season really has turned.

The botanical term *Narcissus* is Latin for the genus of flowers with long, flat, hollow leaves. They are often referred to both as daffodils, which are mainly golden with large trumpets, and as narcissi—usually bearing clusters of fragrant, white or yellow flowers. Just to complicate things further, "jonquil" is a name also applied to yellow forms. But daffodils (*Narcissus* sp.) can be more than yellow and white—they can display pink, orange, reddish, green, or a combination of these colors and be double-flowered.

Like other spring-flowering bulbs, daffodils require a cold period for dormancy. Many varieties naturalize. If

LEFT: *In the big perennial beds the irises, poppies, peonies, lilies, and hardy geraniums have emerged plump and sturdy.*
TOP RIGHT: *Tea roses must be carefully pruned in early spring.*
CENTER: *Before we left New York to live in Connecticut, I ordered the apple trees, which we planted within the poppy border. We pruned them into a very controlled open-center design, creating an appropriately formal appearance.*
BOTTOM: *The hybridization of peonies has made their heads too heavy for their stems; peony rings help them stay upright.*

ABOVE AND LEFT: *Each year I plant a few hundred more daffodils and narcissi amid the perennial borders. Luckily, these escape the attention of rodents and deer, which find the bulbs and flowers offensive. But tulips and crocuses are delicious tidbits for these creatures, and must be planted in protected areas.*

spaced properly and fertilized regularly, bulbs will multiply and not require division for years.

Nursery catalogues offer special combinations of naturalizing varieties. By planting combinations of daffodil varieties, gardeners can expect flowering for about two months. After the flowers are spent, cut down the stems and tidy up the leaves—which must be allowed to yellow and die naturally. Take a handful of leaves and, starting from the top, roll them to the base and tie with two other leaves. Braiding is another option, but I find rolling faster. Some gardeners frown on bunching leaves, saying that without air circulation, leaves will not die naturally or provide the food for next season's flower. I tie neat but loose bunches and have found that the next year's flowering is always admired.

The American Daffodil Society recognizes categories of flowers, and catalogues use many of these categories to describe their daffodils.

TRUMPET DAFFODILS. Hybrid varieties are recognized by a large corona (also called a trumpet or cup) that is as long or longer than the petals; vigorous growers, these bloom early with one flower per stem; excellent for cutting.

LONG-CUPPED DAFFODILS. Cup is more than one-third but less than the length of the petals; one flower per stem, blooms mid-season; excellent cutting flower; varieties with orange or orange-red cup are brilliantly colored; a recent introduction has a pink cup.

SHORT-CUPPED DAFFODILS. Cup is less than one-third the length of the petals; one flower per stem; some bloom in late May. (I am particularly fond of the 'Edward Buxton' variety.)

DOUBLE DAFFODILS. Varieties bloom mid to late season with one or more flowers per stem; two to five rows of petals make the double flowers heavy on their stems.

TRIANDRUS DAFFODILS. One or more drooping, fragrant creamy-white bell-shaped flowers with large cups; petals curve back and sometimes twist; bloom late; foliage is narrow; miniatures with 4- to 8-inch stems; do well in damp locations. ('Thalia' is my favorite.)

CYCLAMINEUS DAFFODILS. Unusual, early deep yellow blooms have bent-back petals and long trumpet; one flower per stem; miniatures with broad leaves; perform best in moist locations.

JONQUILLA DAFFODILS. The 1½-foot stems have two to six small, fragrant clustered flowers with flat petals; deep green leaves; late bloomer.

TAZETTA DAFFODILS. Stems 1½ feet tall with clusters of very short-cupped, extremely fragrant flowers; include paper-whites; late bloomer, when hardy; many used for midwinter forcing (I often give bulbs as a Christmas gift).

POETICUS DAFFODILS. One flower per stem with six white petals and a very short colorful cup—can be yellow, orange, red, even green; fragrant; last to bloom. (I planted 'Pheasant's Eye'.)

SPECIES DAFFODILS. The original daffodils found growing in the wild, existing in the mid-nineteenth century before hybridization. (I like to see these blooming along fences and stone walls, in the perennial border, or in beds at the foot of azaleas and rhododendrons.)

ABOVE: *My forsythia is an ancient variety grown from cuttings taken at the neighboring von Rebay estate 17 years ago. Because of an extremely wet March and April following a mild winter, the forsythia was superb this year, its branches virtually covered with the yellow, bell-like flowers.*
BELOW: *We once had a most magnificent silver Persian cat named Magnolia; when she died, I planted a whole row of pink saucer magnolia trees in her honor. This is a* Magnolia x soulangiana 'Alexandrina', *an excellent and long-lived landscape tree.*

1. Remove sod first in one or two pieces. Dig a straight-sided hole twice as deep as the tree roots. Save topsoil and subsoil in separate piles, and cart away any rocks.

2. Place green sod upside down in the hole, add compost, then mound up some topsoil. Spread roots over dome; set tree 2 inches deeper than it was in the nursery.

3. Clip off any broken roots, then, using a hand trowel, layer the topsoil over the roots. Add a bit of peat moss or compost to lighten the soil if too heavy.

4. Thoroughly water tree, letting the damp soil settle. Add more soil up to 2 inches below the bud union. Press soil firmly down with your foot.

5. Mound topsoil or compost at least 6 inches above garden level. Create a well around the trunk for watering. Do not cover the bud union.

6. Add a 2-inch mulch of straw manure or barky peat. Using a grass rake, clean up loose soil around tree. Water again, filling up the well.

Planting a Tree

A COUPLE OF YEARS AGO, I WAS A guest at the new Southampton home of a young couple. As my housewarming gift, I brought my hosts a lovely, well-branched, four-year-old Bramley apple tree and invited them to help me plant it. By the end of the morning, they and their guests, dressed in pristine Hamptons white, were muddy and disheveled, and smiling. Tree planting is a rewarding task—especially if it's a fruit tree and one can look forward to its harvest.

Choose the best spot for the tree and mark it. If you are siting the tree in a manicured lawn, protect the grass with a tarpaulin before you begin. Using a sharp-edged, round-point, solid-shank shovel, dig a hole and plant the tree following the step-by-step instructions on these pages.

If the roots of a nursery-grown tree are wrapped in burlap, loosen it around the trunk, leaving the fabric around the roots, then set the burlap ball right in the hole. If the tree is balled in synthetic fiber, carefully remove it.

As you refill the hole with soil, take care not to cover the bud union. If the graft, or bud union, is covered, roots will develop above the union and a dwarf tree will revert to full size. If the trunk of the tree is buried, the bark will not be able to breathe, and the tree will die.

Water fruit trees twice each week, at night and again the following morning. Heavy, less frequent watering is much better than constant light watering. After the roots have matured for a year, feed the trees with a general fertilizer.

7. Prune off the top of the tree. Cut lateral branches to two buds—make all cuts on the diagonal just above the bud. Never cut out the central leader if there is one; ideally, dwarf trees should have a well-developed head with a strong central leader and branches (this one lacks a central leader, but is well-branched). In windy areas, stake trees for stability and strong root growth.

8. Next spring I will apply fertilizer around the tree's perimeter. I usually use well-rotted cow manure as a topdressing; it acts as a mulch and also supplies nutrition. Do not let mulch touch the trunk of the tree.

Tulips

HAD I LIVED IN SEVENTEENTH-century Holland, I'm sure I would have been a perfect victim of Tulipomania, the passion that drove prices for this exotic so high family fortunes were ruined.

Tulips brighten my garden from April through May. I plant many varieties in clusters of at least ten for small tulips and six to ten for large-flowered cottage, Darwin, lily, and peony types. For striking displays, I plant monochromatic beds and borders; in my cutting beds, I also plant 2-foot-tall May-flowering tulips. My favorites are yellow- and salmon-pink-colored; these are especially attractive in the house.

Most tulips produce a dramatic bloom the first spring and continue for three to five years with lessening intensity. They require regular fertilizing and cold winters for good flowering. Species tulips come closest to naturalizing and will sometimes form colonies. Most tulip bulbs flower and then die; the food energy from the leaves, which *must* be allowed to die naturally, goes into newly formed bulblets, which may bloom the following year. In spring when the petals start to drop, cut the flower stems to prevent the formation of seed pods that rob energy from newly forming bulblets.

SPECIES OR BOTANICAL TULIPS. Bloom in April, sometimes late March, and are quite resistant to snow damage. They grow from 5 to 15 inches tall, are long-lasting, and often produce multiple flowers—usually red, yellow, or white. Many of the tiny, oddly shaped species are ideal for rock gardens. *Tulipa kaufmanniana*

LEFT: *Beside the old chicken coop (now a tool shed) I created an old-fashioned "cutting garden," where flowers for my house can be raised and picked without disturbing the perennial borders.*
ABOVE: *I don't grow any red flowers (except poppies) in the perennial garden, but I do like to have some for arrangements, so I planted red triumph 'Tambour Mâitre' tulips here.*
BELOW: *These Darwin hybrids, 'Olympic Flame', with their open, saucerlike petals, make wonderful bouquets for the house.*

(called the water-lily tulip because it opens flat in strong light) and its hybrids are the earliest to bloom; *T. acuminata* (Turkish tulip), *T. sylvestris,* and *T. greigii* are other popular species. I am not as fond of *T. fosterana* hybrids (emperor tulips) as they tend to be short-lived.

SINGLE AND DOUBLE EARLY TULIPS. From 10 to 14 inches tall, these late April–early May bloomers are quite hardy. Double varieties bloom before singles and are longer-lasting. These are wonderful tulips for forcing indoors.

TRIUMPHS. Hybrids of the single early and later May-flowering tulips, these bloom in early May after the singles and before Darwins. Strong stemmed, about 20 inches tall, they come in many colors.

DARWIN AND DARWIN HYBRIDS. Up to 24-inch-long stout stems and large, solid-colored flowers make these tulips very impressive—superb for cutting. Brightly colored petals are rounded at the tip. Darwins bloom in May and the hybrids flower slightly earlier in even more brilliant colors with a satiny sheen.

LILY-FLOWERED TULIPS. Narrow graceful flowers have pointed petals that turn backward, resembling those of lilies. These tall late-spring tulips, about 16 inches high, bloom in violet, yellow, white, and more colors.

COTTAGE TULIPS. Oval flowers, often pastel with pointed petals, are borne atop long, flexible stems about 2 feet tall; flowers in May.

PARROT TULIPS. Up to 20-inch stems are often weak. These May flowers, with petals fringed or slashed with odd markings, can be dramatic in arrangements.

REMBRANDT TULIPS. May-flowering with a variegation or spots of color on the petals. This unusual effect is due to a virus that causes no harm to the tulip.

LATE DOUBLE OR PEONY-FLOWERED TULIPS. Many-petalled red, violet, yellow, or white flowers resemble peonies. From 15 to 18 inches tall, these May-flowering tulips top strong stems.

ABOVE: *Tulips make long-lasting indoor arrangements. Cut them after the buds have elongated—just as they begin to open; once indoors, they will twist toward light. To keep the flowers from all facing in the same direction, turn the arrangement in a circle about an inch each day. Here are red and yellow parrot and Rembrandt tulips with forsythia in an oak-splint Arkansas basket.*

ABOVE: *The aptly named 'Flaming Parrot' tulip, with typical fringed petals.*
BELOW: *'Fantasy' is one of my favorite parrot tulips, wonderful in bouquets.*

ABOVE: *I plant tulips in clusters; here is a group of rare, fringed 'Maja' blooms.*
BELOW: *Cottage tulips 'Anne Frank'; monochromatic borders are impressive.*

ABOVE: *Lily-flowered tulips are very graceful: here is a pair of 'Mariettas'.*
BELOW: *I am fond of striped blooms like these 'Union Jack' cottage tulips.*

LEFT: *Whenever I entertain, I try to enlist my daughter, Alexis, to help with the floral bouquets for the house. She has always enjoyed the garden, and has a unique style in her work with flowers.*

BELOW LEFT: *Cut tulips, dogwood, lilac, and azalea branches await arrangement. Flowers will be healthier and arrangements will last longer if the stems are plunged into water as soon as possible after picking.*

RIGHT: *I like to mix the spring flowers in large masses. This early-twentieth-century clear glass vase holds red and yellow Darwin tulips interspersed with long, waving fronds of white bleeding heart.*

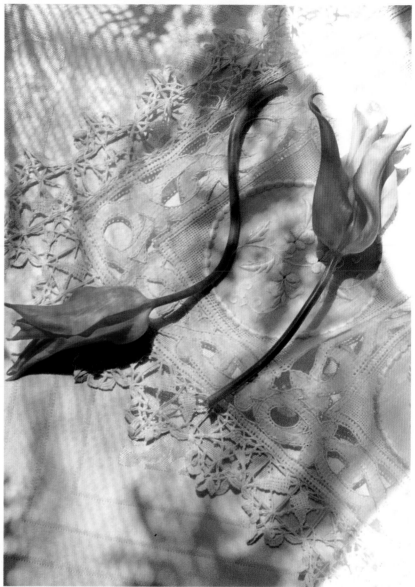

ABOVE: *A shot glass holds an intimate bouquet of Pulmonaria, violas, and spring gentian.*
RIGHT: *I filled an English pansy ring of green glass with old-fashioned flowers (with old-fashioned names): strawberry blossom, pansies, grape hyacinth, spotted dog (Pulmonaria), and garlic mustard.*

ABOVE: *Two lily-flowered tulips, cut for arrangement, on a vintage white cutwork tablecloth.*
RIGHT: *Some of my favorite containers didn't start life as vases: a Depression glass sugar bowl is the perfect home for an arrangement of grape hyacinth, forget-me-nots, and one white anemone.*

Fritillaries

JUST A SHORT TIME AGO, GUINEA HEN flowers—or *Fritillaria meleagris*—were seen only in paintings by Dutch old masters. Now these odd, upside-down checkerboard tulips, just one of the nearly seventy species of *Fritillaria*, are becoming a popular and charming addition to the spring garden.

Fritillaria are not considered as hardy as many other spring-flowering bulbs, and before committing to mass plantings, it is wise to purchase a few to test their hardiness in your area. Plant in a sandy soil as good drainage is very important. Remember, too, that the foliage must be allowed to die back naturally. The scent of *Fritillaria* is singular and sometimes regarded as mildly unpleasant, although I don't find it so.

FRITILLARIA MELEAGRIS. Although modest in size, the checkered lily or guinea hen flower is decidedly elegant and unusual—an early sign of spring. A mixture of purple, yellow, and white form a checkerboard pattern on the drooping bell-shaped flower; there is also a white, a yellow, and a rose variety. Native to Europe, this plant grows to 12 inches and does well in partial shade. I like to plant several hundred to dramatize their effect, along paths and under shrubbery and trees. Their remarkable patterns and shape beautify any arrangement of cut flowers. Pick them just as they begin to open.

FRITILLARIA PERSICA. Called Persian fritillary, this flower, native to the Middle East, produces many tiny bell-shaped rich purple blooms on 2½-foot stems in

May. *Fritillaria persica* is excellent for beds and borders.

FRITILLARIA IMPERIALIS. Crown Imperial is the showiest of the species, growing to 3 feet. I find this late-May bloomer a bit discouraging as I often cut the tops of these slow starters while cultivating other spring bulbs. Always mark where you plant them. When they bloom, a tuft of green leaves tops a ring of bell-shaped flowers—orange, red, or yellow. They have an unusual scent, again regarded by some as unpleasant.

ABOVE: *In the wild, primulas and fritillaries grow in water meadows and on river banks; I grow them in the dappled shade of an apple tree.*
OPPOSITE: *A patch of the garden brought indoors. White bleeding hearts, buds of Oriental poppies, lily-flowered and parrot tulips, irises, the earliest daisy, and several different types of columbine fill a Carnival glass punch bowl in the front hall. In a shallow bowl like this, I use a clay-secured metal frog that will not topple over and that will keep the cut ends of all the flowers in water.*

Bleeding Hearts

I HAVE ALWAYS BEEN FOND OF ANTIQUE flowers, species that have been in cultivation for over a hundred years. The graceful *Dicentra* looks as if it had jumped right out of an old-fashioned flower garden, and its common name, bleeding heart, has wonderful Victorian overtones. It prefers cool climates, and will grow 2 to 3 feet tall and spread a foot or more in spring, fading in the heat of summer.

DICENTRA SPECTABILIS. Wonderfully arching branches display attractive feathery, vivid-green foliage and send out long stems of dramatic heart-shaped pink to red flowers with white tips in late spring. This most popular species of *Dicentra*, a native of Japan, thrives in partial shade; plants in full sun will completely disappear by summer. A cultivar, *D. spectabilis* 'Alba', produces all white blooms and looks particularly wonderful in flower arrangements.

DICENTRA EXIMIA. Native to North America and very hardy, this species grows to 18 inches with lacy gray-green leaves and dark mauve drooping flowers in late spring. Often called fringed bleeding heart; it too has a white-flowering cultivar, 'Alba'.

All varieties of this semishade-loving herbaceous perennial grow best in slightly moist but well-drained soil rich in organic matter. Propagate by division of root clumps in very early spring before flowering. Or take 3-inch sections of roots in early spring from a vigorous plant. Set these in a mixture of moist sand and peat moss and place in a shaded location until new plants appear.

ABOVE: Dicentra spectabilis *'Alba', a rather new cultivar of bleeding heart, has pure white heart-shaped flowers spilling off wavy, bright green foliage.*
RIGHT: *A mass of little woodland flowers—primroses, bleeding hearts, forget-me-nots, grape hyacinths, snowflakes, Poeticus daffodils, parsley, mint, sage, garlic mustard, and squill—nestle in a basket.*
BELOW: Scilla campanulata, *commonly known as wood hyacinths or Spanish bluebells, are lovely harbingers of spring.*

ABOVE AND RIGHT: *A late-April Easter, just warm enough to let the children run coatless, is an opportunity for a garden party.*

ABOVE: *I taught the children an old English Maypole dance, which winds ribbons around a tall, flower-crowned staff.*

GARDENING

76

LEFT: *After the older children have combed the gardens and woods for brightly tinted hard-boiled eggs, they guide the "littles" through the enclosed yew garden where the treasures are more easily found. My friend Monica Pasternak is proud to have graduated to the over-five group.*

CENTER: *Kelly Inabnit knew immediately which basket she was going to choose, its wicker elaborately woven with ribbons of pink and scarlet—her favorite colors.*
RIGHT: *While the children hunt for eggs and pick their pretty baskets, the grown-ups nibble beautifully decorated Easter cookies.*

ABOVE: *Katharine Zaleski found it hard to choose: within each basket, nestled in natural golden straw, lie homemade candies and cookies, and tiny stuffed animals.*
LEFT: *Kelly's basket held a special treat, a little white plush lamb.*
RIGHT: *Treasure trove. Eggs from our chickens are tinted with vegetable colorings—and somewhere in the garden we have hidden a special prize, the gold-leafed egg.*

APRIL

79

Menu

Soft-Boiled Eggs on Breakfast Bread

SERVES 4

On a weekend visit to Connecticut when I was a high school student, I was served peeled 4½-minute eggs on toast. Never had I seen such an elegant thing. I found out later that my hostess actually cooked twice as many eggs as she served to account for broken eggs!

8 large eggs, at room temperature
4 ½-inch slices Breakfast Bread
4 teaspoons unsalted butter

1. Fill a small pot with cold water. Place the eggs in the pot, and bring to a boil over medium-high heat. When the water boils, lower flame and continue cooking for 4 minutes. Maintain a slow boil.
2. Meanwhile, toast the bread and butter each slice. Place 1 slice on each plate.
3. Remove the eggs from the water and carefully peel them. Gently tear 2 eggs in half over each bread slice. Sprinkle with salt and freshly ground pepper.

Breakfast Bread

MAKES 2 LOAVES

I've been baking this bread for my family for many years. It's great right out of the oven, but also as French toast or in bread puddings.

2 cups milk
8 tablespoons (1 stick) unsalted butter
1 teaspoon salt
2 tablespoons sugar
2 packages dry yeast
⅔ cup warm water
6-7 cups all-purpose flour
1 large egg, lightly beaten

1. Scald milk in a small pot. Stir in the butter, salt, and sugar. Cool to lukewarm.
2. Dissolve the yeast in the warm water and add to the milk mixture.
3. Mix 3 cups of flour into the liquid ingredients. Stir in egg. Add rest of flour and knead until smooth and elastic. Add more flour if necessary. Let rise in a buttered bowl covered in plastic wrap until doubled in bulk.
4. Butter 2 loaf pans. Punch dough down, divide in half, form loaves, and place in to pans. Cover with plastic and let rise again until loaves almost reach pan tops.
5. Preheat oven to 350°.
6. Bake for 40 to 50 minutes until browned and hollow-sounding when tapped.
7. Remove from pans and cool on racks.

Breakfast Gravlax

SERVES 5 TO 6

Gravlax is a Scandinavian raw fish cured for 3 days.

1 tablespoon salt
1 tablespoon sugar
2 teaspoons coarsely ground black pepper
1 pound boned filet of salmon (leave skin on)
1 bunch dill or fennel leaves

1. Combine the salt, sugar, and pepper and sprinkle on the fleshy side of the fish. Spread the dill or fennel in a glass dish and place the seasoned salmon, skin side up, on top.
2. Place a smaller dish on the salmon and weight it down with a heavy object. Refrigerate. Turn fish every day for 3 days.
3. To serve, remove salmon from seasoning. Wipe clean and pat dry. Slice thinly on the diagonal. Serve with fresh capers and black pepper.

Orange Pound Cake

MAKES 1 10-INCH LOAF
OR 3 SHALLOW 9-INCH
MOLDS

This pound cake is quite plain, but the addition of orange liqueur and lots of orange zest gives it a satisfying flavor.

1 cup cake flour
1 teaspoon baking powder
¾ cup (1½ sticks) unsalted butter, softened
1 cup sugar
3 large eggs
1 large egg yolk
⅓ cup Grand Marnier or Cointreau (see Note)
Zest of 2 oranges

1. Preheat oven to 350°. Butter and flour loaf pan (or molds) thoroughly. Set aside.

2. Sift together flour and baking powder.
3. Beat together the butter and sugar at medium speed until light and fluffy. Add the eggs and yolk, one at a time, until incorporated. Add liqueur and zest and beat until just mixed. Gently fold in flour mixture in 3 batches, and pour into pan .
4. Bake for 25 to 30 minutes, or until cake springs back to a gentle touch. Carefully unmold, and let cool on a cake rack before handling.
NOTE: Orange juice can be substituted for the liqueur, if desired.

ABOVE: *A basket lined with natural straw is a rustic holder for orange pound cake.*
OPPOSITE ABOVE: *Big slices of freshly baked bread with soft-boiled eggs is my idea of a real farmhouse breakfast.*
OPPOSITE BELOW: *Eggs laid by my own chickens make the most flavorful dishes.*

WITHOUT ANY CONSCIOUS THOUGHT ON MY PART, the garden at Turkey Hill was planted to be at its best in May. This was due in great part to my first friend in Westport, Fred Specht. For twenty years, Fred had been the chief gardener and groundskeeper for the Hilla von Rebay estate, eighteen acres of woods and gardens adjoining my small property. Baroness von Rebay spent only the months of May and June in her Westport home, and she established the most superb perennial borders, boxwood and azalea gardens, and bowers of old-fashioned roses, designing them to be in perpetual bloom during her two-month residence. ❧ It was Fred, after my father, who instilled in me a true love of gardening; with his generosity and patience, he also taught me about the great friendships that come from gardening. Cuttings, divisions, and seedlings from the von Rebay garden gave shape and color to mine; I followed Fred's advice above that of anybody else. He was knowledgeable and gentle, and when he observed a mistake in my technique or in my choice of plant matter, he never was critical, only honest in his funny way. The day I proudly showed him a new planting of cleome amid my beautiful poppies and irises, he merely said: "Oh, you'll have fun with that." For the next two years, it took such effort to rid the beds of the invasive and weedlike plant. ❧

ABOVE: *The perennial borders are planted to bloom in waves of color; here poppies bud in the protective shade of a glorious tree peony.* OPPOSITE: *Fred Specht's 'Von Rebay' poppies about to bloom among the mullein leaves in mid-May.*

MAY

I remember clearly the first time I saw Fred's poppy border in early May. Atop wavy silver stems, furry elongated buds danced in a gentle breeze; bits of bright orange showed amid the gray foliage. The bed was 50 or 60 feet long, a double border split by a fine grassy path, carefully edged. I loved what it looked like then; I couldn't believe what it looked like three days later—with the silver foliage completely hidden by an astonishing mass of ruffled orange flowers, all alike. I couldn't find anything like them in any catalogue, so I wheedled a few plants out of Fred, who called them "Shirley" poppies (they're not true Shirleys, though, so I call them 'Von Rebay' poppies). In 1974, I planted five long tap roots in a cluster near the top of a long border; seventeen years later, I too have an orange poppy border in May.

LEFT: *The woolly leaves and stems of the Oriental poppies 'Carmine' and 'May Sadler' make a gentle backdrop for their bright orange and pale pink petals. Oriental and Iceland poppies make the best cut flowers. Sear the ends with a burning match immediately after cutting, or dip them into boiling water to seal. The dried seedpods of the poppies are dramatic in flower arrangements.*
OPPOSITE: *A lone 'Von Rebay'. The first of my poppies to bloom, they last for two to three weeks, and then fall all at once to the ground; the dried plants are easily scraped up, and other flowers—generally annuals—are planted in their place.*

JOURNAL

Stone edging installed in herb garden.

Kale, beets, cabbage, parsley, and fennel planted in raised beds.

Field and lawns mowed for first time.

Herbaceous peonies supported with peony rings.

Transplanting of annuals and vegetables continued in greenhouse.

Roses fed.

Rhubarb picked for tarts and preserves.

Buckwheat hulls delivered (884 sacks) and used to mulch perennial beds (a mistake, as it turned out).

Eggplants, radicchio, leeks, peppers, and collards planted out.

Nasturtiums planted around yew garden and along paths.

More garden urns planted with ivy, scented geraniums, and pansies.

Weeding continued apace.

Neighbor's car crashed into wall (no one hurt). Knocked down three white pines.

Tractor broken, sent away for repairs.

Deadwood cut from climbing roses.

Fruit trees sprayed right after blossoms fell.

Newly transplanted seedlings fertilized lightly.

Tomatoes, lettuce, and broccoli raab planted.

Sweet peas eaten by rabbits; replanted.

Mâche bed accidently "weeded." (Mâche all gone; weeds remain.)

Huge order of nursery stock delivered.

Planting begun in perennial borders. and herb garden.

Poppies

THE SOIL IN MY GARDEN SEEMS TO BE perfect for poppies. I am attempting to grow at least one of every kind of poppy I find in catalogues, and I have had great luck in growing even the rarest blue *Meconopsis*. The only variety I cannot keep alive is the white giant *Argemone*, or prickly poppy, found in more arid climates like Arizona or California.

Papaver species are the true poppies; other types commonly cultivated are *Eschscholzia* and *Meconopsis*. Poppies can be annual, perennial, and biennial. The tissue-paper petals come in lustrous colors: pink, scarlet, crimson, salmon, or white; many have dramatic black centers. Poppies have long tap roots, and many books warn that they do not transplant well; Fred and I have not had problems.

ORIENTAL POPPY *(Papaver orientale)*. Perennial; blooms late spring. Very showy, large flowers (sometimes 6 inches across). Single, with 4 to 6 petals, and double. Grows 3 feet tall. Fuzzy leaves die back in summer. Divide root mass in mid-August or take root cuttings in late summer. Deeply dig up clumps with spade and take 3-inch cuttings bearing two joints from the thick roots and re-plant each horizontally an inch deep in sandy soil in a flat; keep shaded and moist. Transplant in fall when shoots appear to a permanent sunny location;

LEFT: *An Oriental poppy of palest pink, yet another old flower from next door.*
RIGHT: *'Perry White', a fine, upright Oriental, has bold, straight stems and strong foliage.*

mulch all transplants in late winter with evergreen boughs.

SHIRLEY POPPY, a type of corn poppy (*Papaver rhoeas*). Annuals; 2-inch blossoms in a range of hues from midsummer to mid-autumn. Seeds are edible. In very early spring sow seeds outdoors in well-drained fertilized soil. Loves sun.

ICELAND POPPY (*Papaver nudicaule*). Biennial. Blooms best in the second year. Longer flowering than other poppies; yellow, orange, red, pink, white single and double flowers up to 3 inches. Sow seeds as above. Blooms appear in midsummer and again the following summer. Reseed.

CALIFORNIA POPPY (*Eschscholzia californica*). Perennial (but it's not hardy in Connecticut, so I treat it as an annual). Blooms through summer into fall. Stems and feathery foliage are blue-gray. Flowers, single and double, about 3 inches; yellow, red, orange, or cream. Sow seeds in spring. Full sun. Flowers open in sun and close at night and on cloudy days. Thrives in sandy, poor soil.

BLUE POPPY (*Meconopsis betonicifolia*). Sometimes called "Himalayan poppy." Perennial, difficult to grow in the Northeast—prefers cool, moist summers. Grows over 3 feet high with 2-inch rich blue flowers, 4 or more petals, and oblong 6-inch leaves. Sow seeds indoors in early spring. Partial shade.

Behind the house, the perennial border is in full splendor. The 'Von Rebay' poppies are still in bloom; the Orientals and Iris sibirica are just attaining their peak. I love the garden at this time—just on the verge of unbearable lushness.

Clematis

MY FATHER ORDERED CLEMATIS PLANTS from England, and he was so proud when they finally arrived. Back then, even the best foreign growers offered only the basic types of this hardy, beautiful—and now easily available—climber.

Clematis need shade for their roots, and sunlight for the vine, so choose their spot with care. (If there's too much sun, simply shade the ground around the plant with mulch, groundcover, annuals, or shrubs.) Clematis prefer well-drained but moist soil (give them ample water during summer dry spells) that has a neutral to alkaline pH from 6.8 to 7.5.

Once established, clematis are seldom troublesome, but they can be difficult when first planted as they dislike having their roots disturbed. It is best to plant new vines immediately after purchasing in spring. Dig a hole 18 inches wide and deep. Work compost and sand into the soil well below the plant's roots. Partially refill the hole with garden soil and peat moss before planting clematis. Make a paper collar, about 2 inches around and 3 high, to protect from accidental bumping, and provide a 6-foot or more trellis

LEFT: *An arched trellis wound with two varieties of clematis (the pinkish-mauve 'Nelly Moser' and the white 'Henryii') marks the entrance to the large perennial border, which blossoms with poppies, bleeding hearts, and Siberian irises.*
RIGHT: *'Henryii' clematis is intertwined with 'Blaze' and 'Lavender Lassie' roses; in the foreground, shasta daisies surround a large silver thistle, an interesting interloper.*

or a tepee of stakes if your vine is not close to a supporting structure.

Do not prune clematis until well-established: vines that blossom before June should be pruned right after they have flowered; vines that bloom after June should be pruned in early spring while still dormant to just above a pair of buds about 2 feet from the ground (flowers will appear only on new growth). For new plants, pinch tips in early summer to encourage multiple branching.

Clematis are voracious feeders, but wait until they become established before feeding. Fertilize annually in spring and fall with a handful of bonemeal. Apart from a tendency to wilt, mysterious but not often fatal, these vines are quite hardy. Usually only young plants suffer from wilt; prune out the sagging, withered portion, and discard. (Remember to disinfect your shears.)

Perennial Borders

IT HAS LONG BEEN MY HABIT TO GO to England once a year for a gardening holiday; I like to visit the Chelsea Flower Show, to putter around the garden centers from London to Dorset to Oxfordshire, and to tour some of my favorite gardens, like Hidcote, Upton House, or Kew. It was a visit to an English garden that inspired me to create my long perennial borders. Like trees, they are a true example of planting "for the future," rewarding the planning and patience that went into their early years with incredible beauty every spring and summer.

Perennials are soft-stemmed garden plants that live more than three years; each fall they become dormant and die back to ground level, only to return the following spring. Since they are, therefore, a fairly permanent addition to the garden, their site must be chosen with great care.

When making your border, choose a sunny, well-drained location. Begin in spring; turn the soil with a spade to a depth of at least 1 foot. Mix in organic matter, such as a layer of compost and

LEFT: *The first perennial I planted in Westport was* Aquilegia 'Star McKana', *a columbine hybrid. My father was proud of these free-blooming perennials that he had grown from seed; I still have some of his original plants in my garden.*
RIGHT: Aquilegia vulgaris, *the common columbine, is popular with lovers of antique flowers. Taller than the 'McKana' hybrid, it has smaller, more compact flowers with shorter spurs.*

one of well-rotted manure. Amend the soil so that its pH is from 6.0 to 6.8.

When choosing perennials, consider: height, blooming time, flower color, foliage, light requirements, and which plants grow best in your area. Cultivars, specially bred varieties of specific plants, often have unusual characteristics and disease or drought resistance. If ordering by mail, order early so that plants arrive in plenty of time and your choices are not sold out. Perennials may also be planted in fall with a 6-inch mulch to prevent winter damage. Some gardeners grow their perennials from seed; start them indoors, preferably in a greenhouse, in midwinter, and plant seedlings outdoors in late spring. Seeds can also be sown outdoors after the last frost, though flowers will not appear until the following summer.

Perennial plants can be purchased ei-

ther bareroot or potted. If your bareroot plant looks dry, as it may if it has been shipped, soak it overnight in a pail of water before planting. Dig a hole twice the size of the plant's roots. Fill the hole half full with water. Mix a handful of compost or peat moss with the soil from the hole, and sprinkle a small amount of this back in the hole. Set the plant so that its crown—where the stem meets the roots—is at ground level. Fill in the hole, pressing soil firmly with your foot to eliminate air pockets, which dry out the roots.

To remove perennials from pots, turn upside down in one hand with your fingers across the soil on either side of the stem. Hold the pot with your other hand and gently tap its rim on a hard surface; the plant and its soil will slip out neatly. Place in a hole 2 inches larger than the root ball. Fill in with a mixture of soil

and compost, pressing firmly to remove air pockets.

Deeply water newly planted perennials daily for two weeks unless it rains. Once established, perennial gardens require minimal attention. Most perennials need to be divided every three to four years when they develop overgrown clumps.

In spring, spread bonemeal and well-rotted manure or compost around—but not touching—new growth; work this into the soil to a depth of a few inches,

taking care not to damage roots. Deadhead spent flowers and you will prolong the bloom time of most perennials. I like the look of my bed without a summer mulch; placing plants close, but not crowding, cuts down on the number of weeds to pull. In fact, I have had bad luck with summer mulches of wood chips and buckwheat hulls around my perennials. Slugs seemed to find the wood chips an ideal hideout, and I discovered a mold last year when I used the buckwheat hulls that caused my soil to lose vitality.

In fall, when the flower stalks have turned brown, cut them back to about 2 inches and remove all debris (except diseased) to the compost pile. Apply a fall mulch of compost and straw or hay. When cold weather arrives, I mulch again with a 6-inch layer of evergreen boughs to prevent frost heave.

LEFT: *Two delicate Iceland poppies among plantings of Sweet William ('Dunnets Dark Crimson'). Sweet Williams belong to the* Dianthus *family, which also includes carnations and pinks.*
ABOVE: *The purplish-blue spiderwort, or* Tradescantia, *can be a bit of a garden pest, since it grows only too well anywhere; the new, compact hybrids—white, rosy red, pale blue, or pale pink—are more manageable.*
RIGHT: *The foxglove, a biennial that reseeds itself, is another old-fashioned flower. This healthy* Digitalis purpurea *'Giant Shirley English' has spotted bell-shaped blossoms cascading down a 3-foot stem. Note the buckwheat-hull mulch— excellent for retarding weeds, but also for encouraging mold, I discovered.*

Irises

THERE ARE TWO HUNDRED SPECIES OF iris and thousands of officially named cultivars; I think I have a few unofficial cultivars in my garden, thanks again to Fred Specht, who donated irises from the von Rebay garden that do not seem to match the colors or forms in any catalogue.

These perennials are perhaps most easily categorized as bearded and beardless, growing from rhizome or bulb rootstock. Flowers generally have 3 upright petals, or standards, alternating with 3 downward-curving falls. All prefer a sunny site in rich, well-drained soil.

BEARDED IRIS. Dwarf, intermediate, and tall, often called flags. Bloom late spring to early summer in a wide range of colors. "Beards" or hairs decorate the falls and long flat swordlike leaves form dramatic fan shapes that remain green through the fall. Plant rhizomes or fleshy roots 18 inches apart in slightly acidic or alkaline soil in early fall. Prepare soil and place rhizome horizontally 1 inch deep, spreading the roots over mounded earth. Cover lightly and water well. Fertilize in early spring and after flowering with bonemeal or superphosphate; add an additional sprinkling of potash in spring.

In late fall after leaves have browned, cut them back just above ground level. Every 3 to 4 years in early spring or late summer, overcrowded clumps need to be divided. Cut back leaves to 3 inches. Lift the whole clump and remove soil with a gentle spray of water. Use a sharp knife to divide sections from the central rhizome, with at least one bud or eye and roots on each. Check for iris borer (a cream-colored dark-headed moth larvae). If present, it is best to discard rhizomes. Check soil for larvae and destroy.

SIBERIAN IRIS. Beardless with purple, white, rose, or blue flowers, 2 to 3 blooms on each 3- to 4-foot stem. Tall grasslike foliage. Blooms at the same time as tall bearded iris. Rhizomes (smaller than bearded) need moist, slightly acid soil. Plant early spring when dormant, or early fall. Place horizontally; avoid crowding roots. Rarely needs division. Can be grown from seed. Remarkably pest-free. Fertilize in early spring and summer after flowering with complete fertilizer or bonemeal.

HIGO OR JAPANESE IRIS. Beardless; has been cultivated for 500 years. Blooms later than bearded and Siberian. Flowers,

ABOVE LEFT AND RIGHT: *My bearded iris border was created by accident. I asked my helpers to thin out large iris clumps in another part of the garden; misunderstanding, they dug up every iris in all the borders and presented me with bushels and bushels of rhizomes. So we made a long, narrow border right in front of the climbing roses, and edged it with* Viola *'Lac de Zurich'. The following spring, we had this wonderful garden.*

up to 10 inches across, in blues, whites, pinks, and red-purples, can be crinkled with intricate patterning; petals often overlap; large drooping falls. Single, double, and multipetaled; 3-foot stems produce many flowers. Plant rhizomes in early spring or fall; can grow in bogs or enriched slightly acidic soil with ample watering during the growing season; year-round mulch of well-rotted manure, pine needles, or oak leaves improves the soil and keeps it moist. Divide every 3 to 4 years in early spring into sections with 3 or 4 leaf fans. Keep moist until replanting. Fertilize in early spring with complete fertilizer or bonemeal. Hardier than the bearded; more disease-resistant. Can be grown from seed.

IRIS RETICULATA. Tiny inexpensive bulbs—a miniature species that blooms at winter's end in violet-blue with slender petals. Narrow, upright leaves grow to 1½ feet before dying in spring. Fertilize with 5-10-5 as flowering wanes and water if dry. Allow leaves to die back.

DUTCH IRIS. Bulbous iris with blue, purple, white, yellow, bronze, or bicolored flowers on 2-foot stems. Flowering coincides with bearded. Most famous is the blue 'Wedgwood' with a splash of yellow, sold in florist's shops for cut flowers. Plant in early fall, 3 to 4 inches deep. Not as hardy as other irises, excellent for forcing. Mulch in winter with 6-inch cover of evergreen boughs.

Great clumps of 'New Moon' iris bloom amid spearmint and Icelandic poppies. After their blossoms wane, the irises will be dug up, separated, and replanted so they can flower more extravagantly next May.

ABOVE: *The 'Royal Trumpeter' iris is velvety maroon, exceptionally smooth and silky, with a bronze beard and overlapping standards.*
BELOW: *'Tanya' is a bitone iris. An ocher-yellow standard with purplish-greenish falls, it grows tall—34 inches.*

ABOVE: *'Lacy Snowflake' iris among the shasta daisies. I like the way the pure white petals and yellow beards of the iris reiterate the daisy coloration.*
BELOW: *A closeup of 'New Moon'. When unfurling, the blooming head is quite pointy.*

ABOVE: *'Pacific Panorama' is the 1965 Van Dykes medal winner, as impressive, as the judges said, "as the Pacific Ocean." Its blue-lavender hue is very unusual.*
BELOW: *'Mascara', one of my favorites, is nearly black, silky smooth with very deep blue-black beards.*

LEFT: *I am holding a 'Stepping Out' iris; its extra large, stylishly ruffled blooms make this a spectacular addition to indoor arrangements. Outdoors, the plants are very well branched, and when growing together they can create wonderful groupings. The New York Yankees baseball cap is an excellent sun protector: I always wear sunscreen and a hat in the garden at this time of year.*

OVERLEAF, LEFT: *Bearded irises grow tall and strong, blooming even before the Oriental poppies.*

OVERLEAF, CENTER: Iris sibirica *'Blue Burgee' grow quickly into huge clumps. The annual feeding of superphosphate causes the stems to attain heights of about 30 to 36 inches. The clumps must be dug and divided every four years or so.*

OVERLEAF, RIGHT: *Shasta daisies, Siberian irises, Oriental poppies, and lamb's ears all thrive together in the May garden.*

Peonies

PEONIES ARE DIVIDED INTO TWO groups: herbaceous or soft-stemmed, which die back to ground level each winter, and tree peonies, which are woody-stemmed shrubs. It's a distinction I don't easily forget—not since the year there was a mix-up and all the tree peonies were pruned to the ground. After tearful phone calls to White Flower Farm, I learned that while the trees would never be trees again, they would grow back from their root stock as bushy herbaceous peonies. Indeed they have, and they bloom almost as profusely as before the massacre—albeit with a different growing habit.

Herbaceous peonies grow about 3 feet tall, and have nicely colored and textured leaves throughout the growing season. The mostly fragrant flowers—up to 5 inches across—can be white, cream, pink, red, purple, rose, even yellow. Double-flowered varieties are the most popular, but there are also single, anemone, and semi-double-flowered peonies and Japanese peonies with a single row of large petals.

The double-flowered varieties produce heavy flowers requiring support. A flower ring is excellent for this; be sure to place it in early spring when the plant is still small. To encourage larger flowers, remove side buds and allow just the main flower bud to bloom.

Peonies like neutral soil that is well-drained in a sunny location; they also bloom well in partial shade. Once established, peonies can grow for more than a decade without division. Feed them an-

nually with a topdressing of bonemeal in early spring. The best time to plant peonies is in fall, also a good time to propagate by division if desired. In fall red buds will be visible on the roots. Dig up the clump with a fork, and gently wash with water to remove soil. If you set them in the shade for a few hours they become less brittle and easier to work with. Take a sharp knife and cut off sections of roots with 3 or more buds. Set them with the buds no more than 1½ inches below the surface, 3 feet apart, in a large hole where soil has been amended with well-rotted manure, compost, and a generous amount of superphosphate slightly below root level. Planting peonies too deep may inhibit flowering. Mulch them with evergreen boughs the first winter.

Botrytis blight is most destructive during wet periods. (Single-flowered varieties are less apt to be affected by damp weather conditions.) Sanitation is the best antidote. Remove blackened young shoots, buds, flowers, and leaves as soon

TOP RIGHT: *Siberian irises are an intense foil for the Oriental poppy 'Carmine' and the rose-pink tree peony 'Hanakisoi'.*
CENTER RIGHT: *Tree peonies have a very different growing habit from their herbaceous cousin; the leaves are smoother and more deeply cut, and the buds pointier.*
RIGHT: *A Japanese double tree peony, 'Shinkagura'. I try to pick the blooms before rain; dampness shortens their life.*
OPPOSITE: *Mid-May is a wonderful time to create flower arrangements from the garden: this large blue bowl quickly filled up with blossoms of rhododendron, azalea, lilac, bearded iris, tree peony, allium, wisteria, and columbine.*

ABOVE: *A pressed glass compote filled with herbaceous peonies, 'Bridal Shower', 'Bridal Icing', and 'Chiffon Parfait'.*
RIGHT: *These double pink herbaceous peonies, 'Bessie', were not supported by a peony ring, and the weight of their huge blossoms drags them to the ground.*

as seen; enclose them in a bag immediately to restrict spreading the fungus through released spores, and dispose of the bag carefully.

Tree peonies were once restricted by law to the gardens of those of wealth and position in China. Native to the mountains of western China and Tibet, they have been hybridized, creating an array of colors—from pure whites to yellows, pinks, reds, and lavenders. Cultivars propagated today are grafted on the roots of the more common herbaceous or "perennial" peony.

Flowers are single, double, or semi-double. Petals are crinkly, often fringed, with a silk texture. The foliage is gray-green and deeply cut. In spring the deciduous leaves open reddish-green, continue through summer with a bluish cast and often turn reddish again before dropping in the autumn. Even during winter dormany, tree peonies reveal a beautiful structure of delicate, sometimes twisted branches.

Tree peonies are many-branched shrubs. Woody stems do not die back each autumn, nor should they be cut. Prune only to remove dead or unwanted branches. Growth is slow: it will take 4 or 5 years for a tree peony to reach its full

LEFT: *Single and Japanese peonies are not as lushly heavy as the doubles, but have a more delicate beauty. This is a Japanese peony, 'Fantastic', one of my favorites for flower arrangements. The earlier the peony blooms, and the cooler the weather, the longer the flowers will last.*

size of 4 to 5 feet, but the plants are long-lived. They do prefer protected, sunny conditions in a well-drained, manured soil with a neutral pH; choose a site several feet from other plantings. They do not transplant well; fall is the recommended season to give roots time to become established before the ground freezes. If you must plant in spring, be sure to purchase a container-grown, not bareroot, tree.

Dig a large hole about 2 feet deep and just as wide; mix the soil from the hole with compost before refilling. Set your tree peony so that the junction where the stem is grafted to the roots is well below the soil line—about 5 inches—to minimize the chance of reversion to the herbaceous understock. While becoming established, these slow-growers may bloom poorly. Have patience; they will be worth the wait.

Tree peonies are relatively disease- and pest-resistant; during wet weather be alert for fungal problems. Annually, after they have flowered, sprinkle bonemeal around the plant base without touching the plant and scratch it into the soil. Some of the heavier, double-flowering tree peony cultivars require staking to prevent breakage.

RIGHT: *It takes just two blossoms of a full double pink tree peony, 'Yatsukajishi', to overpower a pottery pitcher. I have successfully stored peony buds, wrapped in cellophane, in the refrigerator for up to a month before placing them in water to bloom. The buds open in two or three days, and the flowers last in cool rooms for up to a week.*

ABOVE: *When I cut peonies, or any flower with very fragile petals, I try to keep the blooms separate until I can arrange them. Here I've used an old wooden bread board.*

LEFT: *'Honey Gold' is perhaps one of America's most sought-after peonies. Strong, upright stems bear double white blooms with butter-colored centers.*

ABOVE: 'Kinshi', 'Kinkaku' and 'Age of Gold' yellow tree peonies are tightly packed into an antique yellowware bowl.

LEFT: 'Bridal Gown', a herbaceous peony with pure white petals, makes a superb cut flower.

TOP LEFT: *Blooming long before less hardy annuals, pansies are a useful, colorful filler for bare spots in the spring garden; this cultivar 'Ullswater Blue' has a particularly attractive face.*
FAR LEFT: *Meadow buttercups* (Ranunculus montanus *'Molten Gold') growing amid California poppies* (Eschscholzia californica) *and early shoots of the bee balm* (Monarda didyma *'Croftway Pink').*
CENTER LEFT: *'Majestic Giants' hybrids grow about 6 inches high and will bloom all summer if dead blooms are pinched off.*
BOTTOM LEFT: *Grown in deeply dug and well-composted soil, these 'Bowles Black' violas* (Viola nigra) *are self-seeding and prolific.*
FAR LEFT: *Many of my brick-edged walkways are planted with violas; these are* Viola tricolor, *also known as Johnny Jump-ups.*
OPPOSITE: *A favorite pottery bowl filled with flowering chives, santolina, dill, nasturtiums, and pansies, all grown in the greenhouse for early blooming.*

Bowls of freshly cut purple rhododendrons adorn the corner of my studio kitchen. The enamel-topped table is covered with an assortment of green and amethyst Depression glass, ready to set a luncheon table. Little glasses hold columbines, pansies, and buttercups.

ABOVE: *A whiteware bowl is filled with long-stemmed pansies from the iris border. The arrangement meets with the approval of Oblomov, the giant blue Persian cat.*
RIGHT: *I use my little office in the house to store all of my flower containers. The shelves hold my McCoy collection, wire and metal frogs, and florists' materials.*

OVERLEAF: *At this time of year, we live outdoors, dining alfresco when we can. By the white wooden gate to the pool garden, the table is set for afternoon iced tea, with opalescent hobnail goblets and heart-shaped cookies. A big copper bain marie is filled with blue and purple flowers: pansies, bearded iris, Siberian iris, and columbines.*

Menu

CAMPFIRE SKILLET TROUT
WITH SAUTÉED VEGETABLES
RHUBARB TARTLETS

Campfire Skillet Trout with Sautéed Vegetables

SERVES 4

I was brought up trout fishing in New Jersey, and I have always liked trout best when they are sautéed, outdoors, right over a campfire in an iron skillet with butter and olive oil. I prefer using slightly unusual ingredients, like imported mushrooms and radicchio, but more common fare like yellow onions and new potatoes tastes equally fantastic.

2-3 small rainbow trout, cleaned with heads left on
   Fresh sage, thyme, and oregano
1 bunch flat-leaf parsley
1 bunch chives
   Juice of 1 lemon
½ cup olive oil
12 small new potatoes, unpeeled, boiled, and cut in half
2 red onions, cut into ½-inch-thick slices
2 Japanese eggplants, sliced ¼-inch thick
6 large shiitake mushrooms
2 heads radicchio, cut in half
   Salt and freshly ground pepper

1. Stuff the cavity of each fish with fresh herbs and sprinkle with lemon juice. Tie trout in three places using kitchen string.

OPPOSITE ABOVE: *You can cook the fish and vegetables together, as we did, if you have a large enough pan (I found this huge cast-iron skillet at an antiques sale). We cooked the meal over an open fire, but the dish is almost as good on the stove.*
OPPOSITE BELOW: *The tarts are decorated with rhubarb "leaves" made from leftover pâte brisée.*

2. In a large frying pan, preferably cast-iron, heat the oil. Arrange the potatoes, cut side down, on one side of the pan and onions, eggplants, and mushrooms on the other side. Sprinkle with additional sage and thyme. As the vegetables brown, turn and brown the other side.
3. Add a bit more olive oil to the pan if needed. Place trout in the middle of pan, add radicchio, and sauté for 5 minutes on each side, or until the fish is tender and the meat is white. Season with salt and pepper. Serve immediately.

Rhubarb Tartlets

MAKES 8 4-INCH TARTLETS

I used 4-inch pans with heavily fluted edges to make these tartlets plump and generous. Stewed rhubarb can be extra good if the fruit is first macerated in sugar for six or eight hours, then gently cooked so the pieces don't fall apart.

Tartlet Shells
2½ cups all-purpose flour
1 teaspoon salt
1 teaspoon sugar (optional)
1 cup (2 sticks) unsalted butter, chilled and cut into small pieces
¼-½ cup ice water

Filling
3 cups rhubarb, cut into ½-inch pieces
¾ cup sugar
3 tablespoons Grand Marnier
   Grated zest of 1 tangerine or orange
   Juice of 1 tangerine or orange
3 tablespoons all-purpose flour

Egg Glaze
1 large egg
2 tablespoons heavy cream

1. To make the tartlet shells, put the flour, salt, and sugar, if desired, in the bowl of a food processor. Add the butter and process for 10 seconds, or just until the mixture resembles coarse meal.
2. With the motor running, add the ice water, drop by drop, through the feed tube. Add enough water so that the dough holds together without being wet or sticky; do not process for more than 30 seconds.
3. Turn the dough out onto a large piece of plastic wrap. Press dough into a flat circle; wrap in the plastic and chill for at least one hour.
4. Lightly spray the tartlet pans with nonstick vegetable spray. On a lightly floured board, roll out the pastry to a thickness of ⅛ inch. Cut into pieces just slightly larger than the tartlet pans. Place pastry in tartlet pans and press into the bottoms and along sides. Trim and crimp the edges. Use any leftover pastry scraps for decorations. Chill until ready to use.
5. Preheat the oven to 350°.
6. Combine all the filling ingredients in a large bowl. Fill individual tart shells with the mixture. Decorate the tops with pastry rhubarb leaves. Mix the egg and cream, and brush the leaves and the pastry edges with the egg glaze.
7. Bake until the rhubarb is tender and the crust is nicely browned, 25 to 35 minutes. Let cool before serving.

FRIENDS OFTEN ACCUSE ME OF WORKING TOO HARD in the garden, of spending too much time on my hands and knees, but to me, this type of "labor" is relaxing and most enjoyable. A real garden is unrelenting in demands on the gardener's time: there is always something that has to be done—another plot to fill, a new bed to dig, a patch to weed. June is the month of most concentrated work: I must be vigilant in protecting the plants from diseases and pests. It is also a time when the true harvest begins, rewarding all our efforts. In June, we gather the early new vegetables, the white, red, and yellow baby beets, the sugar snaps and edible pods, the tenderest lettuces and most delicate herbs. The foxgloves, delphiniums, hollyhocks, and astilbes are at their best; the rose bushes and trellises are weighted with heavily scented blooms. ❧ I try very hard not to travel during this time because I really don't want to miss a thing that is going on. Weekends are for entertaining: I try to have one dinner and one lunch for my friends so they can see the garden. Menus are planned around what is growing; I often send guests home with armloads of fresh fruits, herbs, and vegetables. Just as I love the contemplative, quiet times in the garden during the winter months, I love the sharing in the summer.

ABOVE: *In this quadrant of the vegetable garden, the last to be planted, I grow carrots, chards, and basils; the armload of rhubarb will be stewed, baked with cream, or transformed into pies.*
OPPOSITE: *The vegetable garden is truly a splendid sight. The 'Crimson Glory' hybrid tea climbing roses on the trellis are a superb backdrop for the tall, yellow-flowering dill and the strong-leafed cabbages: 'Early Green', 'Red Drumhead', and 'Saturn Hybrid'.*

J U N E

JOURNAL

Vegetable planting continued.

Nasturtiums and sunflowers planted.

Roses sprayed again (rain has brought black spot).

Herb garden replanted with new seedlings.

Tomato seedlings planted out; surplus given away.

Roses secured to trellises with cord.

General fertilizer applied in perennial borders (too much rain leached soil of nutrients).

New rose garden bordered with bluestone.

Greenhouse emptied and cleaned.

Perennials ordered from nurseries.

Blue flax edging for rose beds planted.

First strawberries, *Fraises des Bois,* golden raspberries, black, white, and red currants picked.

Baby turkeys arrive.

Broccoli picked.

Spent perennials deadheaded and cut back.

Old, infested iris bed replanted with peony, catmint, blue salvia, and pink lavender.

Field mowed twice to bring long grass under control.

First lettuce crop fed to chickens (too mature).

New lettuce seedlings planted.

RIGHT: *The lawns need frequent mowings. In the lower vegetable garden, dirt paths are covered with grass cuttings to prevent the walkways from becoming too muddy.*

Pest and Disease Prevention and Control

LIKE ALL GARDENERS, I DO CONSTANT battle with pests and disease. One year my garden had an intense infestation of whitefly; the next season all the fruit trees were visited by a rusty mildew that made the green leaves appear dusted with gloom. Taken one at a time, these problems were easily solved: the whiteflies were washed away with three applications of soapy water; the mildew was sprayed with a copper fungicide. But a garden that is fraught with too many pests becomes onerous—and I dislike having to use chemicals. (I would prefer an entirely natural garden, but in our congested area, disease and pest control is necessary.) So I practice what I call "preventative gardening," taking great care in the way I grow things, and relying a good deal on my animals—from the bees to the dogs—to help me.

The best way to discourage harmful insects and diseases is to maintain a healthy soil by replenishing nutrients, providing adequate water, never crowding plants, and weeding regularly. If you follow these procedures, your garden will grow vigorously and be better able to resist attacks from insects and diseases.

The ideal garden is one in which nature is encouraged to participate. In winter the chickens are given free range of my garden—their scratching feet and pecking bills vigilantly attack overwintering insects, and they also attract other hungry birds. Dogs are deterrents for deer, woodchucks, raccoons, rabbits, and other woods animals. Cats are natural enemies of moles, squirrels, and other small rodents. Some gardeners introduce beneficial insects, such as ladybugs and praying mantis (both can now be ordered by mail) for biological pest control. Companion planting (putting plants that repel certain pests next to those that attract them) is also to be considered.

Literature abounds on natural control and much new exciting research is being conducted; the more you read about and understand pest and disease problems, the better you will cope. Those concerned about environmental issues will find the many organic books published by Rodale Press in Emmaus, Pennsylvania, a good beginning. If no natural method works for you, ask your local U.S. Cooperative Extension Service, local nursery, or botanical garden for other controls; be sure to understand their potential effect on your environment and what precautions you need to follow.

Garden Diseases

Plant diseases are spread by insects, tools, hands, and smoke. They can be fungal, bacterial, or viral. Some are stress induced—from lack of nutrients or water (use soaker hoses, never overhead spray, to avoid humid conditions which can create fungal problems). Others result after plants have been bruised by people or lawn mowers. Overcrowding and poor air circulation encourage disease.

Good garden clean-up substantially reduces the potential for diseases, which overwinter. Whenever possible, buy disease-resistant varieties. When plants are

ABOVE: *Before transplanting the last lettuce seedlings from the greenhouse to the raised beds, I rake each cultivated square.*
BELOW: *With the handle of the heart hoe as a guide, I dig holes about 8 inches apart.*

BELOW: *Each oak-leaf lettuce is placed gently in its hole; I take care not to disturb the roots unnecessarily. The soil is pulled around each upright seedling to give support as the lettuce grows.*

ABOVE: *When I want to make a straight furrow longer than the hoe handle, I push two stakes into the ground and stretch a cord taut between them.*

ABOVE: *The onion seeds were sown in plastic plug trays in the greenhouse; now 6 inches tall, they are ready to move outdoors to the raised beds, where the soil is being carefully raked and prepared for planting.*

ABOVE: *Dragging a heart hoe along the string, I create a furrow of exactly the right depth for the onions, 3 inches.*

diseased, promptly remove infected portions. In the case of viruses, it is wise to destroy the whole plant. Disinfect pruners and wash your hands after working with infected plants. For some diseases organic fungicides, such as Bordeaux mixture, copper sulfate, or sulfur, can be helpful when sprayed on leaves. These fungicides need to be used with caution; read labels carefully as some can damage plants at certain times of the year, during specific weather conditions, or when used with other sprays.

POWDERY MILDEW is a common fungal disease that thrives in humid conditions. The upper surface of leaves, young shoots, buds, and flowers become covered with a whitish talclike coating. Growth becomes dwarfed. Remove and destroy infected parts. Mulching and soil watering will help reduce this problem.

LEAF SPOT OR BLIGHT, a bacterial disease, causes black or brown irregular spots on leaves, which wither. Humid conditions make plants vulnerable. Rotate crops; prune and destroy affected branches of shrubs and trees in fall.

MOSAIC VIRUS affects many vegetables—cucumbers, tomatoes, lettuce, squash, peppers—and raspberries. Yellowed, mottled foliage and stunted growth are signs of the virus, which is often transmitted by aphids. Remove and destroy infected plants.

LEFT: *By placing the onion seedlings about 3 inches apart and mounding the soil up on both sides, I can guarantee a sizeable result without wasted space. Roscoe the cat, one of my very best garden companions, examines the work closely.*

ABOVE: *Bush bean seeds are planted at 2½-inch intervals, in furrows approximately 1½ inches deep and 8 inches apart.*

ABOVE: *Using my favorite hoe, I cover the seeds lightly with earth by pulling the sides of the furrow inward.*

ABOVE: *I also plant beans in double rows so that the plants support each other.*

ABOVE: *I use a rigid grass rake to tamp down the soil over the seeds; this will secure them in place and make the bed very neat and even.*

ABOVE: *I plant herbs and vegetables in successive waves so as to have a steady supply throughout the summer.*
LEFT: *While seedlings and larger seeds need holes or trenches, the tiniest seeds, like lettuce, do not. The handle of the hoe makes a drill of just the right depth.*
RIGHT: *A ¼ inch of covering soil—just a dusting—is all these lettuce seeds need to germinate quickly and successfully. Roscoe stays by my side for hours in the garden.*

ABOVE: *Borders of Verdura kale, a frost-resistant Dutch variety, surround a portion of the large vegetable garden.*
LEFT: *Lemon-scented basil, sown straight into the ground in late May, must be thinned at about 3 inches tall.*
RIGHT: *Beet seeds are large, and I often sow them directly into the garden. The hardy seedlings sprout quickly; I thin them carefully by hand to encourage larger beets, adding the thinnings to stocks and soups.*

Common Garden Pests

A bit of detective work—checking your garden once a week during the growing season—and a rudimentary knowledge of insects and their habits helps in dealing with pests. Plants are harmed by chewing insects—such as beetles and caterpillars—and by sucking ones—aphids and whiteflies. Examine leaves, especially the undersides, and stems, and points where branches meet stems. Simple hygiene is of utmost importance; always wash your hands thoroughly after touching infected plants and wipe tools with alcohol.

APHIDS are tiny, usually green, sucking insects with an appetite for tender, new growth. They leave a sticky secretion and can transmit viral diseases. Remove with a strong spray of water or crush them with your thumb and fingers, taking care not to harm leaves or flower buds. Natural predators: ladybugs, lacewings, and praying mantis.

WHITEFLIES feed and lay eggs on the undersides of leaves; tiny, sucking insects appear to form clouds when disturbed. Insecticidal soap, a commercially manufactured "organic" control, sprayed directly on the insects is one remedy. Try hanging a yellow card coated with min-

LEFT: *I often transplant during a light rain, but never when it is very, very hot or very sunny: the tender seedlings must be protected from heat. These 'Sweet Genovese' basil seedlings will benefit from the extra sprinkling; transplanted among young cabbages, they will remain in place once the first row of early-maturing cabbages is harvested.*

eral oil in the infested area; whiteflies, attracted to yellow, become mired in the oil. Natural predators: ladybugs and lacewings.

SCALE, brown disk-shaped, waxy shells cover insects that suck sap from stems and undersides of leaves and secrete a sticky substance. Leaves yellow and drop. Rub off scales with a rough cloth. If plants are heavily infested, prune and destroy damaged parts. Natural predator: vedalia ladybug (for cottony cushion scale). Dormant-oil sprays, applied in early spring before leaf growth begins, can smother scale that has become a serious threat.

CATERPILLARS, moth and butterfly larvae, are voracious eaters. Cabbage worm, an inch-long bright green worm with a yellow-green stripe, is destructive to most members of the cabbage family. Look for ragged leaves and deposits of green excrement. In its mature form, it becomes a white butterfly with black spots that perpetuates the cycle by laying eggs at the base of leaves. Home remedies for the worms include regular handpicking or sprinkling cornmeal or a mixture of 2 parts flour and 1 part salt on wet plants, both of which are said to cause feeding caterpillars to swell and die. Natural predators: some birds and yellow jackets. Tomato hornworm is a large green caterpillar, up to 5 inches, with a horn at the rear. Holes in leaves and dark droppings indicate its presence. In spite of their size, they are difficult to spot. Spray with water and they begin to wiggle and reveal their hiding place. Pick off and destroy. Natural predators: grackles, sparrows, and other birds; praying man-

ABOVE: *A row of cabbage seedlings, planted behind the rhubarb just 15 days ago, pokes out of the soil*

ABOVE: *Young Brussels sprouts plants (these are about a month old) look like cauliflowers or loose-leaf cabbages.*

ABOVE: *A Chinese cabbage, 'Mei Qing Choi', ready to be harvested; steamed or stir-fried it will taste delicious.*

tis, assassin bugs, trichogramma wasps.

BEETLES attack flowers, fruits, or foliage, often eating the tissue and leaving only the skeletal veins. Japanese beetles—metallic green with reddish-brown wings—can destroy roses and fruit trees. In its grub stage—a whitish wormlike body with a brown head—it devours roots of lawns, and vegetables, such as beans, onions, and tomatoes.

THRIPS are tiny, slender amber or black sucking insects that cause leaves to scar and blister and flowers to drop; they also transmit viruses. They sprinkle leaves with tiny dark specks of excrement.

OVERLEAF, LEFT: *I plant several kinds of Brussels sprouts: 'Dolmic' (a very tall European type), 'Odette' (medium-sized sprouts in a pale green color that are well spaced on the stalk and easy to pick), and a rather new red type, 'Rubine', a late variety with the color of red cabbage—very hardy in the Northeast.*

OVERLEAF, CENTER: *The crinkly 'January King', a Savoy cabbage, is very hardy and productive and is harvested 115 days after planting; the leaves are excellent stuffed or braised.*

OVERLEAF, RIGHT: *This wavy-leaved 'Grenadier' cabbage, 70 days to maturity, is a very good, dense-headed early cabbage, juicy, crispy, with a sweet and delicate flavor; it is wonderful shredded in salads, sautéed in a bit of sweet butter with caramelized apples, or simmered with red wine and balsamic vinegar. The 'Red Drumhead' cabbage behind it is especially good for pickling. I plant about ten or twelve heads of half a dozen varieties of cabbage so that I have plenty available over many months.*

ABOVE: *The beautiful dark red stalks of 'New Valentine' rhubarb are a far cry from the sour, greenish stems my father grew in Nutley. The new types, reddish and sweet or light pink and delicate, are so good and need so little sugar that I cook it, bake it, or turn it into jams and chutneys regularly.*

ABOVE: *Chives flower during the months of May and June. When the purple ball-like blooms are fully open, I pick them with 6- to 8-inch stems, tie them into neat bunches, and hang the bunches upside-down in a cool, dry, dark place until they are totally dry.*

Remove infected plant parts; use a fine spray of water to dislodge them, concentrating on undersides of leaves. Insecticidal soap can be effective. Natural predators: lacewing.

SLUGS, soft-bodied mollusks up to 2 inches long, appear in early spring leaving slimy silvery trails. In daylight, they hide in moist dark places and feed at night making gaping holes in leaves—especially lettuce—and fruits. Almost every gardener has heard of beer traps; sink a shallow container, half full with beer (or a spoonful of baking yeast in about a quarter cup of water), into the ground. Slugs slither in and drown; replace liquid every few days and after rain. Or simply lay cabbage leaves or old boards in wet areas of the garden. Destroy the congregating slugs you find underneath. Rough surfaces are a deterrent—make borders of sand or scatter crushed eggshells to protect plants. Natural predators: robins, garter snakes, frogs, and toads.

Companion Planting

THIS IS A NATURAL METHOD OF PEST control. Much of it is folkloric, and what works in one area may not work in another due to variations in soil, pests, rainfall, and other weather conditions. But when you find a companion planting that is successful, you will swear by it. This method relies on scent, so crushing a leaf now and then will help deter pests. Here are just a few to test out.

MARIGOLDS perform well for me. I plant them around the perimeter of my vegetable garden. French *(Tagetes erecta)* and African marigolds *(T. patula)* as well as pot-marigolds *(Calendula officinalis)* are said to repel nematodes, tomato hornworm, and whiteflies. Some literature suggests marigolds must be grown in the garden for a few years to be effective against soil-borne nematodes that attack roots and cause bacterial infections.

NASTURTIUM *(Tropaeolum* sp.) is reputed to keep aphids at bay. In my garden I have success with nasturtium and parsley. The results were disastrous when I planted nasturtium with cabbage—both came under siege.

GARLIC *(Allium sativum)* deters aphids and is an excellent companion for corn, carrots, lettuce, tomatoes, and peas. Some gardeners claim it works against Japanese beetles.

MINT *(Mentha* sp.) is recommended with tomatoes to repel tomato hornworm, with radishes to discourage flea beetles, and with cabbage and broccoli to reduce white cabbage butterfly. It is also suggested to deter aphids.

BLUE SAGE *(Salvia farinacea* 'Victoria') planted with leaf crops, such as lettuce and spinach, works for me.

HORSERADISH *(Armoracia rusticana)* is said to keep away potato bugs.

RIGHT: *As 'New Dawn' and 'Blaze' roses cover the trellises, the vegetables are harvested and consumed, and the beds replanted with new seedlings or fresh seeds.*

ABOVE: *An elegant, anise-flavored vegetable of great delicacy, bulb fennel has become very popular in this country in recent years. Thinly sliced it is delicious in salads with arugula and parmesan cheese. I sauté it in olive oil with sun-dried tomatoes and garlic as a simple topping for pasta; sometimes I bake it or braise it in butter. Plant a good bulbing variety: 'Zefa Fino' is reliable, forming solid oval bulbs with a sweet, nutty flavor. Use the ferny, fragrant leaves as a stuffing for fish, or finely chopped in salads.*

OVERLEAF, LEFT: *Toward the end of June, the first planting of lettuces is almost mature. The leaves of the loose-headed types are almost too large, and the buttercrunches and Boston varieties have large roundish heads. Some of the plants have bolted, and they are pulled up by the roots and fed to the chickens, who delight in their daily feasts.*

OVERLEAF, RIGHT: *In the foreground, the dark green arugula has begun to flower. At this point the pungency of the leaves becomes too strong and the texture too tough to enjoy in salads, so that, too, is uprooted for the chickens. The roses bloom all through the month of June, and those climbers that have wintered over well are strong, profuse, and colorful.*

Salad Greens (and Reds)

I FIRST TASTED RADICCHIO IN ITALY, at a little restaurant near Florence's Boboli gardens. The tangy crimson leaves were so beautiful, and so tasty, I searched out its seeds and tried to grow it at home the following spring. All that emerged were spiky, dark green leaves with a bitter taste. I let the leaves fall to the ground; next spring, the first thing to emerge in the garden was a crop of tight round heads with white-veined deep red leaves; it was the 'Rossa di Verona' radicchio that I so much wanted to grow.

Radicchio seeds are now available in the United States, as are many other salad greens. I grow several varieties of lettuce, radicchio, and other greens, sowing them successively throughout the spring and summer. I start with seeds sown in flats in the greenhouse (the seedlings are transplanted at about 3 inches tall, when the weather is more clement), and later plant seeds directly into my raised beds. Always plant lettuces in rich, composty topsoil, and water frequently. The ideal temperature for germination is about 75 degrees; above 80, the seeds will become dormant. Sow the seeds sparsely and cover very lightly if planting directly into the ground, and thin gradually, using the tender thinnings for salad.

LEFT: *Homegrown salad greens so far surpass store-bought, and are so easy to grow, I encourage everyone to try a few varieties of lettuce and other greens, and to experiment with the results in recipes.*

Lettuces come in four basic types: looseleaf, butterhead, crisphead, and Cos or Romaine. 'Sucrine' is a tender-leaved butterhead.

Bibb lettuce, also called Limestone lettuce, is a very old butterhead variety bred by a Mr. Bibb of Kentucky.

Salad Bibb is a larger, more vigorous descendant of the original Bibb, with thicker, smoother leaves.

Mesclun, which I first found in Paris, is a mix of salad greens grown together and harvested young; I sow it every 3 weeks.

Arugula is the new name for Rocket, a strong-flavored old favorite that should be picked when 3 to 6 inches tall.

Mâche, also known as lamb's lettuce or feldsalat, was once a wild green, feasted on by grazing sheep.

'Ballon' is a very heat tolerant, loose-headed, tender Romaine; like all Romaines, it is a relatively slow grower, maturing at 75 days.

Montpelier is another Bibb-type lettuce with large, loose heads, excellent as the base for a big, green summer salad.

'Royal Oak Leaf' is properly a looseleaf or "cutting" lettuce which will form well-defined heads if carefully thinned.

'Winter Density' lettuce is a semi-Cos type, hardy even in very hot weather.

This 'Biondo Lisce' lettuce should have been picked when the leaves were smaller.

'Oak Leaf', a cutting lettuce, has a very delicate taste and texture.

'Black-Seeded Simpson' is one of the first looseleaf lettuces to mature.

Like all cutting lettuces, 'Loose Leaf Garnet' will resprout from a cut stem.

The firm heads of 'Buttercrunch' are excellent for filling with crab, lobster, or corn salad.

'Passion Blond' lettuce is a 'Buttercrunch'-like variety I first found in France.

'Lettuce Couper Salad Bowl' is a curly-leaved cutting lettuce.

'Pirat' is a loose butterhead lettuce whose leaves are mottled bronze at maturity.

In Europe, crispheads like this 'Red Grenobloise' are called "Batavian."

'Lolla Rosa' is an Italian loosehead with crinkly, almost ruffled leaves.

Radicchio, like this 'Palla Rossa' variety, is part of the chicory family.

'Rossa di Verona' radicchio will change color in the fall to the familiar red.

'Rouge d'Hiver' is an old French romaine lettuce, exceptionally hardy and beautiful.

'Red Salad Bowl' is an excellent mid-season looseleaf which will deepen in color.

'Rossa di Treviso' radicchio must be cut back in summer to produce red heads in the fall.

These 'Lettuce Continuity' seedlings are about 3 inches tall, ready for transplanting.

'Blond Passeuse' (foregound) has transplanted well and will form heads.

ABOVE: *Peas should be planted about 1 inch deep at the base of wire fencing; I like to have the seeds in the ground by March 17—St. Patrick's Day—the time when I also plant the flowering sweet peas.*

LEFT: *Bean seeds are satisfying to plant, especially for children, as the plants seem to grow tall and strong immediately. I grow them in double rows, which will appear to be one thick phalanx at maturity.*

ABOVE: *My favorite broccolis are 'Packman' and 'Emperor'; sprouting types include 'Calabrese', 'White Sprouting', 'Purple Sprouting', and broccoli raab. The trellis bears edible podded peas like 'Carouby de Maussane', and taller growing sugar snaps like 'Super Sugar Mel'. I still love the old-fashioned 'Lincoln' shelling pea, and always plant at least one row for summer suppers.*

Shade Garden

THE SHADE GARDEN WAS REALLY designed to experiment with a challenging combination of conditions in one spot on my property. The soil was incredibly rich at the bottom of the hill on the north side of the gardens, and yet, because the trees had grown so tall and densely branched, there was not enough light to cultivate ordinary plants. In addition, this patch borders the nature sanctuary next door, and deer and other creatures constantly came to forage, emboldened by the knowledge that they could easily jump the fence to safety, leaving my chow chow guardians on the other side.

Tree pruners were enlisted to take out small saplings and thin out the canopy of branches enshrouding the ground. What a difference that made! Filtered light shone through, and hostas, azaleas, and ferns thrived. Within three years, a very nice shade garden, really a woodland garden, was established.

Grassy paths and wood chip–mulched beds are easily maintained, and but for small nibblings by the ever-present deer, the plants have all survived, except the rhododendrons, which for some reason are more appealing to the deer than anything else. The chows are learning to keep the large creatures at bay, and the mild winters have made foraging outside of the sanctuary less of an imperative. Each year I add bleeding hearts, or lilies-of-the-valley, or ginger plants, or toad lilies to the garden to see if they will thrive in the shade. Primulas, daffodils, and astilbes all do exceptionally well.

ABOVE: *When I was growing up, hostas were called "plantain lilies" and were ignored by serious gardeners. Nowadays they are valued for their beautifully textured leaves and sprays of delicate flowers, and for their ability to thrive in dense shade.* This Hosta plantaginea 'Grandiflora' *is even somewhat heat resistant; in late summer it will send up tall stalks of sweet-scented waxy white flowers.*
BELOW: *A 'Gilbraltar' azalea; a half day of sunlight and an acid soil will produce a healthy blooming shrub.*

ABOVE: *Hostas love the rich, peaty soil of my shade garden. Hosta fortunei 'Francee' has an especially lovely variegated leaf, with an edge of silver beading. With relatively little care, it will produce lavender bell-shaped flowers toward summer's end.*
RIGHT: *The success of the shade garden leads me to expand it each year. Here are newly planted azaleas, 'Golden Peace' and 'Gilbraltar', flowering beneath the trees.*
BELOW: *Like many other "woodland" flowers, columbines thrive in the shade. 'Dragon Fly' is blooming profusely.*

ABOVE: *Bright pink hydrangeas grow here and there in the garden. These were given as house gifts and planted outdoors after the initial blooming. I never expected them to survive, but these Hydrangea 'Niedersachsen' are thriving.*

RIGHT: *I greatly enjoy filling in the bare spots in my gardens with perennials homegrown from seed. On an overcast day, I divided salvia and foxglove and dug them into the beds around the pool. Tonka, one of the two Tonkinese cats who ultimately went to live with friends (my older cats refused to accept the newcomers), loved gardening and often kept me company.*

OPPOSITE PAGE, TOP: *In June these pool-garden beds are quite spectacular—the geraniums, sea holly, and iris are blooming and the bee balm, phlox, and veronica are just about to attain their prime.*

OPPOSITE PAGE, BOTTOM: *I love perennial hardy geraniums. They are prized in my garden for their summer-long blooming habit and their attractive foliage. Also known as Cranesbill, or more formally as Geranium Wallichianum 'Buxton's Blue', this is the true geranium.*

ABOVE: *Veronica and late-blooming azaleas from the shade garden are displayed in my prized copper lustre decorated yellow ware batter bowl. The tea service in the foreground is also copper lustre, probably early American.*

RIGHT: *In late June, the Higo iris begin to flower atop tall straight stems in an amazingly varied and unusual color palette. Iris Kaempferi, or Japanese iris, Higo strain, are known as the queen of all iris cultivars; the petals have a crêpelike texture, and are often striped and shaded and multitoned. This Japanese iris, Aoi-No-Ue, is arranged with white foxgloves, tiger lilies, pink astilbe, wild white Berteroa incana 'Prominent' grandiflora roses, and blue campanula.*

OPPOSITE: *Another arrangement composed of centifolia roses, astilbe, campanula, phlox, delphinium, larkspur, veronica, yarrow, and scabiosa.*

Drying Flowers

JUNE IS ALSO A BUSY MONTH FOR saving blooms for future use. I have been experimenting with drying—in air and in silica gel—with wonderful results.

For success in drying flowers, gather them right before their prime—when they are not quite fully opened (they will open more during drying the process). Pick them on non-rainy days in the morning after the dew has burned off, but before the sun begins to wilt the blossoms. Treat them immediately. Keep drying flowers out of direct sunlight to prevent fading, and away from humidity. AIR DRY METHOD. The old-fashioned and simplest method is air drying. Cut flowers to desired lengths, and strip foliage from the lower portion of stems. I like to maintain a leaf or two because a flower without foliage looks unnatural. Make bunches of the same kind of flower, three or less, and tie firmly with cotton string—the stems shrink with drying. Too-large bunches can cause mold. Large and multistemmed flowers, such as cockscomb, lunaria, and delphinium, are dried singly.

Hang flowers upside down from attic rafters or in a cupboard or room that is warm, dark, and airy. You can use clothes drying racks or my favorite, antique quilt racks. Different flowers take varying times to dry—anywhere from three to six weeks. Globe amaranth, rose, lunaria, marigold, zinnia, thyme, sage, even poppy seed pods are among the plants I air dry. Dill and statice can be dried simply—upright in a vase. SILICA-GEL METHOD. Certain delicate and more fleshy flowers are best dried in silica gel—water-absorbent crystals. These crystals are usually sold at garden and floral centers and in craft stores. You will need an airtight container; a metal box with a cover is ideal, but you can seal almost anything with heavy-duty plastic wrap.

Strip all but desired foliage from the flower stem. Half fill the box with silica gel (preferably wearing cotton gloves to protect hands). Set the flower, blossom up, gently into the gel. With your fingers, trickle gel slowly on the blossom until it is covered. Using a spoon or a toothpick, separate the petals and allow gel to settle into the flowers. Position the blossom naturally. Tightly close the container and keep it in a dry, warm spot. Flowers feel crisp when ready, in a week or more. Do only one kind of flower at a time, as drying times differ. The crystals are reusable.

Microwaving speeds this process. A glass is an excellent container; fill it about three-quarters full with silica gel. Push the flower stem, one to a glass, into the gel, allowing the blossom to rest on top of the crystals. Gently cover the flower head with more gel. Place in a microwave along with a separate cup of water. Heat at full power for a minute. Larger flowers require as much as three minutes. Experiment with timing. Let stand at least ten minutes before pouring out crystals and removing the flower. Cool gel before reusing.

Carnations, pansies, lilies, daffodils, pansies, roses, peonies, lilacs, chrysanthemums, and clematis are some of the flowers I dry in silica gel.

ABOVE: *I am just now succeeding with silica gel drying, which gives superb results if one has patience and delicate hands. I have dried peonies, poppies, delphiniums, and even single roses.*

ABOVE: *Flowers must be gently placed in the silica gel and little by little additional gel must be spooned between each petal of the flower so that the drying process can occur perfectly. Each flower has an optimum time it can remain in the gel and each bloom must be removed at the correct time or it will become too brittle to pick up. This whole process must be carefully practiced and only by trial and error can one succeed.*
OPPOSITE: *Old laundry racks and blanket racks are great for tying bunches of lavender, salvia, and poppy pods to dry. Flowers should be dried in a dark, warm, airy place (I use the attic) in order to preserve their colors as much as possible.*

ABOVE: *Amid lavender and salvia I also dry poppy pods. Upside down, the stems are straightened by the weight of flower heads.*
LEFT: *I air dry full-blown peonies by hanging them on racks; roses and rosebuds also dry well this way, though the color will not remain quite true and the petals do shrivel a bit.*

Menu

DILL FETTUCINE WITH POACHED SALMON

HERB-ZUCCHINI SAUTÉ

SPICED PEACH ICE CREAM

SPICED PEACHES IN WHITE WINE SYRUP

Dill Fettucine with Poached Salmon

SERVES 4

Flavored pastas are colorful and delicious. Here I've added finely chopped fresh dill to the pasta dough.

Dill Fettucine

3½ cups all-purpose flour
1 teaspoon salt
5 large eggs
1 tablespoon olive oil
⅓ cup finely chopped fresh dill

Poaching Liquid for Salmon

1½ cups dry white wine
1 cup water
3 lemon slices
1 onion, peeled and cut in half
5 sprigs fresh dill
5 sprigs fresh parsley
2 fresh bay leaves
12 peppercorns, white and black
1 teaspoon salt
1 pound fresh salmon filet, skinned and boned
3 tablespoons unsalted butter
2 tablespoons olive oil
Zest of 1 lemon
Thyme sprig, for garnish

1. To make the pasta, combine the flour and salt on a large board. Make a well in the center and break eggs into it; add 1 tablespoon of the olive oil and the dill. Gently mix eggs, dill, and olive oil together with a fork. Gradually incorporate the flour into the egg mixture until the dough comes together. Knead the dough until smooth, about 5 minutes. (If dough seems too sticky, knead in more flour.)

2. Roll out dough to the desired thickness with a pasta machine, following manufacturer's directions. Set the machine to fettucine width and pass dough through it. Store pasta, well wrapped, in the freezer until ready to use.

3. To prepare the salmon, bring all the ingredients for the poaching liquid to a boil in a pot just large enough to hold everything. Lower the flame to a simmer, add the salmon, and cover. Cook for 5 to 8 minutes until just done. Carefully remove salmon to a plate and let cool slightly. Break into large pieces.

4. Cook the pasta in a large pot of boiling water just until tender, 3 to 5 minutes. Drain well and toss immediately with butter, 2 tablespoons olive oil, lemon zest, and warm poached salmon flakes. Garnish with a sprig of thyme and more lemon zest.

Herb-Zucchini Sauté

SERVES 4

I use a mandoline to cut the squash quickly into fine long strips. I choose fresh parsley and thyme as seasoning, but sage and chervil would also be good.

1 tablespoon unsalted butter
2 tablespoons olive oil
1 shallot, finely chopped
5 zucchini, cut into 3-inch pieces and julienned (use a mandoline)
¼ cup flat-leaf parsley, chopped
2 sprigs fresh thyme
Salt and freshly ground pepper

1. In a large frying pan over medium heat, melt together butter and olive oil.

2. Sauté the shallot until tender; do not brown. Add the zucchini and sauté for 3 to 4 minutes, then add seasonings. Toss gently and serve immediately.

Spiced Peach Ice Cream

MAKES ABOUT 1 QUART

Homemade spiced peaches make this rich ice cream especially flavorful.

1½ cups half-and-half
½ cup sugar

3 large egg yolks
8 Spiced Peaches (recipe follows)
½ teaspoon vanilla extract

1. In a heavy stainless-steel saucepan over low heat, heat the half-and-half and sugar, stirring until sugar dissolves. In a bowl, whisk the egg yolks. Pour the warm mixture slowly into the yolks, stirring constantly to prevent curdling. Pour back into the pot and gently simmer over low heat, stirring constantly until mixture coats the back of a wooden spoon. Pour through a fine strainer into a bowl.
2. Remove Spiced Peaches from their poaching liquid. Pit and finely chop the peaches. Stir into the cooled custard and add vanilla. Freeze in an ice-cream maker.

Spiced Peaches in White Wine Syrup

Unusual ingredients and ripe peaches make this a delicious combination.

SERVES 4 TO 6

1 bottle cabernet blanc or rosé
1 cup apple cider vinegar
2 3-inch pieces of cinnamon
6 whole cloves
8 black peppercorns
½ lemon, zest and juice
1½ cups sugar
8 ripe peaches, blanched and peeled

1. Mix together all the poaching ingredients. Bring to a boil, lower heat, and cook until sugar dissolves. Add peaches and poach until tender but not soft, about 5 to 10 minutes. Discard zest.
2. Serve peaches with amaretti cookies and Spiced Peach Ice Cream. Garnish with cinnamon sticks and lemon zest.
NOTE: Refrigerate the poaching liquid in a tightly covered glass jar, to be used again. Leftover peaches should be stored in poaching liquid.

OPPOSITE: *For an outdoor lunch, the table is set with white Wedgewood plates and gold-banded goblets.*
ABOVE: *Poppies and bearded iris complement amethyst-stemmed glasses.*

I CAN REMEMBER PERFECTLY THE DAY THAT my grandmother, Babcia Helcia, introduced me to the fabulous 'Peace' rose that she had nurtured in manure-rich soil in her ultra-neat backyard rose bed; I was quite sure, even then, that someday I would

have my own garden of roses. ❧ Grandma Helen propagated her roses from precious cuttings gathered from the bushes of friends and acquaintances, protecting them with glass "cloches" (really a collection of oversize pickle jars). My father selected his roses from catalogues, purchasing a few bushes each year, and adding them to the ever-expanding rose garden in our Elm Place yard. It was my duty as a child to deadhead the bushes, pick off the Japanese beetles, and cut the most beautiful flowers for my mother or my teacher. ❧ My father preferred tea roses, and chose them primarily for their scent. I inherited his taste; for my first Mother's Day in Westport, my husband bought one dozen sturdy pot-planted hybrid teas, and placed them carefully in the garden as a surprise. It was an exciting and lovely present, affording me many years of pleasure. But my taste in roses remained relatively uninformed until I made my first gardening trip to England. Traveling with friends, I visited Great Dixter, Hidcote, Barnsley House, Sissinghurst, Upton House, Pusey, Rousham Park, Petworth, and Mottisfont Abbey. We arrived at Mottisfont

RIGHT: *I like to pick masses of my roses regardless of color scheme; here are 'Alchymist', 'Blaze', 'Louise Odier', 'Golden Sun', 'White Rose of York', 'Reines des Violettes', 'Jacques Cartier', and other favorites.*
LEFT: *Our old shagbark hickory split in two during a vicious gale, leaving an ugly scar. Following Vita Sackville-West's inspiration of training roses to grow into trees, I planted two roses at the base: a rambler, 'Veilchenblau', and a gallica, 'Tuscany'.*

R O S E S

in mid-July, to be told that we were two weeks too late to see the gardens at their very best. What remained was still, to me, truly astonishing. The garden is a rather new addition to Mottisfont, but in just a few short years the gardeners have grown hundreds of the most beautiful roses in the world. In one afternoon I learned more about roses than I had in a lifetime. All at once I heard about centifolias, gallicas, rosa rugosas, damasks, musks, bourbons, and grandifloras. I had never seen roses in such profusion, and I fell in love with the idea of roses as climbers, wall and trellis trained, as shrubs to be arched and pegged, and as well-pruned bushes to provide cut flowers. I became instantly enamored of the purple, almost black roses, and of those

ABOVE: *The second rose garden was filled with 74 bushes: 'White Wings', 'Belle Blonde', 'Mabel Morrison', 'Madame Zoetmans', 'Charles de Mills', 'Baroness Rothschild', 'Ferdinand Pichard', and 'Variegata di Bologna' among them. Planted in 1984, this bed fills the house with blooms for most of the season.*
BELOW: *The white climber 'Inspiration' and red 'Dortmund' on the pool house.*

exotic roses striped in red, pink, and lavender. I wrote down the name of every rose I saw, and anything I could gather about their habits.

When I came home, I devoured the few good American and Canadian catalogues I had found. I ordered many of those purple roses and the striped varieties, and I could not resist the ponderous, full beauty of 'Constance Spry', 'Paul Neyron', or 'Empress Josephine'. To frame my collection of roses, I commissioned my brother-in-law, Kim Herbert, to create a large trellised garden in which I could grow many of the climbing varieties. I modeled it after the extraordinary, upright garden of Monet at Giverny, and within a year the garden was transformed into a much more defined and elaborate space, with arches and walls, and entrances and exits. The trellised rose garden taught me my first important lesson in landscaping: every garden, no matter how small, needs a plan with vistas and focal points.

After the climbing roses were planted and growing strongly, I dug more rose gardens, planting as many different varieties as possible, mixing the different classifications within each bed, and combining different colors. When we built the stone walls around the pool, I planted shrub roses every eight feet around the inside perimeter, and have pegged and tacked the now massive bushes up and over the walls. Even the chickens benefited from my passion for roses, as I covered their wire enclosures with 'Buff Beauty', 'Moonlight', and 'Charles de Mills' and even trellised their coop to provide space for more climbers.

My latest adventure was to plant two more rose borders from the end of the pool to the large vegetable garden. Here I've mixed moss with musk with rugosa and damask, and the result is a garden of intense variety, wonderful coloration, and delicate, wafting scents. I think Babcia and Dad would have approved.

RIGHT: *The everblooming red 'Blaze' and the small-leafed 'Kathleen', an old-fashioned white hybrid musk that flowers repeatedly, grace the entrance to the vegetable garden. The metal rose trellis is a wonderful construction; covered with blooms of all colors, it brightens the landscape from June to September. I tried to plant only perpetually blooming climbers, but some of the varieties have one strong blooming and then sporadic flowering.*

1. *There was just a bit of unadorned grass leading from the pool garden to the trellised vegetable garden, through the peach and cherry trees, and I decided to transform this space into another rose bed. This south-facing, warm, sunny site, well protected, gently sloping, was a perfect location for roses; in addition, the soil was original to the place, undisturbed during the pool construction.*

2. *You can see how the garden gate to the pool area lines up nicely with the porch of the house. It was important that the new beds have a wide path between them, yet be wide enough themselves to accommodate the great number of roses I contemplated planting in the new new garden.*

3. *I took great care to make the borders correspond sensibly to the other garden spaces they adjoined: the house, the pool, the stone walls, and the trellis. Everything had originally been measured off perpendicularly and parallel to the focal point, the main house; only one small grass path was out of line when the entire rose garden was completed, and that was easily repaired the following fall.*

4. *Using my feet as a measure, I carefully walked off the width of the path, 9 feet. I then went up to the second-story porch of the house to see if this width looked "good" in the garden scheme as a whole.*

5. *It is chancy to transplant a fruit tree in full leaf; this four-year-old semidwarf Black Tartarian cherry miraculously survived its move. Renato first removed the sod around the base, then dug a circle using the circumference of the branches as a guide.*

6. *Thorough initial preparation of the soil is imperative when making a new garden. For the new rose borders, all of the sod was removed first, then the ground was double dug and enriched with peat and compost.*

7. *Once the rosebush is in place and the soil mounded to just below the graft, I create a watering and feeding trench. Even though the soil has been double dug and enriched, I give each bush a cupful of rich food, working it into the soil and then watering it well to spread it to the root system of each plant.*

8. *Each bush must be trimmed of any broken or bruised canes. Use very sharp clippers and cut on 45-degree angles, always above a bud union.*

9. *After all the roses were planted, I decided to add a border of pink lavender plants along each side. Next I underplanted the small bushes with many pink pansy plants to provide color while the bushes took hold and grew. Even in the first year, though, we had beautiful blooms.*

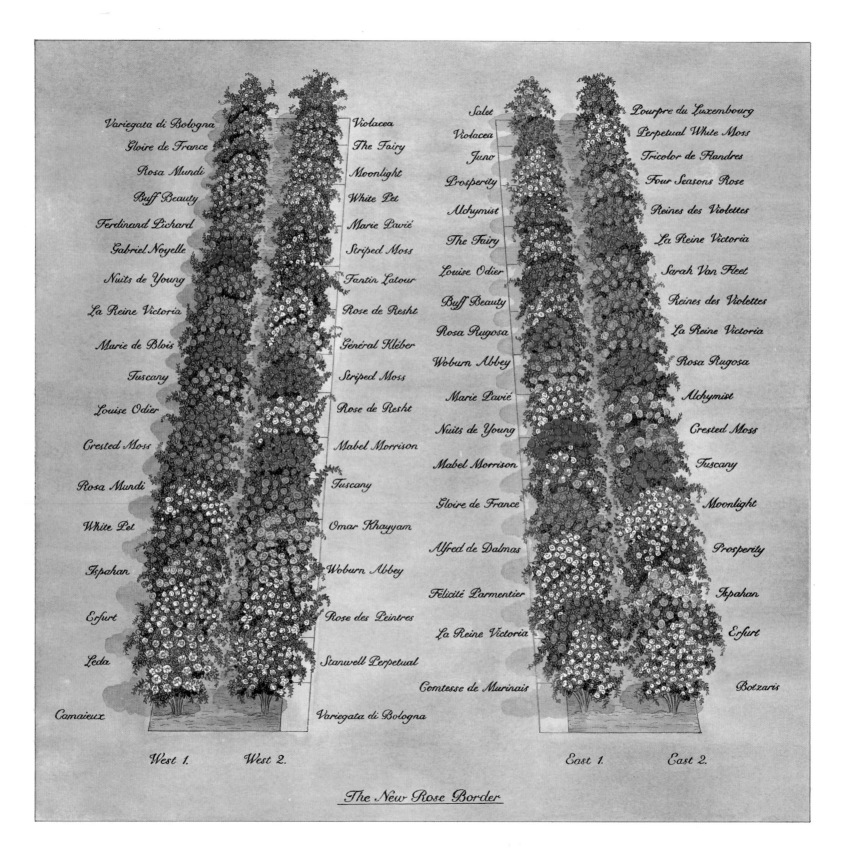

West 1.   West 2.   East 1.   East 2.

Variegata di Bologna — Violacea — Salet — Pourpre du Luxembourg
Gloire de France — The Fairy — Violacea — Perpetual White Moss
Rosa Mundi — Moonlight — Juno — Tricolor de Flandres
Buff Beauty — White Pet — Prosperity — Four Seasons Rose
Ferdinand Pichard — Marie Pavié — Alchymist — Reines des Violettes
Gabriel Noyelle — Striped Moss — The Fairy — La Reine Victoria
Nuits de Young — Fantin Latour — Louise Odier — Sarah Van Fleet
La Reine Victoria — Rose de Resht — Buff Beauty — Reines des Violettes
Marie de Blois — Général Kléber — Rosa Rugosa — La Reine Victoria
Tuscany — Striped Moss — Woburn Abbey — Rosa Rugosa
Louise Odier — Rose de Resht — Marie Pavié — Alchymist
Crested Moss — Mabel Morrison — Nuits de Young — Crested Moss
Rosa Mundi — Tuscany — Mabel Morrison — Tuscany
White Pet — Omar Khayyam — Gloire de France — Moonlight
Ispahan — Woburn Abbey — Alfred de Dalmas — Prosperity
Erfurt — Rose des Peintres — Félicité Parmentier — Ispahan
Leda — Stanwell Perpetual — La Reine Victoria — Erfurt
Camaieux — Variegata di Bologna — Comtesse de Murinais — Botzaris

The New Rose Border

ABOVE: *A long view of the two rose beds, ready to grow and flourish. There were 72 roses planted in 4 rows, north to south, of 18 bushes each. Since the beds were only 2 bushes deep and easily viewed from both sides, I did not have to consider the ultimate height of the various types at maturity. In a deeper bed one would have to plan so that a 3-foot-high 'Marie Bugnet' shrub rose would not be overshadowed by a 6-foot-high bourbon 'Madame Pierre Oger'. Notice the symmetry of the beds and the arch of the garden trellis; the grass path into the garden is off center, but this flaw was remedied.*

LEFT: *All the new rosebushes survived the winter and came into bloom in the spring. The grass edges were replaced with foot-wide bluestone on either side of the center path, which made for easy weeding of the bed and a neater appearance.*

OVERLEAF: *'Charles de Mills', a particularly vigorous and disease resistant gallica, bears its cerise blooms but once in the season; like many of the old roses I love, it is highly fragrant.*

RIGHT AND FAR RIGHT: *When I planted our second rose bed after falling in love with the old-fashioned blooms, I chose the roses as much for the romantic sound of their names and for the extraordinary descriptions in the catalogue as for any other reason. I paid no attention whatsoever to the length of the bloom, or to the real hardiness of the type. As a result, the bed has only one strong flowering period and huge, shrublike climbers and bushes intermixed. Here are the pink 'George Vibert', a compact gallica, and the pale apricot 'Alchymist', a shrub rose. I love all the varieties and would part with none.*

RIGHT: *Tumbling over the raised stone wall behind the barn are the pink bourbon 'Louise Odier', several sprays of 'Alchymist', and two perfect blooms of 'White Rose of York', a fragrant alba.*
FAR RIGHT: *The trellis is covered by 'White Dawn', an excellent trailing climber with camellialike blossoms.*

CLOCKWISE FROM ABOVE:
'Princesse de Monaco', ivory edged with pink, is a hybrid tea, as are the soft yellow 'Golden Sun' and the blushed gold buds of a rose bush from my first Mother's Day garden. 'Madame Delaroche-Lambert' is an exquisite old crimson moss rose. The soft orange 'Royal Sunset' is an excellent large-flowered climber. 'Constance Spry', an English rose named for an inspiring British floral designer, is a pure pink; 'Cécile Brunner', a climbing polyantha sometimes called "the sweetheart rose," is white with a faint rose tinge. The wonderfully luxuriant pink bloom at top left is a hybrid perpetual, bred from Portland and China roses by the Victorians for the perfect combination of huge flowers, heady fragrance, and double blooming: these extraordinary flowers appear in early summer, and again in the fall.

The Name of the Rose

THE OFFICIAL FLOWER OF THE UNITED States since 1986, *Rosa* has been England's royal emblem since 1485. The popularity of the rose has resulted in extensive hybridization—making classification complex and everchanging.

Old garden roses are the first cultivated varieties, dating to earliest civilization. Recently some nurseries have begun stocking these once hard-to-find roses.

Prior to the eighteenth century, European cultivated varieties were gallicas, damasks, albas, centifolias, and moss roses. Admired for their fragrance, these old garden roses generally bloomed only once in a season. Hybridizers were able to extend that flowering period by crossing them with roses from the Far East. These less hardy but longer-blooming roses began arriving in Europe in the late 1700s. The cross-breeding of European and Eastern garden roses resulted in bourbons, musks, noisettes, damask perpetuals, and hybrid perpetuals, also classed as old roses.

In 1966 the American Rose Society established that "a rose is an 'old' rose if it belongs to a group which existed before 1867." That year 'La France'—regarded as the first authentic hybrid tea rose—was introduced. The best-known modern rose classifications are hybrid tea, polyantha, floribunda, grandiflora, and miniature. Shrub roses, climbers, and ramblers are also recognized categories.

LEFT: *'Variegata di Bologna', a midsummer-blooming bourbon, sometimes offers a few flowers in the fall.*

HYBRID TEAS: Certainly the most popular in the United States; hardy, but some require winter protection in Connecticut. Blooms prolifically from early summer until first frost. Height: from 2½ to 5 feet; strong stems. My favorite is still Babcia Helcia's 'Peace'.

POLYANTHAS: Native to China; low growing, hardier than hybrid teas; clustered flowers and fine-textured leaves.

FLORIBUNDAS: Cross between hybrid teas and polyanthas. Profuse flowering and minimal maintenance. Worldwide favorite. Height: about 3 feet. Suitable for hedging.

GRANDIFLORAS: Cross between floribunda and hybrid teas, displaying the best of both. Everblooming and hardy. Height: to 6 feet or more.

MINIATURES: Hardy everblooming; can be grown in pots, even indoors. Height: usually no more than 12 inches.

SHRUB ROSES: Closely related to species roses, sharing many characteristics. Incredibly hardy; require little maintenance. Height: up to 8 feet, spreading habit. Flowers, generally with only 5 petals, sometimes fragrant. Attractive foliage. I'm fond of 'Constance Spry'.

CLIMBERS: Long, stiff canes; everblooming, somewhat resistant to disease. Often tied onto walls, trellises, arches, or lattice. My favorite is the crimson 'Blaze' and 'White Dawn.'

RAMBLERS: Long, pliable canes; vigorous growers. Can be trained to cover fences, trellises, and pergolas.

RIGHT: *'Rosa Mundi', a very old gallica (it was even described by Pliny), has a sprawling habit, perfect for covering a wall.*

LEFT: *After we built the Palais de Poulets and surrounded the yard with stiff, sturdy wire fencing, I planted climbers here and there to offer some romance and fragrance to the chicken yard. The roses grew rapidly and bloom extraordinarily—probably because of their proximity to rich and natural nutrients from the chicken manure. The pink rose is a centifolia 'Cristata', also called 'Crested Moss'; the white is 'Madame Hardy', a hardy bush damask rose with but one spectacular flowering.*

BOTTOM LEFT: *Next to the pool gate leading to the vegetable-garden walk, I planted a pink centifolia 'Fantin Latour'.*

TOP RIGHT: *'Rosa Complicata' is a single, once-flowering gallica of extreme delicacy and beauty.*

BOTTOM RIGHT: *'Cornelia' is a hybrid musk rose with a vigorous, spreading habit.*

OVERLEAF, LEFT: *This deep rose-crimson 'Étoile de Hollande' is a climbing hybrid tea growing up to 12 feet; it has an unsurpassed damask fragrance and produces long-stemmed blooms for most of the season.*

OVERLEAF, CENTER: *The original 'Blaze', a hardy, long-lived climber with abundant blooms of bright scarlet that repeat themselves throughout the summer months, was the first rose to be granted a plant patent.*

OVERLEAF, RIGHT: *The pale apricot-yellow of 'Buff Beauty', a many-flowered hybrid musk climber, is beautiful in flower arrangements.*

ABOVE: *'Raubritter' shrub roses with beautifully cupped bright pink blooms and bachelors' buttons in the same shade fill a compote to brimming, decoration for one of the fifteen tables at a garden tea party.*

ABOVE: *A mass of English 'Emanuel' roses makes a beautiful, highly scented arrangement for the table.* LEFT: *Small glass compotes, yet more trophies from a tag sale, are filled with an abundance of roses and other June flowers from my garden.*

LEFT: *In the parlor a nineteenth-century bronze urn is filled with roses: 'Blaze' climbers, 'Marchioness of Londonderry' hybrid perpetuals, 'Mutabilis' species roses, 'Botzaris' damasks, 'Étoile de Hollande' climbers, 'Windrush' shrubs, and 'Crimson Glory' hybrid teas. The formality of the arrangement is offset by handfuls of phlox, astilbe, peony, and digitalis.*
RIGHT: *Another figural urn is filled with masses of 'Alchymist' roses in all stages of bloom, from tight buds to full-blown flowers.*
PREVIOUS PAGES: *A glorious mass of roses. On the table: 'Arillaga' hybrid perpetuals, Rosa soulieana, 'Crimson Glory' climbing hybrid teas, 'Alchymist', 'Baroness Rothschild' hybrid perpetuals, 'Grootendorst Supreme' hybrid rugosas, 'Général Jacqueminot' hybrid perpetuals. In the basket: Rosa rubrifolia species roses, 'Madame Alfred Carrière' and 'Louise Odier' bourbons, 'Elegance' hybrid teas, 'Canterbury' English roses, 'Royal Sunset' and 'Inspiration' climbers.*

ABOVE: *I love yellow roses, but they are not nearly as hardy in my garden as the pink, purple, and crimson types. These large hybrid tea 'Golden Sun' roses mix well with Higo iris, scabiosa, phlox, astilbe, and digitalis. The container is a cut-glass compote, one of a pair that I bought from a local antiques dealer.*
LEFT: *A combination of crimson hyrbrid teas ('Grande Duchesse', 'Crimson Glory', and 'Charlotte') in a small silver bowl, one of many I bought at a tag sale for a dollar each.*

RIGHT: *A simple blue ware kitchen bowl makes an informal arrangement of roses look "comfortable" anywhere in the house. Included in this mixed bouquet are 'Catherine Mermet' teas, 'Ferdinand Pichard' hybrid perpetuals, 'Rosette Delizy' yellow hybrid teas, 'Étoile de Hollande', 'Comte de Chambord' pink Portlands, 'Cornelia' hybrid musks, 'Madame Hardy', 'Michèle Meilland' hybrid teas, and Rosa chinensis mutabilis, an old species rose from China.*

LEFT: *A sterling silver Revere trophy bowl, one I won years ago in a contest, is filled with bright yellow roses ('Honorine de Brabant' bourbons, 'Golden Sun', 'McGrady's Sunset' teas, 'Buff Beauty' musks) accented by just a few 'Crimson Glory' hybrid teas.*

BOTTOM LEFT: *A pink ware kitchen bowl, fitted with a large metal frog to hold the flowers securely, is filled with red and scarlet 'Duchesse de Brabant', 'Henry Nevard', 'Grand Duchesse Charlotte', and 'Général Jacqueminot'. One or two peach and pink roses relieve the monochromes.*

RIGHT: *My daughter, Alexis, created this arrangement of noisette, centifolia, and hybrid tea roses combined with peonies, snapdragons, astilbe, and cornflowers. She arranged more than twenty bowls filled to brimming—centerpieces for a garden party.*

Caring for Roses

ROSES DEMAND GREAT COMMITMENT of time and energy. Given the joy they bring, as ornamentals, in fragrant bouquets, in dried-flower arrangements and wreaths, and for potpourri, I make the commitment willingly.

Every spring and fall I liberally spread triple phosphate on the beds. Summertime, when we enjoy the benefits of these flowers, also finds us with hectic work schedules in the garden. Deadheading and pruning climbers are just a few of the activities. I give my roses plenty of water using a network of soaker hoses and avoid overhead sprinkling to discourage fungal problems.

Every three weeks I feed with 5-10-5 fertilizer or manure water "tea"—the magic my grandmother doused her perfect roses with. To make this, place about a cup of dried or bagged dehydrated cow manure in 2 gallons of water; allow it to steep for a few days before using. Dilute to the color of weak tea and, as with other water-soluble fertilizers, apply only to

ABOVE LEFT: *In October and November, the roses must be put to rest for the winter months. Tall shrub roses are tied with treated cord into bundles. This prevents the canes from breaking under weight of snow or force of wind. I cut out any damaged canes at this time, but I believe that the more bush left for winter, the better.*
ABOVE RIGHT: *Each rose-bush crown is liberally covered with rich compost to protect the base from winter heaving.*

a moist soil, never one that is bone dry. Following clean-up in late fall, I mound compost and dried manure around the crown of each bush. The entire rose garden is then screened with burlap to protect it from the winds.

Roses in Connecticut, like those in almost any climate, are more susceptible to disease and pests than a lot of other perennial plants. Some of the more common diseases, caused by fungus, are blackspot, powdery mildew, and rust. Blackspot and powdery mildew are the most threatening in my garden.

BLACKSPOT. Often caused by late-

afternoon watering, blackspot first appears on lower leaves. Yellow spreads out from the dark spots; eventually the entire leaf yellows and drops prematurely. Remove and destroy diseased leaves at once. Here garden clean-up is imperative as the fungus will overwinter on diseased leaves left on the ground and in cane lesions. Roses downwind from an infected plant must be watched carefully. Blackspot spores are transmitted by insects, through contact with contaminated tools or clothes, and by rain splashing nearby plants. The most promising research in organic control involves a solution of baking soda—5 tablespoons of baking soda in 5 gallons of water, with a few drops of soap added for adhesion. Spray as a preventative, or on diseased leaves—but only in the morning and be careful of leaf burn.

POWDERY MILDEW. Watch out for warm days followed by cool nights—especially in areas with poor air circulation. You may see young leaves, buds, fruit, or shoots coated with a fuzzy white or grayish film. Powdery mold has begun to set in; it will stunt and distort growth but will not usually cause defoliation. Drought-stressed plants are more susceptible. This disease overwinters on fallen leaves.

RUST. Reddish-brown spores appear on undersides of leaves, usually those closest to the ground; the tops are speckled yellow. Leaves wilt and drop. Pick off and destroy diseased leaves.

After handling diseased plants, thoroughly wash your hands, tools, and clothes. To keep disease and pest problems to a minimum, make certain roses are disease- and pest-free before you purchase them. Choose resistant hybrids whenever possible, and keep up with garden chores. A regular schedule of fertilization, watering, and garden clean-up will do far more than a blitz of chemicals, which kills beneficial insects along with the disease or insect pest you are attacking.

TOP RIGHT: *First 4-foot stakes are driven into the ground around the individually planted bushes and around most of the rose and perennial borders. Then 36-inch-wide burlap is stapled onto these stakes to create protective surrounds.*
BOTTOM: *The newest rose borders are surrounded with burlap. Rose beds are beautiful in themselves, but they can be greatly enhanced with borders of stone or brick, and planted with edges of lavender, teucrium, sage, or even tiny boxwood. I chose to plant these edges with 166 six-inch pots of pink lavender ('Rosea'), and with a second row of blue flax inside.*

ABOVE: *I try to dry as many of the fading rose blooms as possible for use later in the season in my homemade potpourri. Dry the blooms on coarse screens in a dark, dry, cool place, or in silica gel.* LEFT: *Once the rose beds are surrounded with burlap and the ground is frozen, raked-up leaves are mounded around the bushes.*

YELLOW CHINA ROSE.

S

U

Drawn by J. T. Hart,
at the Garden of Mr. Stark, Thistle Grove,
Little Chelsea.

M M E R

I SUPPOSE I HAVE BEEN INFLUENCED by the English school of gardening more than by any other; I am constantly amazed at what fine and thoughtful gardeners that small country

LEFT: *Max, the black chow chow, is my constant companion in the garden. Like the cats, he is curious about what goes on and I always wish that these dear animals could tell me what they think of the flowers, fruits, and vegetables.*
RIGHT: *Thompson and Morgan offers more than thirty varieties of sweet peas. Every January I order one packet of each (varieties vary from year to year) for planting out in late March.*

produced. It is where I have found much inspiration, as well as more practical things—I know that when I take a trip to England I buy more seeds and tools than in all the other places I go combined. ❧ On one visit I had the opportunity to view several experimental vegetable and fruit gardens, to study the amazingly clever ways the English propagate fruit trees and berry bushes, and to taste many of the products that had been grown. I filled my suitcases with jam pot covers (the rounds of cellophane the English use instead of messy paraffin), feltlike strainers for clarifying fruit and berry juice to make crystal clear jellies, old glass jars that were so much more decorative than the new ones we could find at home, and many books describing new old ways to grow and harvest and use all the berries and fruits that I planned to have at Turkey Hill. ❧

I was so enthusiastic about what I saw and ate that I came right back to Connecticut and began my search for the best raspberries, the most unusual currants, and the most fragrant and delicious strawberries. It was not easy to locate a source for the black currants that I wanted to transform into in jam and syrup. (I use black currant syrup year round to make

J U L Y

JOURNAL

Wooden tomato stakes painted cupboard blue.

Much watering required to combat dry spell.

Raspberries and gooseberries picked (one result—10½ pints of golden raspberry jelly).

Entire garden weeded almost daily.

Currants transformed into syrups (4 gallons black, 3 gallons red).

Edges of all gardens dug and trimmed.

Compost heaps turned, aerated, and moved.

Cucumbers and squash planted.

Climbing roses pruned to encourage second blooming.

Chickens allowed to scratch in rose gardens to combat Japanese beetles.

Remainder of vegetable gardens planted with carrots, parsnips, etc., for fall harvest.

Chive borders trimmed.

Cabbages and kale picked.

Overgrown vegetables fed daily to poultry.

Lavender rotted.

Part of old orchard cut down; new rose bed dug.

Lettuces, baby string beans, beets, radicchio, eggplants, Swiss chard, red onions, and a bowl of blueberries picked.

RIGHT: *When planting sweet peas, I group the seeds of each color together so that at picking time I can gather harmonious clusters. Bright crimson red is an unusual sweet pea color, and I love these 'Winston Churchill' blooms.*

sorbets and ice creams of the most amazing color.) White currants were even harder to find, but I did not give up: I found them in Makielski's catalogue. What a glorious clear jelly they make—it looks like the sourwood honey that my brother Frank collects in South Carolina, but tastes like nothing else on earth.

My search for gooseberries was not as successful. In England I ate in pies, preserves, and fools the giant green gooseberries one sees in pictures; alone or mixed with blackberries or raspberries, these fruits are extraordinarily delicious. Yet here in the United States I seem to be able to grow only the small gooseberry that ripens to a purplish color. The taste is good, but it is not the same.

Now that I am growing white, red, and black currants, golden, purple, red, and black raspberries, gooseberries, blueberries, blackberries, and strawberries of all kinds, I am going to experiment with the beautiful growing methods I saw in several English gardens: topiarylike bushes, bushes trained along wires for easy picking, special wire and cloth netting to discourage birds from picking the berries before you do, and different ways of pruning to encourage immense fruits and better fruit production.

We like to use the garden a lot for entertaining in the summer months. It is the best time to invite guests for a swim, a stroll, and an alfresco lunch. The garden is at its peak: it provides me with the ingredients for simple, quick but delicious fare for as many guests as I want. During July I rarely have to go to the grocery store except for staples like flour, milk, or cream for the berries.

ABOVE: *A tall spiked cutting basket is filled with sweet peas in amazing colors: the blue-violet 'North Shore', ivory 'Royal Wedding', scarlet 'Red Ensign', rosy 'Royal Flush', and palest pink 'Grace de Monaco'.*
OVERLEAF, LEFT: *'Grace de Monaco' is a lovely, soft pink with white centers.*
OVERLEAF, RIGHT: *'Wiltshire Ripple', the sweet pea that first enchanted me and started me on my collection, bears three to four richly scented blooms on each stem. The petals are a snow white, striped and dotted with rich brownish-claret markings; arranged alone in a tiny antique bottle, these flowers are extraordinary.*

Sweet Peas

ONE OF MY FAVORITE PARTS OF THE garden is the sweet pea patch. It began with a packet of 'Wiltshire Ripple' seeds, bought one February at Scott's Nurseries near Dorchester, in England. That led to more expeditions to England in search of other hauntingly beautiful varieties (my family used to estimate the cost of the patch based on my plane trips), but now Thompson and Morgan, one of my favorite English mail-order seed suppliers, offers more than three dozen varieties, and I can be a spendthrift at home.

Sweet peas *(Lathyrus odorata),* Italian natives long loved and nurtured by English gardeners, are annual vines, but hybridizers have created dwarf and bush forms. Soft-colored flowers are lavender, salmon, pink, white, rose, and blue, and can be deliciously fragrant—especially the old-fashioned varieties. (There is also a distant relative of the Italian *odorata* which grows wild along the roadsides of the Northeastern United States; it has dense pealike foliage and pinkish-lavender blossoms on short stems.)

Sweet peas are cool-weather lovers. I start sowing mine on St. Patrick's Day, rain or shine, and I continue with successive sowings until April 15. Sweet peas perform best in a moist, but well-drained, deeply dug and fertile soil that is just a bit alkaline. Organic matter, such as manure or compost, will enrich the soil, which—because of the very early planting date—is best prepared in autumn.

To construct a simple trellis for the vines, sink 4-by-4 posts into garden soil every 4 to 5 feet in a north-south direc-

tion. Attach heavy gauge galvanized wire fencing, 6 feet high, to the posts. Separate the rows by 3 feet.

Twenty-four hours before you sow your pea-size seeds, soak them in water to help soften the hard coating. (I find custard cups, labeled with the variety name, work very well as containers.) Because of the vagaries of spring weather, we sometimes lose the first seedlings to frost (germination is about two weeks). Spring is most often rainy, but if a dry period does occur, water sweet peas well; they do not tolerate dry conditions.

Sweet peas are wonderful in cut flower arrangements. Deadhead what you don't pick; never let them set pods or they will stop blooming. Keeping their roots cool with mulch can lengthen their blooming time. Heat-intolerance is one of the few drawbacks of this graceful, delicate flower; as soon as hot weather arrives, blossoms disappear.

LEFT: *With a few last clusters of lavender 'Harmony' and the dappled 'Wiltshire Ripple', the cutting basket is ready to be taken indoors.*
RIGHT: *This unusual pink McCoy container holds sweet peas in assorted pink shades. Displayed in front of this American painting of viburnum, red buddleia, and purple lilac, the flowers almost vibrate with beauty.*

Berries

WITH REGULAR MAINTENANCE MY berries—strawberries, raspberries, black-berries, blueberries, gooseberries, and currants—are prolific bearers, rarely troubled by disease or pests; hungry birds are my biggest headache. The raspberries grow in beds, but others like currants and gooseberries are lovely enough to be planted close to the house as ornamentals. July is the most plentiful month for my berries, but we are still picking them in autumn. Whatever is not eaten is frozen whole or as juice or puree.

Berries are sun-lovers and demand good quantities of water for quality fruit. Each spring and fall all the small fruits are top-dressed with manure and compost; they are given a winter protection of a hay mulch in late November. When choosing varieties, find out from your local nursery which berries perform best in your area and select disease- and pest-resistant varieties.

RASPBERRIES. The everbearing red and golden varieties that I grow multiply by root suckers and will spread rampantly if left unchecked. They are hardy perennial plants and thrive in a slightly acidic soil

FAR RIGHT: *Ten years ago, I was given ten plants of 'Charles V' Fraises des Bois, or woodland strawberries; I've since divided them hundreds of times to create edgings for my brick-lined grassy paths. The neat round clumps of foliage bear tiny white blossoms, followed by a wonderful crop of intensely perfumed, dark red fruits that bear little resemblance in taste or texture to the commercial American berry.*

ABOVE AND BELOW: *The upright growing habit of* Fraises des Bois *produces much tidier plants than the sprawling cultivated strawberry plants.*

BELOW: *I planted 'Guardian' strawberries in rows, allowing runners to set plants until all the spaces were filled. Soon the entire patch, including the paths, was overgrown with berries.*

ABOVE: *'Latham' red raspberries, hardy, disease resistant, and abundant, are a perennial favorite among berry growers.*

ABOVE: *Golden or yellow raspberries have a sugary flavor, very different from most of the reds.*

with a pH of 5.6 to 6.0. Iron deficiency will occur when soil pH is above 7.0. Choose a sunny site with fertile, moisture-retentive soil and good air circulation—away from any wild raspberries or blackberries that could transmit diseases to nursery-grown stock.

Prepare the site well ahead of planting. Dig to a depth of 12 to 18 inches and work in plenty of compost and manure; dust with bonemeal. Purchase bareroot plants and plant in autumn. Soak in a bucket of water overnight before setting in the soil. Make a hole large enough for the roots to spread comfortably. Add water to the hole and set the crown 2 inches below the soil level; fill in and water well. Cut each cane back to 6 inches to help underground growth. Set plants 3 feet apart and, for ease of picking, in rows spaced 6 feet.

During the first season, only allow two or three robust canes to grow; in following seasons, maintain eight or nine strong ones. Everbearing raspberries produce in early summer and again in fall. Prune canes to ground level in early summer after they bear; also thin new canes and any that are far from the mother plant. Remove diseased and dead canes and any that are crowding or rubbing. Fruit is produced on new canes in autumn and again on these same canes the following summer.

Propagation of raspberries is easy, but not recommended because of the potential for virus in the mother plant. To propagate, dig up newly formed suckers, roots and soil, in very early spring just as they appear. Transplant in prepared soil.

BLACKBERRIES. Choose a site for blackberries carefully. They can become invasive quickly if unattended, sending out suckers as far away as 10 feet from the plant. Blackberries will be more easily controlled if you loosely tie them to a fence or wire support. Wires drawn at 1-foot intervals through 4-by-4s placed 10 feet apart make excellent supports for these bushes.

Prepare bed site and plant as for raspberries. Members of the same plant genus *(Rubus)*, their needs are similar although blackberries tolerate sandy soils. To minimize the risk of disease, do not plant in beds that previously contained raspberries or blackberries.

Blackberries, with upright growing habits, produce stiff canes that live for two years—bearing leaves the first and berries the second. Each year new canes appear. Remove fruited canes at ground level after they have borne berries. Thinning discourages disease problems. The plants are extremely vigorous and productive, and need annual pruning and staking to keep them manageable.

CURRANTS AND GOOSEBERRIES. As hosts for part of a disease cycle that attacks white pine, currants and gooseberries (*Ribes* sp.) have been restricted in certain parts of the country, particularly near evergreen forests: check with the Cooperative Extension in your area. These fruits produce abundant amounts of delicious berries; I grow red, white, and black currants and gooseberries.

Prepare soil with an abundance of compost and manure well before planting. Sun, good drainage, and a soil pH from 5.5 to 6.5 are important. Plant these hardy bushes in October to establish good roots before growth begins in very early spring. Dig holes large enough to adequately accommodate roots, with the crown about 3 inches below soil level. In early spring these fruits require extra potassium to encourage quality fruit.

Prune currants and gooseberries after they fruit. These plants bear near the base of year-old shoots and on fruiting spurs produced by two- and three-year-old wood. Remove dead and diseased branches and those over three years old. Maintain six to eight strong canes in an open, airy form. Heading the main branches (cutting back by one-third) stimulates the growth of fruiting spurs. Thin new growth if it begins to crowd.

STRAWBERRIES. Most varieties of strawberries (*Fragaria* sp.) are perhaps too prolific—self-propagating by throwing out runners which take root and form new plants. One self-contained kind, *Fraises des Bois,* produces no runners. These tiny but ever-so-sweet berries from the Old World are my favorites.

Prepare a bed with manure and compost in a sunny location; soil pH range should be between 5.5 and 6.5. If drainage is a problem, mound the soil. Plant strawberries at the end of July; any later will diminish the next year's crop by one-half. Set 8 inches apart in rows 18 inches apart; cover roots well but do not bury the crown; water generously.

The more common runner-type strawberries fall into two categories— standards producing more berries but only once a season in spring or early summer and everbearing varieties that bear in early summer and again in early fall. If plants are allowed to set too many runners, the quality of berries diminishes.

To encourage strong growth, remove all blossoms the first season from standards but only until mid-July on everbearing varieties, which will then produce a vigorous late-summer crop. Strawberries perform best when they are grown for two seasons, and then replaced. For sweeter berries, dress with manure in early summer.

BLUEBERRIES. Highbush varieties (*Vaccinium corymbosum*) can be more than fruit producers in the garden. They can be beautiful ornamentals, with clusters of creamy blossoms in spring and flaming red foliage in fall.

Because blueberries are slow growing and long lived, I start with good-sized bushes. Plant them at least 4 feet apart in a sunny location where the ground is moist but never flooded.

A soil high in organic content with a 4.0 to 5.2 pH is ideal. Work well-decomposed cow manure into soil several months before planting; add peat moss and compost at planting time. Fertilize in spring with a complete fertilizer, such as 10-10-10, or use a water-soluble acid fertilizer. Mulching with pine needles or oak leaves will increase soil acidity.

Prune mature bushes lightly to shape and remove any dead, diseased, weak, or crossed wood. I usually cut mine in fall after they stop producing; they can also be pruned in early spring while still dormant—when fruit buds (larger than leaf buds) can be identified.

Because we grow early-, mid-, and late-season varieties, there are always blueberries to pick starting in June and continuing through September.

ABOVE: *Even newly planted, a blackberry bush shows its wild growing habit.*

ABOVE: *This 'Bristol' raspberry will ripen to a deep purplish black fruit with a mild, sweet flavor.*

ABOVE: *Thornless, suckerless blackberries are now available.*

'Heritage' red raspberry bushes bear firm, delicious fruit in July, and then another big crop in late September; 'Fall Gold' is sweet, juicy, delectable, and prolific, producing crops in July, August, and again in September.

I planted my first blueberries near the main house eighteen years ago, and now the bushes are quite large and amazingly abundant, and still beautiful enough to serve as a border between the lawn and the flower gardens. I tried to choose a range of types with different bearing schedules: in June, 'Earliblue' produces excellent, large berries with mild sweet flavor; 'Bluecrop' is a bit later; 'Jersey', whose beautiful foliage and upright growing habit make it a lovely shrub, bears through August.

ABOVE: *Red currants are perhaps the most beautiful of all garden berries—fully ripe and plump on the bushes in July, they look like clusters of the finest cabochon rubies.*
LEFT: *I take very good care of my currant bushes, pruning out any dead wood and keeping the plants well formed for good health and high production.*
RIGHT: *When the entire cluster is red, I will cut off these racemes with small scissors, or pinch them off with my fingers.*

GARDENING

ABOVE: *Black currants are dense, blackish purple when ripe, retaining the remains of the flower on the bottom of the berry.*
RIGHT: *I planted two kinds of black currants: 'Crandall' and 'Consort'; both produce huge numbers of smooth fruits. One of the best sources for vitamin C, black currants are used in my kitchen for jam, jellies, syrups, ice creams, and sorbets; some day, I may learn to make cassis.*
BELOW: *I have attempted to grow figs more than once: now I have several large fig bushes, 'Celeste' (violet skin with white to rose flesh) and 'Brown Turkey' (very hardy, producing violet greenish fruits). Depending on the way they've been wrapped for the winter and the severity of the cold, I'll harvest bushels or merely a basket or two. I love to eat them dead ripe, right off the bush, or poached in white wine; fig preserves are also delicious.*

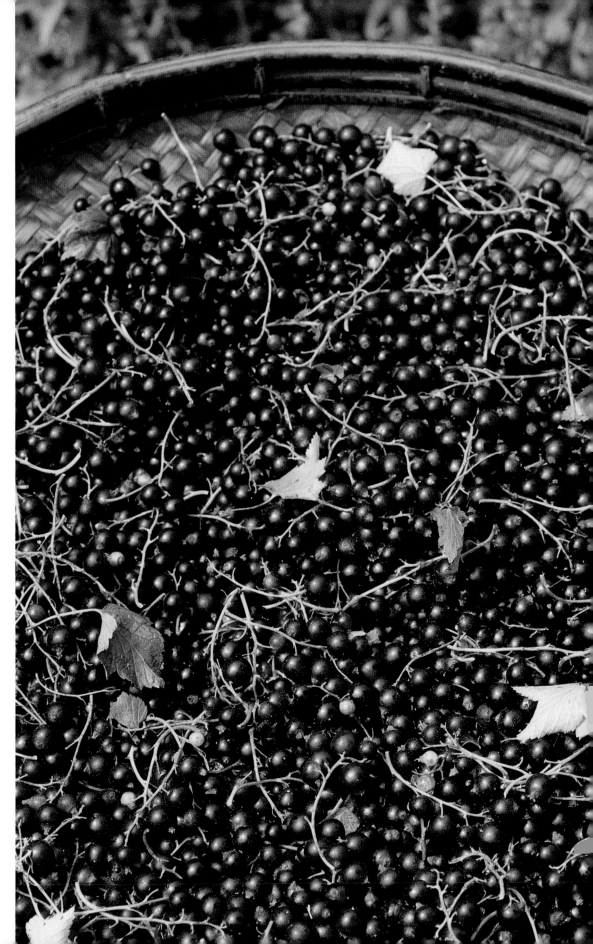

Daylilies

TO ANYONE WHO GREW UP IN THE eastern United States, the orange-yellow flowers of roadside daylilies *(Hemerocallis)* are the ultimate sign of summer: these were the flowers we saw from the car window as the family drove to the shore.

Native to Asia and southern Europe and naturalized in the U.S., daylilies have been augmented with a rainbow of colors and forms. Hybrids also produce huge flowers on branched clusters at the top of 3-foot stalks. Perhaps the one drawback of daylilies is that flowers bloom, as their name suggests, for just one day, but each flower is followed by others on the same stalk. By judicious mixing of hybrids, gardeners can expect blooms from late spring through midsummer. Foliage is grasslike and profuse, and will provide a dense cover that reduces the need for weeding if plants are close. Flowers tower above the foliage and can make successful cut flowers; pick just as buds begin to open. Often daylilies are lightly scented.

I prefer the pure colors—the rich velvety reds, golden yellows, and deep pumpkin hues—and grow the great big varieties with fluted edges on curled petals. These look enchanting massed at the base of the stone wall or fence.

LEFT: *Delphiniums, coreopsis, and orange Asiatic lilies brighten the July borders.* RIGHT: *The Siberian iris are not quite finished blooming when the hollyhocks begin to flower. In the upper garden's large perennial borders, shrub roses, lilies, and monarda begin to bloom at the same time.*

Daylilies maintain a richer color in partial shade. Most garden soils are fine with the addition of compost. Keep high nitrogen fertilizers away from these flowers; too much promotes foliage and adversely affects the quantity and quality of blooms—use superphosphate or 5-10-10 in spring and fall. Plant new lilies in early spring, 18 to 24 inches apart depending upon the height. Set the crown slightly below soil level. Established plants will survive some drought conditions, but watering enhances blooming. Cut off the flower stalks after all blooms are spent; foliage will stay green for some time and then yellow with the advent of cooler temperatures. After the leaves have died naturally, remove and compost.

Once established, daylilies will grow untouched for years. Division is necessary only when the vigor of blooms diminishes. Propagate by dividing root clumps in early spring. Or take 3-inch root sections in early spring and place in a medium of moist sand and peat moss in a shaded site. When new plants begin to grow, transplant to a permanent site.

RIGHT: *Each spring, my father planted jumbo-size gladioli corms, and in July and August he filled big vases with showy flowers. Gladioli fell into semi-disfavor about twenty years ago, appearing only as a funeral flower, never for happy occasions. Since then, amazing things have happened: colors range from silky blackish red to true ruffled green. There are bicolors and tricolors, and stalks are tall and heavily laden. With successive plantings, almost continuous blooming can be guaranteed for July and August.*

Tomatoes

A RICH SOURCE OF VITAMINS C, A, and B complex, tomatoes are given high priority in my garden. Once thought poisonous and only suited to ornamental gardening, they are now solely appreciated for their delicious fruit. Their beauty is often overlooked, and gardeners with limited space might consider growing a dwarf bush variety among the flowers.

Tomatoes are of two types: indeterminate, with stems that lengthen and produce fruit as long as the weather allows, and determinate, which bear a set quantity of fruit all about the same time. Indeterminate varieties yield far more but require some mode of support.

Hybridizers have been attentive to the diseases affecting tomatoes, and gardeners are advised to look for resistant strains. Each year I rotate crops to prevent the spread of disease and to avoid depleting nutrients.

Natives of South America, where they are perennials, tomatoes (*Lycopersicon* sp.) are grown as annuals in our colder climate. I grow all mine from seed, sown indoors in March to get a head start on our short New England growing season. By early June they are all moved outdoors to the garden.

I grow a wide selection: red, yellow, orange, and white, round, plum- and pear-shaped, big and tiny. Some plants are tall and some dwarf. Because of the many varieties, both early and late, they produce all summer until the cold weather returns. I am always experimenting with new varieties and ways to grow these fruits. The indeterminate

ABOVE: *These wire cage supports are good for small fruiting tomatoes; within a month the plants will fill the cages and start producing fruits. Planted in raised beds about 30 inches apart, each plant has plenty of room. I use large gauge hog wire for the cages. The spaces are narrow at the bottom, which discourages small animals, but larger near the top so there is room for a hand to get in to pick the ripe tomatoes.*
BELOW: *My father always grew 'Big Boy' tomatoes in his Nutley garden; fertilized with compost, manure, and fish heads, his soil was perfect for growing the extra-large juicy red New Jersey variety tomatoes. I still grow a couple of 'Big Boy' plants each year, but my fruits never attain the size, or the flavor, of my dad's.*

ABOVE: *'Big Boy' was hybridized in 1949 to produce the disease-resistant 'Better Boy', which bears large uniform fruits.*
BELOW AND OPPOSITE ABOVE: *I have experimented with growing tomatoes on wooden trellises, in wire cages, and on wooden stakes. Each method has its benefits and drawbacks: stakes require severe pinching back of the plants.*
OPPOSITE BELOW: *'Marmande' small beefsteak tomatoes, Burpee's 'Big Girl Hybrid VF', Burpee's 'Big Boy', 'Early Girl Hybrid', 'Basket King Hybrid' large sweet cherry tomatoes, 'Tiny Tim' ¾-inch cherry tomatoes, 'Yellow Pear', sweet and juicy 'Red Pear', and the 'Principe Borghese' cherry tomatoes that are so very good for drying.*

"vine" types are trellised or staked and some I surround with tall over-6-foot cylinders made from heavy-duty wire mesh. Staked and trellised, they require tying as well as pruning. Pruning means removing the side shoots, when they are small; these shoots sprout from the intersection where leaf branches join the main stem. Removing these allows the plant to devote more energy to fruit production for larger fruits and also creates a more manageable plant.

Looking at the lists of tomatoes in seed catalogues can be overwhelming. Although I always try new ones, I plant my old favorites year after year. There is nothing quite so deliciously sweet as the 'Better Boy', 'Big Boy', and 'Beefsteak' varieties in sandwiches. 'San Marzano', a plum variety, is one of my preferences for tomato sauce, which fills the freezer at the end of each season. 'Alicante', a small red cherry tomato, is my choice of the smaller ones, which I usually eat right off the vine. I love 'Tigerella' with its unusual orange-yellow striped markings.

When the weather begins to cool, many of my tomatoes are still producing copiously. We use armloads of unripe green ones to make mincemeat, and sometimes when frost is imminent they are taken inside to ripen in the attic under newspaper; it is warmth, not light, that reddens these fruits.

LEFT: *Blocky, thick-skinned yellow tomatoes grow from a packet of seeds sent by an Italian friend. I use them peeled, seeded, and coarsely chopped for an unusual pasta sauce.*

LEFT: *Pointed 'Super Roma' plum tomatoes grow full of flesh with barely any cavity or core.*

RIGHT: *Ripening on a sturdy, healthy vine, this well-formed round tomato is 'Burpee's Big Girl Hybrid VF'.*

BELOW: *'Golden Sunrise' produces medium golden fruits of very good flavor. I serve these thickly sliced with fresh mozzarella and opal basil.*

LEFT: *Small-fruited 'San Marzano' plum tomatoes will ripen to red to make wonderful sauces and purees—or to be sun dried for use in fall and winter.*

RIGHT: *Grown in a wire cage, the prolific 'Principe Borghese' plant produces bright red cherry tomatoes, excellent for drying.*

FAR LEFT: *Mild or "sweet" onions cannot be found as sets, but must be grown from seed.*
LEFT: *I try to pick beans young and thin; if they become large, they are stringy and tough.*
ABOVE: *Blue* Salvia farinacea *'Victoria' and* basilica fino *(an oramental dwarf variety basil that is ideal in salads and superb in pesto) grow thick and green and purple as a border around this quadrant of the garden; onions grow well next to the wires, in front of the climbing beans.*
BELOW LEFT: *Pole beans are beginning to climb up the strings and poles of a homemade tepee in the upper vegetable garden; these constructions add height and additional interest to a garden while serving a utilitarian purpose.*
BELOW RIGHT: *I pick peas early and often; the more I pick, the more the vines produce.*

ABOVE: *I plant four or five varieties of potato each year in well-prepared beds (with no manure), and dig them "new," right after the plants flower. My favorites are 'Yellow Finn', 'Red Bliss', 'Red Pontiac', 'Yukon Gold', and 'White Cobbler'.*

ABOVE: *A square of mesclun, or mixed salad greens, that has grown a bit too large. I prefer to pick it smaller, when it is at its tenderest best; Weeny, the seal point Himalayan cat, likes it big, all the better for chasing real and imaginary foes.*

ABOVE: *One of the first "homegrown" meals we had in Westport was a delicious spinach salad. I re-create that salad every June and July with the tender baby spinaches; then, as the plants mature, I stir fry, sauté, or steam the leaves.*

ABOVE: *Chervil likes shade and grows well under other plants like this curly kale. Some plants do seem to thrive in the company of others: blue salvia does well near tomatoes, for example, while dill and cabbages do well together.*
BELOW: *Another of the old-fashioned greens I like to grow, Swiss chard is delicious steamed or sautéed.*

ABOVE: *Beet seeds should be planted sparsely, a little less than an inch deep in rows 5 to 8 inches apart. As the beets grow, thin them twice, taking every other beet.*
BELOW: *Careful planning results in a garden with few bare patches—and occasional overlaps. Here sweet peas are intertwined with the tomato vines planted to overtake their space on the trellis.*

ABOVE: *Fred Specht always told me to plant the carrots when the ground is totally free of spring's chill; I start on June 1, and make successive plantings every two weeks, assuring me of a good harvest until frost.*
BELOW: *Snow peas, with their wonderful sweet pods, grow on 3-foot-tall vines; I space my pea wires about 2 feet apart for good growing and picking.*

GARDENING

214

ABOVE: *Broccoli 'Romanesco' is unimpressive in July, but will develop one conical head of bright chartreuse-colored florets that look to me like the hats worn by the Siamese dancers in* The King and I.

ABOVE: *I plant several types of pole beans: 'Romano', 'Zefa Fino', and 'Annelino'.*
RIGHT: *I like to pick most of my vegetables on the young side; these Brussels sprouts in the foreground of the lower garden are just ready. Behind, varieties of salad greens at different stages fill the raised beds.*

The Easter Field

ALL PASSIONATE GARDENERS LOVE TO experiment. Every season the catalogues show some new plant I cannot wait to try, or I spot in a friend's garden a variety with a color or petal shape I cannot resist. At the same time, I am, at last, very content with the gardens around my house: the combinations of flowers and forms seem just right, and I am reluctant to disturb the happy balance. In our Easter Field (so called because it's where we usually hold our Easter egg hunts), I created my "laboratory" gardens, where new plants can be tried out each spring—and removed if they are not pleasing.

Both Easter Field gardens were created in July; the earth can be easily worked at this time, and new plantings can be made quickly. The first one—370 feet long and 12 feet wide—we dug completely by hand. We removed the sod and composted it, then double dug the soil, adding well-rotted goat and cow manure and compost. Within a year the garden was thriving with all kinds of perennials.

Two years later, I decided to dig another border, of the same size, to the north; this time I encouraged my friend Victor Perkowski to help with his bulldozer and backhoe, and the work was done in a couple of days. Victor also in-

Victor Perkowski has always helped me when I needed an expert with a backhoe or bulldozer or some other monstrous piece of huge machinery. For the Easter Field border he used the backhoe to dig out a trench, saving the topsoil and using the subsoil to fill in low areas at the rear of the property.

ABOVE: *With the backhoe and a ditch-digger attachment, Victor dug a narrow, deep trench for water lines.*
BELOW: *In my part of Connecticut the lines and the hydrants must be placed deeper than 3 feet, preferably at 4 feet, to prevent freezing during cold spells. These frost-free lines are not just for the garden: they are invaluable if you keep backyard livestock that need constant watering, and they are very useful in case of fire.*

ABOVE: *It was very important to make this second border exactly parallel with the first. Tightly drawn cord marked the new edge and a deep, clean cut with a square spade separated the garden from the grassy area (this was reseeded, and within a few weeks good new grass was growing in this wide central walkway).*
BELOW: *The original border in early summer is well planted, with plenty of spacing between the new perennials.*

stalled a deep water line the length of the garden so that we would have year-round running water via hydrants placed deep below the frost line—it has been a great help during dry spells.

This garden took a little longer to thrive because of one error: trying to avoid ruining the grass path that runs between the two gardens, I asked Victor to drive the bulldozer out over the newly dug soil. This caused too much compacting, and for the first two years we had trouble with the drainage. Lots of the initial plantings were lost; after two years, I dug up the entire bed and tilled and aerated the soil until it was workable.

These borders are planted with a vast array of color and variety. Inspired by Christopher Lloyd's garden at Great Dixter, I planted shrub roses and other flowering bushes right in the borders. Pussy willows, various hydrangeas, and hibiscus grow near hollyhocks, asters, and daylilies. In these gardens I have discovered new and wonderful varieties; I have also learned useful lessons: clumps of ornamental grasses, pretty at first glimpse, are terribly invasive in a flower garden, and not to my liking. Some asters sound good in catalogue descriptions but have rather gigantic growing habits and tiny flowers—not at all attractive. Phlox must be monitored carefully in case hybrids revert to the common mauve type. On the other hand, *Achillea* is carefree and heat resistant, and best of all, its blooms, traditionally yellow ('Moonshine'), are now available in shades of apricot, pink, white, cream, and even red: 'Red Beauty' flowers profusely in the Easter Field border.

ABOVE: *Siberian iris, digitalis, euphorbia, and some perennial grasses are among the first flowers to bloom in the Easter Field. Note the buckwheat-hull mulch that is thickly covering the ground: it was an effective weed control, but I did not like its inert, dry appearance, and as in other parts of the garden, I found it created unhealthy conditions.*

BELOW: *As I learn more about the many genera available for the home garden, I am astonished by their variety and their individual characteristics. Sea Holly, for example, with its serrated foliage and thistlelike flowers on pincushion centers, is an exciting perennial for the flower border. These sea holly flowers are bluish at maturity, and when cut, the lacy blooms last in water for more than two weeks.*

ABOVE: *Both Easter Field gardens are in view: the south border, two years old, blooms with phlox, coreopsis, and astilbe, while the north border is newly planted with large perennials.*

BELOW: *Astilbe were unknown to me when I first moved to Connecticut, then I discovered a huge planting and fell in love with its feathery, fernlike flowers and its attractive foliage. 'White Plume', light pink 'Erica', and dwarf deep red 'Etna' are a few available varieties.*

ABOVE: *Single hollyhocks are often overlooked, replaced by fully double "powderpuffs," but the simpler flowers (tucked here behind the astilbe) retain an old-fashioned charm.*
BELOW: *Within a month of planting, the new Easter Field border already begins to look good. However, even with the buckwheat-hull mulch, weeding is an enormous task—in the height of the summer we sometimes hire another helper just to pull weeds and cut grass.*

ABOVE: *Ornamental grasses became popular a few years ago, and I planted some in the Easter Field southern border. Within three years, great clumps were threatening everything around and have been dug up and replaced. Grasses such as these should be planted in great grassy beds, where they can be viewed and enjoyed without jeopardizing the garden.*
BELOW: *I have used the Easter Field borders to more closely examine variegation, a phenomenon that can look quite beautiful in the catalogues, and not at all attractive in reality. This Iris pallida 'Alba-variegata' is one of the successes: it first emerges as a great fan of wonderfully striking, spiky green, white, and cream leaves; lavender blue flowers appear in early summer and have a delicious fragrance.*

Hollyhocks

LONG BEFORE I HAD A GARDEN OF my own, I was collecting garden books. My favorites are the old ones, found in boxes at tag sales, or under the tables at flea markets. I love to find in them illustrations of flowers that have gone out of fashion, and now that I have a garden, I love to search out those flowers to grow for myself.

The strangely tall, thin, and distinctly large-flowered hollyhock *(Althaea rosea)* is more familiar in images than real life. The hollyhock, a garden staple in Shakespearean England and a popular floral motif in Chinese art, is of unknown origin. It is thought to have developed in cultivation, perhaps in China, as it is not known in the wild.

Modern hybridization has ruffled, fringed, and doubled many hollyhock flowers. My favorite is the single English maroon-black variety—*Althaea rosea* 'Nigra'. Hollyhocks grow to 6 feet with huge, hairy, somewhat heart-shaped leaves; dwarf varieties reach only 2 feet. Flower buds open from bottom to top, and peak in early summer, when the whole stalk is nearly covered with blooms. Flowers, up to 3 inches or more in diameter, can be white or shades of yellow, pink, or crimson.

True sun-lovers, hollyhocks do not perform well in shade. They are more particular than some perennials, requiring good air circulation but not too much wind and a quite fertile, well-drained soil. Because of their towering stature, hollyhocks look best at the back of a flower border or next to a wall or a fence. They frequently require staking.

Sow seed indoors in February, and flowers may bloom the first season. Transplant seedlings outside in the perennial border only after danger of frost is past. Space them 18 inches apart. Seeds started outdoors in May will not flower until the following summer. Once established, this prodigious self-sower continues to reproduce. So long as varieties are not mixed, seeds will have a chance of breeding true to variety.

Although a perennial, hollyhocks are treated as biennials. They are apt to be afflicted by a rust that mars the leaves with orange markings and reduces flower quality. Some plants on the market have been bred for resistance to the fungus. By growing plants for two years and then discarding, you reduce the likelihood of being troubled by the fungus. If the undersides of leaves show rusty spots, remove and burn. Allow only healthy plants to continue in your garden from season to season.

TOP LEFT: *The single pink hollyhock* (Althaea rosea) *is classically charming.*
CENTER LEFT: Hemerocallis, *better known as daylily, is another old-fashioned flower that has developed in recent years into a widely collected species.*
BOTTOM LEFT: *Delphiniums are perhaps the quintessential border flower, tall and imposing, very colorful, with a long blooming period. Determined to have them in my garden, I obtained seedlings from Mr. Askenback, a Westport gentleman who has experimented with the English strain, Blackmore and Langdon. I have had only minor success: this is a second-year plant, badly in need of staking.*

ABOVE: *Higo iris, yarrow, allium, lupines, sweet William, bee balm, astilbe, lamb's ear, and veronica for a summer bouquet.*
LEFT: *Many dandelions find their way into my field of grass; I pick them as soon as they are fully open and make dandelion wine. I try to never let the flowers go to seed, fearing a more serious encroachment.*
RIGHT: Achillea *(milfoil, or yarrow).*

Berry Tartlets

MAKES 30 TO 40
TARTLETS

*Use the freshest, most beautiful berries
you can find for the tartlets.*

1 recipe Pâte Brisée (page 347)
1 cup Black Currant Curd
1 cup Lemon Curd
2 pints fresh raspberries,
    blackberries, strawberries, or a
    mixture

1. Make Pâte Brisée. Chill thoroughly
before rolling out.
2. Assemble two 1½- to 2½-inch tartlet
pans for each shell you plan to bake.
Spray the insides of half the tartlet pans
with vegetable spray.
3. On a well-floured board, roll out the
pastry to ⅛ inch. Press a piece of pastry
into each oiled pan and remove excess
with your thumb. Press a second, un-
coated pan into each shell to act as a
weight while baking. Place the pans on a
baking sheet; chill for at least 30 minutes.
4. Preheat the oven to 375°.
5. Bake pastry for 10 minutes, or until
edges begin to color. Remove the liner
pans and continue to bake until the shells
are golden, 5 to 7 more minutes. Cool
on racks.
6. Spoon filling into shells and top with
fresh berries.

LEFT: *Ranging from 1 to 4 inches in
diameter, these delectable berry tartlets are
wonderful for tea. I serve them with herbal
infusions or special teas like Rose Pouchong
or Fortmason (from Fortnum and Mason
in London). I like to set the table outdoors
with white linens and a French porcelain
tea service decorated simply, pink on white.*

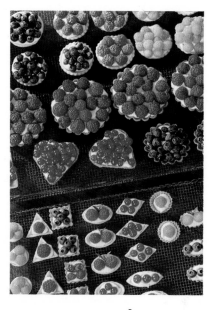

Black Currant Curd

MAKES 1 PINT

6 large egg yolks, lightly beaten
1 cup sugar
½ cup black currant juice
½ cup (1 stick) unsalted butter, cut into small pieces
1 tablespoon cassis

1. Strain egg yolks through a sieve into a medium saucepan over low heat. Stir in the sugar and black currant juice. Cook, stirring constantly, for about 10 to 12 minutes, until the mixture thickens and coats the back of a wooden spoon. Do not allow the mixture to boil.
2. Remove from heat and whisk mixture until slightly cooled. Stir in butter, a piece at a time, until fully incorporated. Add cassis. While still warm, pour into sterilized jars, cover tightly, and refrigerate until ready to use.

Lemon Curd

MAKES 1 PINT

6 large egg yolks, beaten
1 cup sugar
½ cup freshly squeezed lemon juice
½ cup (1 stick) unsalted butter, cut into small pieces
1 tablespoon grated lemon rind

1. Strain egg yolks through a sieve into a medium saucepan over low heat. Stir in the sugar and lemon juice, and cook, stirring constantly, for about 10 to 12 minutes, until the mixture thickens and coats the back of a wooden spoon. Do not allow the mixture to boil.
2. Remove from heat and whisk mixture until slightly cooled. Stir in butter, a piece at a time, until fully incorporated. Add the rind. While still warm, pour mixture into sterilized jars, cover tightly, and refrigerate until ready to use.

ABOVE AND LEFT: *I now cultivate all types of raspberries—golden, red, purple, and black—each unique in flavor and size. Currants for topping tartlets such as these should be the 'Red Lake' (bright red) or white varieties. Black currants are not very good for eating in the raw state— they are much better cooked and pureed or juiced (as in the black currant curd used to fill the tartlets). Woodland strawberries,* Fraises des Bois, *are very different from the ordinary garden-variety berries—smaller, sweeter, more tender, and immensely more fragrant.*

A U G U

WHEN MY DAUGHTER, ALEXIS, WAS A CHILD, she sometimes set up a stand on the street to sell our excess August harvest to neighbors and commuters who drove past our house on their way home from the train. It was fun to create a little market, to weigh and add and make change. It was also an extremely sensible—and ecological—way to use up the plethora of the garden. ✿ Now I just show a few close friends how and what to pick, and their families are provided with vegetables all summer long that are infinitely more varied and fresh than store bought. ✿ I greatly enjoy the long days of summer and start very early, at sunrise, to weed and to plant. Some days I don't go inside at all until dark, choosing instead to answer the phone in the garden, eat my lunch in the tomato patch, and pour cold iced tea from a pitcher brought into the garden by Necy, or by Mother if she happens by for a swim. I encourage my young nieces and nephews to use the pool and they often help me harvest: we have blueberry-picking contests and hunts for the largest tomato. A garden

ABOVE: *José Arcadio Buendia, a member of the parrot family, is the noisiest bird on earth—his strident voice was heard even above the lawnmower.* LEFT: *If I'm working at home I'll often stroll through the garden; I'll stoop to pull a weed, see a flower that should be picked, or a herb, like this fragrant basil, that should be snipped.*

S   T

should be a place of life and laughter. I love to share its pleasures, as well as its bounty of good harvest.

My garden in August, although amazingly prolific, still creates problems. The hot weather causes many plants like the basils and lettuces to bolt; once this happens they must be pulled and their space replanted. The flower beds and borders, so lush and colorful, now fade, many of the perennials finished blooming for the year. I am attempting slowly to make all of these gardens true perennial gardens, planted for continuous, luxurious bloom, but I fear that I will disturb the character of the garden if I replace too many May- and June-flowering plants with those that will bloom in August and September. So I am proceeding slowly, fitting in an aster or two here, and there a grouping of sedum, a stand of monkshood, and five or six anemones near the poppies or lilies.

ABOVE: *In hot weather, the chicken coop is cleaned out every three weeks, the old bedding carted off to the compost heap. Clean surroundings are very important when backyard livestock are kept.*

RIGHT: *In August, lettuces and cabbages go to seed, as do dill, basil, chervil, even broccoli, cauliflower, and rhubarb.*

JOURNAL

Lettuce seeds planted on 4th; germinate on 6th.

Beans, peas, squash, herbs, spinach, mâche, arugula planted in succession.

Friends instructed in rules of picking.

Basil picked; several kinds of pesto made.

Garden helpers start at 7 in the morning because of heat wave.

Water hydrant next to garden shed breaks; entire unit dug up to find leak at bottom.

Red, golden, white beets replanted.

Collards and kale planted for fall.

Weeding and watering are a way of life.

Mom strings little red hot peppers.

Chicken coop cleaned and washed.

Birds eat unopened sunflowers.

Turkeys finally sexed: two males, two females.

Phlox mildewed.

Roses get more black spot, must be sprayed.

Euonymous, yews, and boxwood given light shaping.

Flowers deadheaded and topdressed with bonemeal and compost.

Lots of lettuce varieties planted as beds cleared out.

Sweet pea vines fed to chickens; runner beans planted in their place.

All fruit trees fed.

Roses given systemic root feeding.

Grass paths edged and reseeded where worn.

Manure added to all new gardens.

Soap-based spray applied to tomatoes against whitefly.

Young Brussels sprouts harvested.

RIGHT: *I make successive plantings of onions, starting from seed so as to have the greatest variety. The seedlings are planted out about 3 inches apart; in less than one hundred days, most of the onions have reached maturity and must be picked. While the tops are still green, I bend the leaves down to the ground, just above the crowning point of the onion.*

ABOVE: *I let the onions sit like this until the tops are dry and brown (up to five days); they are then ready to be picked.*

BELOW: *Once pulled, the onions are left to dry in a cool, dark place until I can rub the loose skin and dirt from the surface. I try to leave the coppery inner skin intact on these sweet 'Fiesta' Spanish onions; it will act as protection.*

Onions

ALTHOUGH MANY GARDENERS PREFER planting onion sets (small bulbs), I find sowing seed works best for me. I begin as early as February and March with successive sowings in small peat plugs. Once a strong root has developed, my onions are planted in trenches outside in the garden as early as April—3 to 4 inches apart, in rows or squares. They can withstand a mild spring frost.

Day length is very important when growing onions—if you want bulbs and not just scallions. The number of hours of light triggers bulb development in onions, and I plant the "long day" varieties that do best in northern locales.

Most of today's cultivated onions are varieties of *Allium cepa*. I grow many of these yellow, white, and red onions. All onions can be harvested almost immediately as scallions (though specific scallion seeds are also available), and I always enjoy the thinnings. I feed my onions with my own homemade "manure tea." To make this, let 1 cup dried cow manure stand in 2 gallons of water for a few days and then dilute to the color of weak tea.

OPPOSITE ABOVE: *'Rossa di Milano' are excellent storage onions.*
OPPOSITE BELOW, LEFT TO RIGHT: *After the outer skin has been rubbed off, the onions are braided. Starting with three onions, plait the tops, adding a new onion every inch or so. For sturdiness, twist a piece of natural twine into the braid; this can be looped at the top for hanging.*
RIGHT: *'Red Mac' onions, set out late, must be supported with earth until mature.*

Eggplants

EGGPLANTS ARE NOT THE EASIEST vegetables to grow in my climate, but I persist each year in trying many varieties, always looking for those that are not bitter or seedy, with tender skins that require no peeling.

Eggplants (*Solanum melongena* var. *esculentum*) are tropical natives with centuries-old roots in Africa; Arab traders probably introduced them to the Middle East. They require a longer growing season than their tomato relatives. I start them in my greenhouse in March for an outdoor planting date of May 15. Eggplant does not transplant well, so I sow each large seed in its own peat plug and then move them into $2\frac{1}{4}$-inch reusable plastic pots. When the seedlings are strong, healthy, and about 6 inches high, they are hardened off for about a week in my cold frame before going into the ground. The soil should be rich in organic matter, and I feed the plants once a month with a well-balanced fertilizer.

Weather dictates success: eggplants must be protected when early summer nights are too cool—lower than 55 to 60 degrees. Some varieties with large, heavy fruit require a bamboo stake, but most grow unsupported.

Harvest eggplants after the skin becomes glossy (overripe, they lose their shine), usually when the fruits have reached about 4 inches. Cut with a knife, leaving about an inch of stem.

LEFT: *If I'm lucky, August brings masses of eggplants to be used or given away; we cook ratatouille and many Moroccan dishes.*

ABOVE: *'Black Beauty' is broad and blunt; fruits are large and flavorful.*
BELOW: *These anonymous fruits came from seeds I found during a trip to Japan.*

ABOVE: *'Violetta Lunga' is excellent for slicing into narrow strips for grilling.*
BELOW: *Just picked 'Black Beauty' and 'Ichiban' eggplants.*

ABOVE: *'Little Fingers' bears early and continues throughout the season.*
BELOW: *These perfectly round eggplants also came from Japanese seeds.*

ABOVE: *I grow several different varieties of Swiss chard, including red 'Charlotte', the crinkly-leaved 'Paros', and a silvery-ribbed dark green 'Argentata'.*

ABOVE: *Planted in May and early June, 'Rossa di Verona' radicchio first forms these beautiful, round heads with bitter, tough leaves. Cut back in September, they will return next year as delicious dark red heads with white veins.*

RIGHT: *These rows of lettuce should have been transplanted at 3 inches tall. Now too large to take well to moving, they will not form heads, but can be used as leaf lettuce.*

Beets

MODERN BEETS ARE VARIETIES OF A European native, *Beta vulgaris*. They are cool-season vegetables, growing best in my garden in spring and late summer into fall.

I start large varieties as early as February in the greenhouse with successive sowings in flats and transplant outdoors in April. Miniature ones are sown in the ground, as is the second crop in August. I grow red as well as yellow and white ones.

The seeds are really fruits containing many seeds. Don't be surprised to find multiple seedlings where you planted one "seed." Thinning is important; I eat the leafy tops of even the tiniest of thinnings, which, when less than 2 inches tall and close together, are best pinched off; pulling disrupts others nearby. Like other root crops, beets require soil where manure has had ample time to decompose. The roots are harvested forty to fifty days after planting; the green tops can be picked for salads at any time.

RIGHT: *Underused and underestimated, beets are one of my favorite vegetables. They hold well in the soil for extended harvesting, but I still stagger their planting. I start with seeds sown in plugs in the greenhouse for later transplanting, and continue with seeds sown directly in the ground for thinning as they grow. White 'Albina', 'Golden', and red 'Early Wonder' beets are harvested with bright tops rich in vitamins; I often serve both the leaves and the beets in the same salad. I am particularly fond of the 'Golden' beets, which do not "bleed" in cooking.*

ABOVE: *Beets are relatively simple to grow, doing best when planted before and after the heat of midsummer.*

ABOVE: *The soil must be moist to prevent roots from turning woody. Beets that erupt from the ground must be picked quickly.*

ABOVE: *In Paris street markets, I saw beets roasted like this in foil packets; the skins easily slip off the cooled roots, and vitamin content and flavor are preserved.*

ABOVE: *A sweet 'Gypsy Hybrid' pepper.*
LEFT: *'Anaheims' are quite pungent.*
BELOW: *'Hungarian Wax', mildly hot.*

ABOVE: *These are both four-lobed 'Bell Boy Hybrid' peppers; the green will eventually turn to scarlet.*

ABOVE: *'Torito' peppers are hot enough to mandate gloves while picking.*
BELOW: *We dry cayennes for ristras.*

ABOVE: *Peppers that turn yellow (as these 'Sweet Bananas' will) are natural; the purples or chocolates are specially bred.*

ABOVE: *'Gedeon Hybrid' peppers are extra large, with thick walls—excellent for stuffing. Pepper plants are started in the greenhouse; after 8 to 10 weeks, they are planted out into warm, rich soil, 16 to 24 inches apart, and heavily mulched. Full-grown plants are upright if staked, and very pretty, with dark, glossy leaves and bright white flowers.*

ABOVE: *A small harvest. Peppers are classed in two groups, hot and sweet. Both can be stuffed: I will vary the fillings— mild for the hot peppers, spicy for the sweet—and then bake them separately in olive-oil-rubbed dishes, covered, until they are tender. Served hot or at room temperature, stuffed peppers are delicious. We also dry hot peppers for winter use.*

ABOVE: *I begin cucumber seeds indoors, hardening them off in cold frames. 'Green Knight' will produce 18-inch cucumbers.*

ABOVE: *This is broccoli 'Calabrese', which forms tender little shoots rather than the more common clustered heads.*

ABOVE: *When "curds" appear in the cauliflower, I tie the leaves over the crown with raffia or a rubber band, and harvest when the heads are 8 or 9 inches in diameter, before they get a greenish tinge.*

Beans

SNAP OR STRING BEANS (PHASEOLUS *vulgaris*) are the most recognized bean species in this country. These New World natives are mostly grown for their edible pods, but I also like to harvest them dried, when they are loaded with protein, B vitamins, iron, and potassium.

Lima and kidney beans are also species of *Phaseolus*. The fava or broad bean (*Vicia faba*), the most tolerant of cold temperatures, is an Old World native, and soybeans (*Glycine max*) come from the Orient. All are legumes—part of the pea family or Leguminosae.

Beans are categorized loosely by use: snap beans have edible pods, shell beans immature seeds, and dried beans ripe seeds. They are also classified by their growing habit—pole or climbing and bush or dwarf. Bush varieties don't need support, bear beans earlier, and have a shorter season than pole beans. The pole varieties produce more beans, bearing throughout the season.

An excellent crop for first-time gardeners and children, beans are extremely resilient with few disease problems, provided they are not planted too early. One precaution to bear in mind is never work or walk near beans when they are wet as you risk spreading any minor problems that might exist. Rotating the crop each year also further reduces disease risk.

Plant snap beans when the ground has warmed to 60 degrees. Bean seeds will rot in cold soil. If you start them indoors, do so three weeks before the last frost date in your area. I also make successive sowings, in rows and squares, of bush snap beans 1 inch deep and 4 inches apart throughout the summer. This ensures a continual supply of the crisp, cool pods. Climbing snap beans grow on the same poles, arranged in tepees, that served to support my earlier cool-weather pea crops. Plant snap bean seeds around the base of each pole, 1 inch deep and 6 inches apart. Space bush lima bean seeds 8 inches and pole limas as much as 10 inches; both are sown 2 inches deep. Limas are less tolerant of cold than the snap and go into the garden after the ground has warmed.

All kinds of beans grow prolifically in my rich garden soil, and I dry some of the more unusual and colorful varieties right on the vine, including 'Swedish Brown', 'Fiamata Flageolet', 'Yellow Eye', 'French Horticulture', 'Vermont Cranberry', 'Christmas Lima', and 'Jacob's Cattle'. Once the plant leaves have browned, I begin harvesting the pods. Once picked, they are allowed to dry completely for a few more weeks in an airy site. Then they are shelled and stored in clear glass jars, their decorative coloring and unusual markings making them attractive until we are ready to use them.

A quicker method for shelling dried beans requires a burlap bag, two buckets, long rope, and a stick, such as a broom handle. Place the dried bean plants in the bag, tie it, and hang at about shoulder height from a sturdy wall. Beat the bag with the stick. Place the bucket under one corner of the bag and cut a small opening to allow the beans to flow out— into the bucket. On a windy day, pour the beans back and forth from one bucket to the other; the chaff will fly away.

ABOVE: *Here are some of my bush and pole beans: 'Camile', a high-yielding filet bean; 'Dragon Tongue', a flat waxy bean; 'Royal Burgundy', a purple bush bean; 'Dorabel', a tender yellow filet bean; 'Bush Romano', which should be harvested just as pods begin to fatten; 'Green Annelino', with the flavor of a romano; 'Slankette'; and 'White Knight' runner beans.*

LEFT: *It is important to harvest beans at just the right size and age for optimum flavor and tenderness. This is a handful of one of my favorite bush beans, 'Tendercrop': picked before pods filled out (as all bush beans should be), these are crisp, tender, and truly stringless.*

ABOVE: *Most of the larger fruits are just starting to swell to mature size. These yellow freestone peaches are still green, but will ripen to golden yellow blushed with red.*
LEFT: *This three-year-old dwarf 'Red Bartlett' tree should produce many more pears, but a late-spring frost has reduced the harvest significantly.*

ABOVE: *Though only 7 feet tall, this dwarf apple is a good producer. Its apples can be picked in late August.*
BELOW: *I recently planted golden and white cherry trees, including this 'Napoleon'. With the exception of the new multivariety grafts, cherries are not self-pollinating, and it is imperative to plant two or more of each variety.*

Containers

WALLS, GATEWAYS, POOLS, AND terraces are always more beautiful when adorned with unusual urns or containers planted with combinations of flowers, ivies, and herbs.

I like to plant most of the containers early in the season with plants that will grow all season: ivy, scented geraniums in standard or topiary form, vinca minor, and prostrate rosemary or thyme. These I interplant with other, less-long-lived plants, beginning in early spring with pansies. When these become leggy in June or July, I replace them with lobelias, petunias, or nicotiana. Some containers are planted with only one kind of flower: the large terra-cotta urns were filled one year with pale peach bearded iris, another year with huge tuberous begonias. I planted two large Chinese egg jars with blue flowering agapanthus, and they have flourished, blooming from April through June; smaller pots are planted with white agapanthus.

Cast-iron containers require paint; many people antique cement containers; and wood needs paint or some treatment against rotting. Soak clay pots overnight before filling and planting. All containers require holes for drainage; however, it is possible to use terra-cotta or plastic pots within a nondraining container that has been lined with 2 inches of gravel or coarse pebbles.

Before adding your growing medium, line the bottom of all containers with an inch or more of gravel. Use more gravel for taller containers. A rich growing medium consists of one-half good quality

potting soil, one-quarter coarse builder's sand (or perlite), and one-quarter compost (or peat moss). Mix thoroughly with a hand trowel.

Container plantings have a lower tolerance for neglect than do plants growing in garden soil. Containers will dry out faster, making regular watering a must. Feed plants with a water-soluble fertilizer every three weeks to ensure they have enough nutrients to keep them happy and healthy.

ABOVE: *Cast-iron urns, pots, and pedestals, like this one, should be wire-brushed clean and sprayed with a good outdoor enamel paint. The finish can be left plain or antiqued with shadings of paint. Cement and terra-cotta containers can be aged by applying buttermilk, water-soluble plant food, beer, yogurt, or manure tea to the surface and placing the container in a shady spot until a mossy green patina appears. Cast iron and cement can be left outdoors (empty and covered) during the winter; terra cotta must be brought indoors.*

CLOCKWISE FROM TOP: *Fresh Garden Salad, Yellow Beet Salad, Arugula and Red Oak Leaf Salad, Harvest Salad, and White Beet Salad. I like to serve these salads on colorful Fiestaware bowls and white or green glass platters; each creation appears artfully arranged without looking as though every item was touched and fussed with.*

Harvest Salad

SERVES 6

This is an excellent main course salad. Serve with hot crusty French bread and a wedge of ripe Italian Fontina or creamy Toma. The sun-dried tomatoes add special flavor, as do the baby okras.

12 red new potatoes, of uniform size
 4 tablespoons extra-virgin olive oil
   Salt and freshly ground pepper
12 whole shallots, unpeeled, of uniform size
12 peeled cipollata onions (or other small, white onions)
½ pound green beans, strings removed, soaked in warm water for 30 minutes
18 pieces baby okra, 2 to 3 inches long
 3 tablespoons canola oil
 2 tablespoons red wine vinegar
 1 tablespoon balsamic vinegar
¼ cup chopped parsley
 1 tablespoon fresh thyme
¼ teaspoon ground cloves
12 sun-dried tomatoes, either oil-packed, or dried

1. Preheat the oven to 375°.

2. In a shallow pan, toss the potatoes in 2 teaspoons olive oil, and salt and pepper to taste. Roast for 20 minutes, or until a fork just pierces a potato to the center. Let cool and cut into quarters.

3. Toss the shallots in 1 teaspoon olive oil and a pinch of salt. Roast in the oven until soft, about 30 minutes. Let cool, and partially remove skin, leaving them connected at the root.

4. In simmering salted water, cook onions for 12 minutes, or until they feel soft throughout. Let cool thoroughly.

5. Cook the green beans in boiling salted water for 5 minutes, then immediately plunge into ice water to stop the cooking process. Drain and set aside.

6. In boiling salted water, cook the okra for 3 minutes, or until just tender. Plunge immediately into ice water to stop the cooking process. Drain and set aside.

7. In a large bowl, whisk together remaining 3 tablespoons olive oil, the canola oil, vinegars, herbs, cloves, and salt and pepper to taste. Add all the vegetables and sun-dried tomatoes, and toss gently. Serve immediately.

Yellow Beet Salad

SERVES 4

Sherry wine vinaigrette subtly flavors the tender yellow beets and bitter radicchio. Orange and yellow calendula flowers have a unique flavor and also add a bright coloration to this salad.

4 medium yellow beets
1 head radicchio, leaves separated, washed, and dried
1 head oak leaf lettuce, washed and dried
4-6 calendula flowers, for garnish
 Sherry Vinaigrette
 ¾ cup extra-virgin olive oil
 ¼ cup sherry vinegar
 2 tablespoons Dijon mustard
 Salt and freshly ground pepper

1. Cook the beets according to the White Beet Salad method. Arrange the peeled and sliced beets with the greens on a serving platter.

2. Just before serving, whisk the dressing ingredients together and pour over the salad. Garnish with calendula flowers.

Fresh Garden Salad

SERVES 4

Use one handful of washed and dried salad greens per serving if salad is served with a meal, a bit more for a main course salad. Don't drown greens with dressing—about a tablespoon per person is enough.

Sherry Vinaigrette (see Yellow Beet Salad)
4 large handfuls salad greens (we used radicchio, oak leaf lettuce, ruby lettuce, basil leaves, flat-leaf parsley, nasturtium flowers)

Whisk together dressing ingredients. Reserve 3 tablespoons and pour the rest into a resealable jar for later use. Toss salad greens with reserved dressing and serve immediately.

Arugula and Red Oak Leaf Salad with Flowering Chervil

SERVES 4

Arugula is best when its leaves are 3 inches tall, but larger homegrown leaves are still superior to store bought. Chervil flowers are a bit milder than the leaves.

3 tablespoons hazelnut oil
1 tablespoon champagne vinegar
 Salt and freshly ground pepper
3 handfuls fresh arugula
1 handful baby red oak leaf lettuce
1 cup flowering chervil, or fresh chervil with stems removed

Whisk together oil, vinegar, salt and pepper in a large bowl. Add lettuces and chervil, and toss well. Serve immediately.

White Beet Salad

SERVES 4

White beets are perhaps the sweetest beets one can grow, and in combination with onion and beans they create a colorful and fine salad. The opal basil, which is purplish in color, sometimes veined with green, adds a unique flavor and appearance.

4-6 medium white beets
1 pound baby green beans (haricots verts)
1 medium red onion, thinly sliced
 Rice-Wine Dressing
 ½ cup extra-virgin olive oil
 ¼ cup rice-wine vinegar
 2 tablespoons Dijon mustard
 Pinch of sugar
 Salt and freshly ground pepper
1 small bunch opal basil, for garnish

1. Trim the beet tops, scrub well, and seal them in large pieces of aluminum foil. Bake until beets are tender, about 45 to 50 minutes. When the beets are cool enough to handle, slip off the skins and slice.

2. Trim the stems off the green beans. Blanch in boiling water for 3 minutes; the beans should be bright green and slightly crunchy. Drain and immediately plunge them into ice water to stop the cooking process. Drain well.

3. Whisk together the dressing ingredients and season to taste. Toss the beans, beets, and onion with the dressing.

4. Arrange on a platter and garnish with opal basil.

ABOVE: *I love to make small-container herb gardens, but I recently realized a long-held wish to build a full-scale herb garden behind my barn.*

I HAD ALWAYS WANTED TO CREATE a big herb garden in Westport, the formal kind one sees at historical restorations such as Williamsburg or Deerfield. I wanted to grow at least one of every kind of herb I had ever read or heard about. And I wanted the garden to be large, and walled, and orderly, with room for knots and borders and even a thyme "lawn" like the one at Sissinghurst. ❧ When my husband and I built the barn, we constructed a large, walled parking area behind it, and paved the space with crushed stone. When we had finished, I realized that we had made a mistake. It was a grand and visible space, surrounded by a beautiful four-foot-high stone wall. To devote it to cars seemed an important waste. With Renato and Renaldo, I dug it up and made my herb garden. It took three months to dig the beds, another three to fill them with rich loam, compost, and manure, and yet another to plant hundreds of herbs. Yet even the first season was a total delight to the senses. It was a beautifully scented garden, colorful in a subtle way, and totally useful. ❧

H E R B S

The design of my garden was adapted from a wonderful book, Herb Garden Design, *by Faith H. Swanson and Virginia B. Rady. Scores of herb gardens are presented, along with scale drawings, planting plans, and lists of herbs. I was particularly inspired by one chapter, "Using Standards and Maypoles," though I did not follow the planting plan, preferring to create my own.*

1. The herb garden was built right below the cantilevered deck of our reconstructed 1900 tobacco barn; to give the garden a more structured background, I added a bluestone terrace and four architectural stone pillars. A wonderful crew of stone masons finished this part of the job in just seven days of very hard work.

2. To protect the stone terrace from freezing, thawing, and cracking, we laid a 16-inch-deep cement base; the large paving stones were set atop this base and grouted with ¾ inch of gray concrete.

3. Vinnie, chief of the masons' crew, spread the cement with the help of his six-year-old son. Since this phase of the construction required heavy machinery, it had to be completed before work on the garden itself began.

4. The terrace floor was made of huge pieces of local bluestone, laid in an irregular pattern. An electric stone mason's watersaw cut the edges to size.

5. I marked the boundaries of the beds with strong stakes and heavy twine, and then we dug the rectangles right out of the parking lot. The crushed stone, which was on top of densely compressed "hardpan," was dug to a depth of 30 inches.

6. It was back-breaking work; as each bed was excavated, the gravel and stone was hauled away with the Gravely tractor and used to build up a low area along the property line. Paths, part of the original parking area, were retained.

7. For the new beds, we used four truckloads of Mr. Bulpitt's special enriched compost, two loads of rotted manure, and one load of sand. In addition, I was given three truckloads of good loam, and I enriched the mix with 400 pounds of triple superphosphate, 200 pounds of granular lime, and 200 pounds of 5-10-10 fertilizer.

8. Six of the completed beds, dug and filled. Paths were kept wide to enable me to bring in a large garden cart or wheelbarrow. Two special areas were created in the design for the urns.

Belgian Fence of Apple Trees

Grey Gravel Walks

Bluestone Edging

Bluestone Paving

Herb Garden Design

Garden 1: Hyssop, Flat-leafed Parsley, Bush Basil, Chives, Garlic.

Garden 2: Catmint, Sweet Marjoram, Tarragon, Horehound, Spike Speedwell.

Garden 3: Silver Thyme, Oregano, Bay trees, Grey Santolina, Chamomile.

Garden 4: Curly Parsley, Rosemary, Love-in-a-Mist, Yarrow, Sage, Salvia "Superba".

Garden 5: Chives, Variegated Sage, Winter Savory, Green Santolina.

Garden 6: Bee Balm, Scented Geraniums, Lemon Thyme, Salad Burnet.

Garden 7: Purple Sage, Salvia "Victoria", Lovage, Miniature Chives, Golden Oregano, Creeping Rosemary, Meadow Clary.

Garden 8: Chervil, Pennyroyal, Munstead Lavender, English Lavender, Spike Lavender, and Eight Kinds of Basil: Piccolo Verde Fino, Anise, Lemon, Dark Opal, Purple Ruffles, Genova Profumatissima, Napoletano, Broadleaf.

Garden 9: Seven Kinds of Thyme: Lemon, English, Common, Silver, White, Creeping, and Mother-of-Thyme.

ABOVE: *We installed a bluestone edging to give the beds more definition, and then I allowed the soil to settle.*
LEFT: *After about three weeks I dressed off the beds, raking them carefully and preparing them for the initial planting.*
RIGHT: *To make the furrows for the basil fino seeds, the first to be planted, I drew a heart-shaped hoe along a cord; once the seed is planted, the same hoe can draw the soil right over the groove, covering it to the correct depth.*

LEFT AND ABOVE: *Because we dug the beds right out of the parking-lot crushed stone base, the paths remained hard and even. I dressed them with ¼-inch round gravel, 1 inch deep.*

BELOW: *After all that hard labor, I wanted some "instant gratification," and so ordered a large selection of 1-quart potted herbs from some of our local plantsmen.*

ABOVE: *The rooted santolinas came in peat pots. After tearing away most of the pots, I loosened the roots and placed the plants in deep holes with 1 or 2 cups of water.*
BELOW: *Along the edge of the bed behind, I had planted violet spiked* Salvia x superba. *As each of these plants fills out and is clipped, the intersecting gray and green lines will be more defined.*

RIGHT: *To create equal spaces between the santolinas, I used my Japanese hand trowel (one of my favorite tools) as a measure.*
BELOW: Santolina virens, *a verdant green, contrasts nicely with silvery 'Nana', a charming deciduous dwarf lavender cotton* (S. Chamaecyparissus), *and with the catmint* (Nepeta), *a treat for the pets.*

ABOVE: *On top of the stone walls surrounding the herb garden, I placed several terra-cotta urns. These fragile antiques are not for planting, just for show.*

ABOVE: *Spaces were left in the center of the garden design for two huge, beautifully shaped composite stone urns, which were planted with miniature Alberta spruce.*

ABOVE: *In its first season, my new herb garden needed careful nursing, but the herbs' exuberant health—and scent and taste—was almost instantaneous reward.*

Thyme

OF THE MORE THAN 60 DIFFERENT species and varieties of thyme, garden thyme (*Thymus vulgaris*) is the easiest to grow. A much-branched perennial herb, it can reach about a foot in height and is native to the Mediterranean and Europe. Small, narrow oval leaves, about $1/8$- to $1/4$-inch long, seem to grow directly out of the stems with almost no stalk. Their scent is somewhat clovelike. Small flowers appearing in July and August are white to lilac. As the plant matures, it tends to become woody.

Other varieties of thyme, decorative and good for edging, smell like citrus *(T. x citriodorus)* or caraway *(T. herba-barona)*. Both have dark shiny leaves with white or lavender flowers. They are also grown for culinary use. Mother-of-thyme, or creeping thyme *(T. praecox arcticus)*, is a 2-inch-high groundcover, dense and moundlike with tiny rose-purple flowers; *T. praecox arcticus* 'Coccineus' is a cultivar of creeping thyme with redder flowers. Not good for cooking, both are well suited for rock gardens and as a groundcover, especially attractive between paving stones or bricks.

Thyme thrives in full sun but tolerates partial shade. Well-drained soil is crucial for prevention of fungal problems, and where winters are harsh, thyme requires cold weather mulching.

Sow seed directly in the garden in late spring. Cover lightly with a layer of fine soil and keep moist until germination— about a week. Then water when dry. Seeds can be started earlier indoors in a mixture of sand, peat moss, and sterile potting soil. After seedlings are several inches high, move them outdoors to a warm protected location to "harden off" for at least a week before planting. Thyme will often reseed itself.

Thyme is also propagated by root division. Dig up established plants in mid-spring and separate carefully. Replant. Cuttings from new, green stems, never woody ones, will root in about two weeks. Layering, another propagation technique, takes longer but is very reliable. In spring choose a long, flexible branch coming from the base of the plant. Bend it to the ground and strip off leaves and any smaller branches from the section where it touches the soil. Push this section gently into the soil and secure with a paperclip or U-shaped wire pushed into the ground on either side of the branch. Roots will develop where it touches the soil. At the end of the season, sever the branch that connects the newly rooted plant. Dig up, transplant, and mulch the first winter.

Leaves and sprigs can be picked all summer. The best quality harvest, however, is before thyme flowers in midsummer. Frequent cutting will help keep your plants from becoming woody too fast.

I grow the following varieties of thyme in my herb and vegetable gardens:

T. praecox arcticus
T. praecox articus 'Coccineus'
T. x citriodorus 'Argenteus'
T. vulgaris
T. x citriodorus
T. 'Alba'
T. Serpyllum

The longed-for thyme lawn, in which many different varieties of the herb
were planted as tightly as their growing habits would permit.

Basil

BASIL IS ONE OF MY FAVORITE HERBS. I grow many, many kinds in my garden, and am thrilled when I discover a new variety. I use the leaves liberally in cooking, especially in pestos and tomato-based sauces, and also as a pungent addition to the salad bowl.

Basil *(Ocimum basilicum)*, not hardy in northern climates, is grown as an annual. A culinary favorite, sweet basil can reach 1 or 2 feet in a season, producing aromatic, dainty white flowers and then tiny seeds. Varieties have diverse characteristics—some have dark purple foliage ('Dark Opal'), some textured foliage ('Green Ruffles'), others display large leaves ('Crispum'), and one is lemon scented ('Citriodorum'). A dwarf variety ('Minimum') is often planted in pots by Italian cooks. It grows into a pleasing globe shape and is said to repel insects.

Seed is the only method for reproducing this herb. Some basil self-sows directly in the garden; I always shake some of

the dried seeds back into the garden at the end of the season. Seeds can also be saved for the following year's crop; if you grow different varieties together, the seed produced will be of mixed lineage.

Basil requires warmth, plenty of water, and well-drained soil with a relatively low pH, around 6.0. Sun is preferable, but it will grow in partial shade. Once all danger of frost has passed and the soil has warmed to about 50 degrees, sow seeds directly in the ground no more than ¼ inch deep. Cover with a layer of soil and water with a fine spray. Germination

ABOVE: *Like my vegetables, the herbs are sown in successive plantings: here is another, younger row of broadleaf basil.*
BELOW: *I try to mark every plant in my garden carefully, but mix-ups do happen. This 'Purple Ruffles' basil has been labeled 'Red Ruffles,' but 'Green Ruffles' is correctly marked. Both are slow starters.*

takes about 2 weeks. Pinching back the tops of young plants encourages bushy growth.

For a head start, sow seeds indoors in a medium of equal parts sand, peat moss, and sterile potting soil about 6 to 8 weeks before the danger of frost is passed. Full sun, good air flow, and a dryish atmosphere are important for indoor germination. Too much humidity as well as overcrowding will cause fungal problems. Transplant, if necessary, to individual pots only after three to four leaves have appeared. When 3 to 4 inches high, plant outside.

When flower buds appear, pinch them off. Once basil begins to flower, the leaves become more pungent and no new ones will be produced.

Basil can be harvested all summer from the time the plant is large enough to spare a few leaves until the first frost, as long as flowers are pinched off. I plant successively to have tender plants all season. It is such a wonderfully prolific herb, I always have enough to give away.

ABOVE: *From left, purple basil, sweet basil, and broadleaf sweet basil. The broadleaf is one of the most productive basil varieties, and the one most familiar to us from produce stores and greenmarkets.*

ABOVE: *Among the chard, lettuce, and onions, another row of 'Purple Ruffles'.*
OPPOSITE: *From left, 'Purple Opal', 'Fino Verde', 'Greek Mini', salvia, and more 'Purple Opal' basil.*

I have 15 varieties of basil growing in the herb and vegetable gardens. From left to right, sitting on the windowsill of my barn, are:

Fino Verde Compatto
  'Piccolo'
Licorice basil
Purple basil
'Fino Verde'
'Purple Opal'
'Sweet Genovese'
'Green Ruffles'
Broadleaf sweet basil
Sweet basil
'Purple Ruffles'
Basil Napoletano
Fino Verde Compatto
Cinnamon basil
Mammoth basil
Lemon basil

It is wonderful to have such a selection to snip from as I cook. The cut ends of the herbs are in water and will last about a day unrefrigerated, or two days in the cooler. If the plant is uprooted and placed in cool water it will last even longer.

Dill

SINCE I AM OF POLISH BACKGROUND, dill—much used in many Eastern European dishes—is an important and familiar herb to me. I use it fresh, finely chopped, sprinkled on top of boiled potatoes, or over plates of beet or carrot soup. I use the dried seeds in the preparation of pickles, or in biscuits or bread.

A member of the carrot family, dill *(Anethum graveolens)* develops one long tap root—making it difficult to transplant successfully. It is an annual herb, native to the Mediterranean. Not only the leaves, with their subtle flavor, find their way into the kitchen, but the seeds as well have long been used—most famously for pickling. I grow two kinds of dill for these two purposes: bouquet dill, for seeds, and dukat dill, for a large supply of feathery, aromatic leaves.

Full sun and well-drained soil are a must for dill. Unlike many herbs that thrive in poor soil, dill prefers moderately rich soil with plenty of water.

Sow seeds in early spring once the danger of frost has passed; space them at least 8 inches apart. If you wait much later, you may not see flowers the first season. Dill seed germinates readily and once established will self-sow year after year if you allow a few of the flowers to go to seed.

Begin harvesting fresh leaves once the plants are established. Some gardener-cooks say the flavor is best when plants are in bud, just before flowers open. Fresh dill is quite delicate; pick it right before using—it lasts but a few days in the refrigerator.

Rosemary

I AM EXTREMELY FOND OF ROSEMARY, and use it when sautéeing fish, grilling lamb, or in a tomato-cream-saffron sauce for pasta. The blue flowers are tender and an excellent way to obtain the taste of the herb without using the tough, leathery leaves.

Rosemary *(Rosmarinus officinalis)* is a perennial evergreen shrub with needle-like dark green leaves. Varieties have either an upright or prostrate habit; the prostrate or horizontal-growing ones are ideal for planting in urns; I grow the upright varieties, which can reach 5 or 6 feet tall, in my gardens. The herb produces clustered flowers, powder blue, pink, or white, in early summer; I use them as garnish in my cooking.

Rosemary prefers a well-drained, slightly acid to neutral soil in a sunny location, but will also grow in partial shade. Not being reliably hardy below about 10 degrees, rosemary will not survive Connecticut winters. Every fall, I dig up a few plants and make stem cuttings and bring all into my house and greenhouse to overwinter.

Rosemary seeds have a poor germination rate, and plants produced this way do not seem to be nearly as vigorous as those propagated from layering or cuttings. Take 3-inch cuttings from new growth—a greenish soft, not woody, stem; and strip the leaves from the lower half or third of the stem. Fill a shallow container (with a drainage hole) with a rooting medium of half sand and perlite; wet and pack it down. Push the bottom part of the stem into

the medium; make certain no leaves are below the surface, as these will rot and can cause fungal problems. Mist cuttings daily—in the morning, never at night. After three weeks have passed, gently pull stem to check on root development. Once rooted, replant in a small pot with sterile potting soil or a mix of equal parts sterile soil, sand, and peat moss. Mist regularly. A few weeks after transplanting, you should pinch back the top growth for a fuller plant.

The leaves can be picked any time of the year; cut short sections of new growth from branch tips.

Sage

PLACED UNDER THE LOOSENED SKIN of chicken or turkey, or chopped and sprinkled in the sauté pan with thin slices of liver, sage can add amazing flavor to many foods. I love to use it, and do so frequently.

Garden sage *(Salvia officinalis),* native to Mediterranean hillsides, is very easy to grow. Its velvety, grayish-green leaves are about 2 inches long, very aromatic, and a culinary staple. This perennial grows to about 2 feet and in summer produces lovely purple flowers, which will add color to salads. Varieties can have leaves showing green, white, and purple ('Tricolor'), or purple ('Purpurea'), or gold variegated foliage ('Aurea'); a dainty dwarf variety ('Nana') has also been hybridized.

The pineapple sage *(S. elegans)* has dazzling scarlet flowers and a pineapple scent. About a foot taller than the garden variety, it is not hardy in Connecticut

ABOVE: *Not officially a herb,* Salvia farinacea *'Victoria' is one of my favorite annual flowers, and I use it frequently to border edges in the vegetable gardens.*

ABOVE: *I use delicately flavored chervil for flavoring fish, and garnish with its flowers.*
BELOW: *Coriander* (Coriandrum sativum) *likes cool weather, and must be sown before mid-June. The seeds are peppercorn-size, with a nutmeg-citron scent. Known as cilantro, it has a pungent smell and taste, indispensable in Oriental cooking.*

ABOVE: *Gilbertie's, my local herb specialist, sells 23 types of sage. I try to grow at least 8 for variety in color as well as taste. 'Tricolor' sage and purple sage* (Salvia officinalis *'Purpurea') look especially well combined in the herb garden; both plants are compact, strong and very fragrant. The smallest, tenderest leaves are wonderful sautéed with fish; small branches can be sautéed in olive oil with peppers.*

ABOVE: *Angelica* (Angelica archangelica), *a herb not often grown in the U.S., is treasured in Britain, where its stems are candied and give delicate scent and taste to cakes and buns. Easily propagated, it grows tall, with big, round clusters of greenish-white flowers.*

ABOVE: Salvia officinalis, *a strongly scented herb with small, tender leaves; the purple flowers are delicious in salads and with pork or poultry.*

ABOVE: *Rows of 'Bouquet' and 'Dukat' dills; both varieties must be picked before flowering for the best flavor.*
BELOW: *Behind the salvia, calendula blooms, whose bright yellow petals are excellent in salads, breads, biscuits, and for flavoring egg dishes.*

but can be overwintered indoors. Clary sage *(S. sclarea)* is even taller, up to 5 feet, with large heart-shaped leaves and dramatic two-toned lilac or white flowers. The seeds of this biennial sage are best sown annually if flowers are to bloom every year.

Pale yellow flowers are an added attraction to Jupiter's distaff *(S. glutinosa),* which is often grown just for its lovely foliage. About 3 feet tall, this perennial variety is native to Europe and Asia. Another European native is meadow clary *(S. pratensis),* growing to about 3 feet with brilliant sea-blue flowers.

Blue sage *(S. clevelandii),* 3 feet tall with blue flowers, is native to North America. This variety is an excellent culinary substitute for ordinary garden sage, although it is not reliably hardy in colder areas.

Sages require well-drained soil; too much water can be detrimental to established plants which are remarkably drought resistant. They perform best in sun, but they will grow in partial shade. Propagate sage by seed, division, cuttings, or layering. As with most of my herbs, I let sage go to seed at the end of the season and shake the seeds back into the soil. Late spring is the time to plant purchased seeds. Since sage spreads, transplant young seedlings so they are spaced about 1½ feet apart. Pinch off the tops of young plants for bushier growth.

Divide established plants; transplant the younger, newer growth at the outside of the plant. Sage gets woody with age and is best replaced every 3 to 4 years.

A perennial, sage maintains leaves throughout winter. I harvest sage from my garden all year long.

Storing Herbs

I HARVEST HERBS EVEN IN FREEZING weather—from the sage still showing leaves in the garden to herbs brought indoors to overwinter. I also freeze my own herbs, store them in oil, and even dry them; while dried herbs do not really compare to fresh, the homemade variety is infinitely better than the commercial.

Drying herbs is remarkably simple. The prime time is midsummer just before the plants begin to flower. Collect leaves or sprigs on a sunny morning before the heat of the day when oil content is highest and flavor at its peak.

Wash, if needed, in cold water and pat dry. Perhaps the easiest method is to tie sprigs—no more than three—in a bunch with cotton string and hang in a warm, dark airy room in the same manner as flowers. Leaves and sprigs can also be dried on cloth (I use fine muslin) stretched over a roasting pan, allowing air to circulate above and below. Herbs dry rather quickly—most in about two weeks. I store them in opaque containers, labeled and dated. Clear glass jars will allow you to check if moisture is still present, but they must be kept away from light.

The microwave is the twentieth century's drying rack. Rinse and completely dry leaves or sprigs. Place a layer on a paper towel or paper plate in the microwave with a bowl of water. Set the microwave on high for about 3 minutes. If herbs are crumbly, remove. If still damp, reset the microwave for 2 minutes and try again. Continue on 1-minute settings until completely dry.

Freezing is another modern method.

Rinse sprigs or leaves and dry thoroughly. Seal in plastic bags; press out any air and freeze. Do not thaw; simply take whatever portion is desired and add to your recipe. I also freeze chopped herbs in water in ice cube trays—remove cubes and store in dated plastic bags. Simply add whole cubes to recipes or drinks.

Basil is notoriously stubborn when it comes to preserving. It tends to lose its green color when dried, and many gardeners recommend microwaving as a way to preserve the color. My method for keeping basil green is to freeze the herb, finely chopped, in olive oil, stored in a sealed plastic sack.

Dill is one of a few herbs prized by cooks for seed. To collect seeds, pick flowers after they have browned, about two weeks past their bloom. Place them headfirst in a paper bag and hang the bag until seeds loosen, or suspend flowers upside down in a dark location with paper underneath to catch seeds as they drop. Store in airtight containers.

Herb sprigs can be extremely decorative and flavorful bottled in good vinegar or fine olive oil.

RIGHT: *When I am about to begin cooking, I pick a big bowl of the best culinary herbs in the garden. Here is an assortment of golden oregano, sage, chives, tarragon, lemon thyme, French thyme, parsley, marjoram, rosemary, and basil.* OVERLEAF, LEFT AND RIGHT: *In the herb garden's first summer, the beds were fragrant and colorful, with a good assortment of all kinds of herbs. Heavy rains caused some of the santolinas to perish in the autumn, but the next spring, they were replanted with much greater success.*

SEPTEMB

MY GARDENS EXPERIENCE A KIND of rejuvenation in September. Whatever reservations I felt about their condition disappear as the August replantings take hold and the vegetables and fruits put on their last flourish. ❧ I see a lot of my mother in September. Now that she has left teaching she has again the time to make preserves; I love to see her leave the kitchen with buckets and trays to pick the last berries or the first freestone peach. Not a single tomato will go to waste: Mother is here, transforming any excess into sauce, paste, or plain canned tomatoes with basil. If we've planted corn, she is wise enough to come the evening before the day I say it should be picked, rescuing it from the raccoons who surely would have outsmarted me, again. ❧ Alexis makes basil and parsley pestos; I spice peaches and seckel pears. We freeze berries and purees and juices; we fill jars and jars with jams, jellies, pickles, and chutneys for winter and spring use, and for giving as gifts. The garden is bountiful; as responsible gardeners, we should not waste its great generosity. ❧

ABOVE: *In the shade of the pergola, I grow American hybrid rhizomatous begonias. I start them in the greenhouse in May, and they begin to bloom in August. By pinching off the side buds, I sometimes get 6-inch blooms.*
LEFT: *Summer-blooming plants are cut down to make room for asters, dahlias, anemones, sedums, calendulas, zinnias, monkshood, and roses.*

E R

JOURNAL

Ripe peaches ('Redhaven', 'Golden Jubilee', 'Elberta') picked and spiced.

Lawns still mowed weekly.

A few spots in grassy paths reseeded.

'Big Boy' and 'Better Boy' tomatoes canned daily.

Max and Zuzu sent to Easter Field to ward off deer.

More dill, parsley, winter lettuces, coriander planted.

Tag-sale garden furniture painted.

Driveway and garden gates washed and painted.

Mildew on north side of house washed off with diluted bleach.

Fruits and vegetables harvested for canning, pickling, and relish making.

Driveways edged and weeded.

Dried beans harvested.

TOP LEFT: *The large perennial bed needs lots of attention after the hot and humid month of August. The phlox is suffering from mildew, and the ligularia, rudbeckia, and lilies must be cut down. But the grass paths, not too heavily trodden in August, are bright green and healthy.*
LEFT: *Cosmos, daisies, coreopsis, and gaillardia appear in place of earlier blooming plants.*
OPPOSITE: *A lone sedum, 'Autumn Joy', blooms amid a bed of green. After the blaze of color earlier in the season, this more monochrome garden is a refreshing respite.*

Lawns and Grassy Paths

MY FAMILY CLAIMS THAT I AM doing my best to eliminate lawns in preference for gardens of all kinds. There is a grain of truth in this: I do think that the mowing time for great grassy areas can be much better spent creating and maintaining gardens of fruits, herbs, vegetables, and flowers.

I do, however, like grass when it is a wide path through the perennial borders, a green relief in the orchard, or a smooth carpet for croquet. My lawns and paths are treated with the respect lavished everywhere else, and the resulting thick grass is a testimonial to that care.

We lime the grass early each spring. The entire lawn and every path is aerated with a power machine that pulls plugs from the soil. A light reseeding is done, and the entire area is watered. Paths are tied off from traffic until the grass is reestablished. We fertilize in April with 20-10-15 (a slow-releasing fertilizer is best), and again in September and in November (right after the grass has stopped growing, but before a hard freeze). Mowings are begun in late April, and continued every seven days throughout the growing season. All clippings are picked up after mowing and added to the compost heap; left on the grass, they may cause mildew or disease. We do some weed control (crabgrass is a problem in Connecticut), but I find that a healthy lawn is not too prone to disease.

Grass in a path is more demanding in its care than it is in a lawn. The width of paths is crucial; anything less than 3 feet will force traffic to follow one trail, causing irreparable damage. Drainage is critical. Working sand into the soil improves drainage, but the height of the path is also significant. With all the watering my perennial beds get, if the paths were lower than the bed soil level, water would drain onto the grass and make puddles.

Another consideration with grass paths is edging. Without it, foot traffic will grind down the borders. Edging keeps soil in the beds and the invasive roots of grass out. I use bricks set upright on the diagonal sunk halfway into the soil, creating a pinking-sheared look.

The grass in my paths is a patented mix called Trail Blazer Hybrid Dwarf

Fescue—a blend of tall fescue, Kentucky bluegrass, and perennial rye grass. Anyone who knows grass may recoil at tall fescue, which in the past was known as durable but coarse. But I find it holds up nicely with regular maintenance. This hybrid mix has a fine blade resembling Kentucky bluegrass. The tall fescue, grass, roughly 40 percent of the blend, remains green in hot weather and is quite drought tolerant. The Kentucky bluegrass, making up 10 percent, has the potential to fill in bare patches, eliminating the need for frequent reseeding. Perennial rye grass is a tough fast-grower that is more wear- and disease-resistant than the other two.

SEEDING A NEW LAWN. Test soil; a pH range between 5.5 and 7.5 is best.

Work the soil to a depth of 6 inches; add sand, if better drainage is required, and lime and fertilizer depending on soil-test results. Summer's end—not later than early October—is ideal for seeding new lawns in Connecticut.

Rake flat and broadcast seed; use a seed spreader to ensure even coverage.

Flatten seedbed with a lawn roller.

Water with a *fine* spray and keep moist until seeds sprout.

If you decide to take a short cut and use sod, prepare your bed exactly as for seeds. Choose a sod that is a blend of grasses; lawns with more than one grass species are more resistant to disease.

LEFT: Hibiscus moscheutos *hybrid 'Southern Belle' grows 4 feet tall with attractive, bushy foliage, and produces huge papery blooms in the latter part of summer and early fall.*

ABOVE: *Along one edge of the vegetable garden I planted annual asters, 'Totem Pole', 'Fluffy Ruffles', and 'Dwarf Border' mixed types. No garden should be without these excellent cutting flowers.*
LEFT: *A planting should consider texture as well as color. This border of* Artemesia schmidtiana *'Silver Mound',* Sedum *'Autumn Joy', and* Aster x frikartii *looks almost soft to the touch.*
RIGHT: Salvia farinacea *'Victoria' and some droopy second-blooming digitalis together in the perennial border.*

Compost

I FIND IT AMUSING AND WONDERFUL to see compost become fashionable, part of the great recycling wave. It has always been part of our garden routine. Frugality, a necessity during my childhood, has become so ingrained in me I cannot bear to see anything go to waste, and compost—wherein garden and kitchen leftovers become rich food for future gardens—is the ultimate in recycling.

Compost improves soil structure, and if manure, bonemeal, or fertilizer are added during decomposition, compost enhances soil fertility as well. The process is simple. The ratio of nitrogen to carbon is key: one-third nitrogen-rich to two-thirds carbon-rich plant materials will create a good balance for bacterial decomposition. Chopping or slicing all materials before composting speeds decomposition; never add diseased plants or kitchen scraps that contain meat or fat.

Choose a location on level ground near a convenient supply of water for your compost bin. Many gardeners select a concealed, partially shaded site in or near the vegetable garden. A good size for a half-acre yard is roughly 4 feet square and 4 to 5 feet high.

Building a bin is easy and inexpensive. Sink untreated 4-by-4 posts about 4 feet high into the ground at the corners. Bolt 2-by-6-inch boards to these posts, leaving space between each board for air. Keeping the front of your bin about 18 inches lower than the other walls allows ready access for shoveling in debris. Heavy-gauge wire, bricks, or even cinder blocks may also be used, so long as there is allowance for air movement. A cover made from wire or burlap will discourage animals from digging.

Line the bottom of the bin with 6 inches of coarse twigs, cornstalks, wood chips, or chopped brush—to aid air circulation at ground level. Add a few inches of plant materials rich in nitrogen mixed with twice that amount of carbon-rich waste (maintaining the $\frac{1}{3}$ to $\frac{2}{3}$ ratio). Sprinkle on well-rotted manure or bonemeal or fertilizer. Continue layering—never make layers more than a few inches. Moisten, but do not soak. A depression in the center of the pile will help catch rainwater.

Turn your compost about every eight weeks. If it starts to smell wretched, it is

ABOVE LEFT: *A "mistake" I made was interplanting the clematis and roses with many vines of morning glory* (Ipomoea). *Prolific and voracious plants, the morning glories almost took over the trellises; this all-white* I. *'Moon Child' seems about to overwhelm the arch.*
RIGHT: *Vigorous, but so beautiful:* I. nil *'Early Call Mixed', an early bloomer.*
FAR RIGHT: *I planted some morning glory on the pea and bean tepees, and the vines almost choked the weaker vegetables.*

almost certainly from lack of oxygen. Simply stir it again. If you want speedier decomposition, turn it every few weeks, moisten regularly, and add sprinklings of garden soil. Within several months to a year, you will have compost, or "black gold." This earth-smelling organic matter will be rich, dark, and hopefully crumbly. But don't worry if it's a bit lumpy. Just work it, lumps and all, into your garden soil.

INGREDIENTS FOR COMPOST
Nitrogen sources: kitchen vegetable scraps, grass clippings, houseplant trimmings, soft prunings, eggshells, coffee grounds, and tea leaves (even tea bags).
Carbon sources: autumn leaves, chopped cornstalks, paper egg cartons, and fireplace ashes.

TOP RIGHT: *The terrace off the kitchen was always a bit hot, so we designed and built this pergola. Its dappled shade allows me to serve meals outdoors even at high noon, and to grow potted plants like begonias, African violets, and agapanthus.*
BELOW RIGHT: *The porch stairs were given over to the begonias. A roll-down awning offers adequate shade.*
OPPOSITE TOP: *I grow many types of hydrangea (this is* H. paniculata*) along the southernmost border of the Easter Field. They give height to plantings and provide superb cut flowers in the fall.*
OPPOSITE BELOW: *The terrace looks bright and cheery, with orange and red begonias, purple agapanthus, and a large arrangement of decorative* H. paniculata *'Grandiflora'. This semishady place is also a perfect location for summering over my collection of indoor topiaries.*

ABOVE: *I recently discovered a wonderful type of clematis: C. montana rubens is a remarkably vigorous and fast growing species with beautiful rose-pink blooms that look like anemones. I planted these all around the pergola; within one growing season they should reach the tops of the columns and begin to cover the lattice roof. Clematis likes sun for the vine itself, but the roots prefer a moist shady spot. I think planting them at the base of the yew hedge was a perfect choice.*

LEFT: *I dug generous holes and enriched the soil with compost. The well-rooted and sizeable vines were placed carefully in the holes, making sure that the level of the new ground matched that of the container.*
OPPOSITE: *Almost devoid of color, the gardens are serenely beautiful. I continue to use the pool, even though it is unheated (our ecological statement), well into October. The dark, unpainted concrete helps to absorb the warmth of the sun and, in turn, warms the water.*

ABOVE: *I was captivated by the name 'Love-lies-bleeding' on a packet of* Amaranthus caudatus *seeds and planted far too many of these very invasive Victorian favorites.*

ABOVE: *In these last days of summer a bumble bee enjoys the nectar of a morning glory. The ruffly, citrus-yellow blooms are yellow marigolds, a native American flower introduced to Spain by Cortez.*

LEFT: Amaranthus caudatus *seeds itself annually, which is how a 'Viridis' somehow got into the eggplants.*
CENTER LEFT: *One year I planted dahlias amid the eggplants and peppers, and they loved the sunny spot, compost-rich soil, and extra moisture. I pinched this bicolored 'Decorative' to keep it bushy and productive; for giant specimen blooms, most of the buds would be removed and the plant allowed to grow tall and supported by stakes.*
BELOW LEFT: *The chicken coop garden is surrounded by a low yew hedge which, in turn, is surrounded by a narrow border in which I plant spring-flowering bulbs (*Anemone blanda *and* Muscari, *or grape hyacinths), and lots of French marigolds and zinnias for late-summer cutting. They are colorful and are said to ward off some insects.*
RIGHT: *Strawflowers (*Helichrysum bracteatum) *are cheerful in the autumn. I grow 'Bright Bikini' and 'Tall Mixed', and group them without regard to color in unusual containers like this McCoy vase.*

ABOVE: *I planted several rows of sunflowers in various parts of the garden.* Helianthus giganteus *grows 12 feet tall with foot-wide flowers, but smaller varieties are available. 'Luna', 5 feet tall, produces multitudes of brown-centered yellow flowers; 'Maximilian', a perennial sunflower, grows 6 feet tall and blooms with scores of 3-inch blossoms in the late summer; 'Mammoth' is another very tall type with thin-skinned seeds that are plump and meaty.*

LEFT: *There are still some roses blooming on the trellis in September. The vegetable garden itself is amazingly lush; every member of the* Brassica *family—broccoli, cabbage, kale, collards, cauliflower—thrives after most other vegetables have given out. The ferny green in the foreground is fennel.*

ABOVE: *After the dry bean pods are harvested, I shell them onto a large strainer. This mix of varieties (some of which came from friends in an antique-seed exchange) will be used in soups, baked beans, and Tuscan salads: 'Chevrier' (a pale green flageolet-type bean), 'Masterpiece' (a red flageolet bean), 'Cannelone' (a white shelling bean), 'Red Runner' (a speckled mauve bean), and 'Royal Burgundy" (a shiny dark purple bean).*

ABOVE: *If I forget to pick the pole beans while they are young and tender, they can be left on the vine to dry; they will lose no nutritional value in the process.*

LEFT: *Hog wire, galvanized wire woven into 4-inch-squares, is good for growing runner or climbing beans; finer mesh makes removal of the vines quite difficult. Always chop up the vines after harvest and before putting the material into the compost heap.*

ABOVE: *My French "potirons" (pumpkins) have unpredictable growing habits. Some grow round and pale yellow or orange, others flat and pale peach or bright orange; some are smooth, others very deeply ribbed. One year a potiron weighed 30 pounds, the next year 5 pounds. It is easy to grow pumpkins and squash if the ground is properly prepared and rich in organic material. I try to manure that part of the garden early, and to include different varieties of pumpkins, summer and winter squash, and zucchini.*

ABOVE: 'Gourmet Globe Hybrid' squash will have a delicate flavor at maturity. Cultivated by Central American Indians, this 4- to 6-inch bush squash is delicious steamed, baked, stuffed, or breaded.

ABOVE: Spaghetti squash first appeared a few years ago as a novelty and has become a staple in my garden. We boil it whole for 25 to 30 minutes, then pull the inner flesh from the skin, like strands of pasta.

ABOVE: 'Sweet Mama' is a winter squash with a dark green skin and bright yellow flesh. It is excellent steamed and pureed, and grows on compact vines, requiring very little space in the garden.

ABOVE: The 'Jack-Be-Little' pumpkin will taste mild, like a squash, when stuffed and baked. Only 3 inches in diameter, it is excellent for individual servings.

ABOVE: This winter potiron is maturing nicely into an orange, flat fruit with a thick, tough skin; it will be wonderful steamed and pureed for a soup or pie.

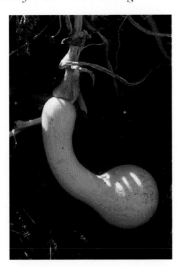

ABOVE: 'Butter Scallop' at maturity is bright golden yellow. It should be eaten while tender and young.
LEFT: The 'Melon' squash grows on a rampant vine and ripens after harvest, its sugar content increasing for three months.
RIGHT: A mystery squash: shaped like a butternut, but colored like a marrow or zucchini. Every year some of the markers are missing, and we are left to guess.

ABOVE: *These round, brown, applelike fruits are Chojuro pears; the flesh is juicy, crisp, and translucent—applelike in texture, but pearlike in taste. The tree is not self-pollinating and must be planted with another Asian pear or a Bartlett. The greenish pears are Beurre d'Anjou. These were picked a few days early because of a hurricane warning; they did ripen off the tree, and were delicious, sweet, and juicy.*

RIGHT: *We planted the new orchard in 1988, fifty-two trees in all. I wanted to try trees from Miller's of Canandaigua, New York, a grower that sells dwarf and semidwarf fruit trees because they found such trees to have a better, longer yield—and to be easier to pick. I have had success with their Compspur trees, which have almost twice as many fruit-growing spurs as regular semidwarfs and often produce in the second year. These apples, for example, are ripening on a Compspur McIntosh tree.*

ABOVE: *A lone apple on a newly planted semidwarf. Northern Spy ripens to a bright red with an overbloom.*

ABOVE: *Empire apples are similar to McIntosh, but keep longer. They ripen to a bright red and are uniform (medium) in size; I like them in tarts or baked.*

ABOVE: *Golden Russet is an old variety, producing medium-large apples that are very good for cooking.*

ABOVE: *Within a few weeks, this Canada Reinette will be crisp, fragrant, and juicy, with russet-splashed yellow skin. This is a wonderful eating apple.*

ABOVE: *A partial view of the old orchard. Some of these trees were planted in 1975; others were added later at the perimeter. At the end of summer the trees are extremely bushy, and lots of new top growth is evident. Much of this new growth must be pruned in early spring to shape the trees and make them more productive.*

ABOVE: *Roxbury Russets grow in abundance on a shapely, full tree. Very good "keepers," yellow and firm-fleshed, they are flavorful and good for pies, sautéed with cabbage, or caramelized as an accompaniment for roasts or birds.*

LEFT: *Some peaches continue to ripen as late as September. Hale Haven produces yellow freestone peaches with high red cheeks. The trees are generally very good producers and the fruits are large and delicious.*
ABOVE: *Lady apples ripen to beautiful miniature golden yellow fruits with red blushes. They are somewhat sour-sweet, and I find they make excellent jelly (they are very high in natural pectin). They are also most decorative in large flower arrangements or by themselves displayed on the branches.*
BELOW AND RIGHT: *I now have nine quince trees on the property and I think that is too many: quince trees are very, very productive. Each September the green fuzzy pearlike fruits turn a deep gold; we harvest bushels for baking and for jelly and preserve making (like lady apples, quinces are very high in pectin and can be used to thicken preserves made from other fruits, like raspberries). I also use sweetened quince juice to thicken whipped cream, and I love to make quince paste to spread on toast.*

Menu

GRILLED HALIBUT

FRESH CORN SALAD

PEACH SHORTCAKE

Grilled Halibut

SERVES 4

Rather than serving whole slices of grilled fish, I sometimes try breaking up the fish into large, tender flakes. Served with fresh corn salad, this halibut is delicious and inexpensive.

Marinade
2 tablespoons extra-virgin olive oil
¼ cup freshly squeezed lime juice (juice of 1 lime)
1 tablespoon fresh basil, chopped
1 tablespoon fresh cilantro, chopped
½ teaspoon kosher salt
½ teaspoon freshly ground pepper

2 center cut halibut steaks (½–¾ pounds each)

1. Combine the marinade ingredients in a baking dish. Add the halibut and coat well. Cover with plastic wrap and refrigerate for 2 to 3 hours. Turn fish once.

2. Heat the grill, allowing it to get very hot, and then cool down slightly. Brush the grill with vegetable oil and immediately place the fish on the grill. Grill each side for about 7 to 8 minutes, until dark grill marks appear. Remove the fish and let cool slightly. Carefully break it into 2-inch chunks. Serve with Fresh Corn Salad.

ABOVE: *Sliced red and yellow tomatoes garnish the fish. The table is set with a peony-patterned tablecloth and blue-banded Pyrex dishes. The amber-colored flatware is Bakelite I found at a tag sale.*
OPPOSITE: *Tender, flaky biscuits are a must when making shortcakes such as these. Use shortening instead of the butter for even lighter biscuits.*

Fresh Corn Salad

SERVES 4

8 ears fresh corn, blanched and cut off the cob
10 tomatillos, blanched, peeled, and sliced into ⅛-inch rounds
1 medium red onion, diced
3 tablespoons fresh whole cilantro leaves
1 tablespoon rice-wine vinegar
2 tablespoons fresh lime juice
⅓ cup olive oil
Salt and freshly ground pepper
Cilantro sprigs and lime wedges for garnish

Mix together all the ingredients except the garnishes. Season to taste with more lime juice, salt, and pepper. Garnish with lime wedges and cilantro sprigs.

Peach Shortcake

SERVES 4

Use the sweetest, ripest, unblemished peaches for the topping. I prefer freestone peaches because they can be easily cut into slices right from the pit. For extra flavor, warm the peach slices in a tiny bit of Sauternes until they are tender (about 5 to 7 minutes). Cool the cooked peaches before using.

Shortcake
¾ cup (1½ sticks) unsalted butter
3 cups all-purpose flour
⅓ cup sugar
4 tablespoons baking powder
1 tablespoon salt
1½ cup light cream

Egg Wash
1 large egg yolk
1 tablespoon light cream

4 ripe but firm peaches, cut into 1-inch slices
1 cup heavy cream
2 tablespoons confectioners' sugar

1. Sift together all the dry ingredients for the shortcake. Cut in butter using a pastry blender. When the mixture resembles coarse meal, stir in the cream. When the pastry comes together, knead it with your hands and form it into a rectangle on a floured board. (If dough is very sticky, knead in a bit more flour.)
2. Preheat oven to 425°.
3. Roll out dough to ¾ inch. Cut out biscuits using a 3-inch round cutter. Cut the scraps into small heart biscuits, creating a garnish for each dessert plate.
4. Place biscuits and hearts on a parchment-lined baking sheet. Beat the egg yolk with the light cream. Brush the biscuits with the egg wash and sprinkle the tops lightly with sugar.
5. Turn oven down to 400° and bake the biscuits for 15 to 20 minutes, until barely brown.
6. Transfer the biscuits to a rack. Beat heavy cream with confectioners' sugar until soft peaks form. While biscuits are still warm, split and fill with whipped cream. Top with peach slices and garnish each plate with a heart-shaped biscuit.

THE GRAVENSTEIN APPLE.

A U T

Drawn by J. T. Hart, at Mr Lee's Hammersmith.

Published by Thomas Kelly, Paternoster Row Aug. 1. 1828.

U M N

O C T O B

MY TWO FAVORITE GARDEN SEASONS are mid-spring, when sowing seeds and transplanting seedlings proceed at a rapid pace, and autumn, when planting spring-flowering bulbs keeps me almost as busy. ❧ Each October I try to make up for all the years I planted no spring flowering bulbs. Last fall I put in thousands of tulips, narcissi, hyacinths, snowdrops, snowcaps, squill, grape hyacinths, Dutch iris, fritillaries, brodiaea, and allium. The task is hard, but because the weather is cool, and the sun warm, being outside is a real treat. ❧ The days shorten perceptibly; the night air sometimes drops below freezing. Still the garden is amazingly productive, and I pick giant pumpkins, colorful gourds, and baskets of apples and pears. The 'Fall Gold' raspberries are savored, and the crabapples gathered on the bough are unusual additions to the huge urns of dried flowers placed around the house. Long walks with the dogs and cats give me time to reflect on what has passed in the summer gone by and what is to come in the approaching winter. ❧

ABOVE: *China Cat, now fifteen, single-handedly keeps the mice from boring holes in the giant pumpkins that we grow each year for jack-o'-lanterns.*
LEFT: *The chill air quickly turns the New England landscape into a blaze of color. The swamp maple is a deep gold, the sugar maple a blaze of orange, and the Japanese maples dark red or gold. The lawns suddenly become thick and green before lapsing into dormancy.*

E R

JOURNAL

Last fruits harvested.

Leaf raking begins.

All plants from outdoor urns repotted and brought into greenhouse.

Cuttings made from large urn plants, like scented geraniums; new rooting encouraged.

All urns emptied and washed.

Terra-cotta urns brought inside.

Spent perennials cut back.

Dead and dying annuals uprooted and composted (if healthy) or thrown out.

Old vegetables given to chickens.

Hydrangeas that have dried on bushes cut and arranged for the house.

Soil prepared for bulb planting.

Sophie Herbert and Monica Pasternak help me to plant crocuses and narcissi outside the garden wall; in spring they will see their flowers on their way to school.

Roses tied up; dead wood or weak shoots cut back.

Thousands of bulbs planted.

Three 25-cubic-yard trucks of rich mulching compost ordered.

Pumpkins picked, carved, and displayed on steps and dinner tables.

ABOVE RIGHT: *The perennial beds take on the earthy tones of autumn; Sedum 'Autumn Joy', late-flowering hibiscus, and monkshood add a bit of color.*
RIGHT: *The ash trees are among the first to drop their leaves, while the nectarines and apples retain their foliage longer.*

ABOVE: *Nicotiana, or tobacco plant, is a great favorite among English gardeners. Lemon balm borders the garden walks, offering fragrance.*
BELOW: *This new squirrel faucet looks like an old ornament, and is more charming than ordinary hardware-store stock.*

BELOW: *The large tree is a sycamore maple. It is beautiful, but sheds myriad fluffy panicles and seed pods in the spring, hosts moth larvae in summer, and loses its leaves weeks after every other tree. I have learned much about trees of late. One rule: never plant, so near to a residence, such a "messy" tree.*

Leaf Raking

ALWAYS ONE OF THE RITES OF autumn, leaf raking is often considered a dull chore. I well remember being drafted into the effort as a child—and being paid five cents for each garbage can full of leaves gathered. (I also recall that for every three dandelion roots, we were paid one cent by Billie Shoop's dad. Luckily he had a big lawn with many weeds.)

Leaf raking seems to drag on forever. I sometimes wish that everything would become bare all at once, but then I remember those childhood afternoons spent jumping into piles of leaves, and I relent.

If one approaches it with a sense of humor and a firm belief in the value of cardiovascular activity and upper-body aerobic exercise, leaf raking can actually be fun. It certainly is essential: a cover of unwanted leaves can breed fungus and other diseases, and can cause mold on existing plants. A set of good leaf rakes, a large tarpaulin in which to gather the leaves, and a large cart with wire sides in which to carry them away are all the equipment you really need. A child's bamboo rake is useful to remove leaves from fragile plants or from the vegetable garden. Leaf blowers do make the job easier, and are almost a necessity if you have a large area and a lot of deciduous trees, but they must be used with due consideration for friends and neighbors. Whichever gathering method you use, do not dispose of the leaves by burning, which is wasteful and polluting, but compost them: I compost all the leaves from the trees on the property in big composting bins in the Easter Field.

Monkshood

AN EXTRAORDINARY HERBACEOUS perennial with curious hooded flowers, monkshood (*Aconitum* sp.) is a special favorite of mine: one of the last fall flowers to bloom, I treasure it for its late show of color in the garden. However, these enticing characteristics must be weighed against its potential danger—the plant is poisonous in all its parts and not to be carelessly grown in areas where inquisitive young children may easily come upon it. The potent poison was used by early Greeks to tip their spears. The strange hood on the upper portion of each flower represented the helmet of gods in mythology before it came, in the Middle Ages, to denote the headgear of monks. The plant is also known as aconite and wolfsbane.

These exceptional flowers can stand partial shade; in fact, their native habitat is the cool mountainous regions of Europe and northern Asia. A member of the buttercup family, to which peony and delphinium belong, monkshood produces a similar deeply cut attractive dark green foliage. It makes a superb cut flower and accents fall arrangements of chrysanthemums and hydrangeas. I do not cut this perennial back in fall; it

LEFT: *The pool shed, where filters and pool equipment are stored out of view. The pile of leaves has been raked from under the apple trees in the boxwood border, and the giant blue flowers are my nicest monkshood. The trellis, constructed to serve both decorative and utilitarian purposes, supports five climbing roses.*

maintains some color and a quite lovely silhouette on the winter landscape.

Plants develop clumps that can be divided in early fall every three or four years; but so long as they are prospering, it is wise to leave them undisturbed. Grow them in semishade in a well-drained but moist garden soil enriched with organic matter and slightly acidic— a pH from 5.0 to 6.0. Water thoroughly during dry spells.

I allow my monkshood to go to seed; I shake much of the seed back into the soil and when overcrowding occurs, I carefully transplant into other areas of the garden. Monkshood grown from seed will take three years to bloom.

Aconitum Napellus is a European native, naturalized in North America. Growing to 3 feet or taller, its many vibrant midnight blue flowers display ¾-inch arched hoods that seem to shroud the rest of the bloom. A variety, *A. N. album*, blooms with white flowers; *bicolor* with blue and white.

Aconitum Carmichaelii, also known as *A. Fischeri,* is commonly called azure monkshood. Another rich blue-flowering species, this one is native to China and sends up 5-foot stems loaded with large-hooded flowers. Leaves are lacy but quite thick and leathery.

RIGHT: *Three years ago, I planted nine different kinds of crabapples, and each produces beautifully colored fruit and varied leaves; these dark red crabapples are from a tree just two years old. The old wooden wheelbarrow is still as sturdy and useful as the day it was built, probably in the late nineteenth century.*

Autumn Bulbs

THE NUMBER OF BULBS I HAVE PLANTED over the years is staggering, yet there always seems to be room for more. This is due in part to the natural diminishing of the blooms (tulips are most impressive the first spring after planting, daffodils the second season), to destruction by predators (rabbits, deer, moles, squirrels), and to other factors, like flooding (which will rot the bulbs), frost heaving, or unwarranted digging.

I have discovered that there are several ways to plant bulbs, but all are labor intensive. The task is easiest if the beds are well prepared in advance; spring-flowering bulbs must be planted after cool weather has set in and before a hard frost makes the ground unworkable.

Bulbs prefer a well-drained soil with a pH of 6 to 6.8, but most will perform in heavy or sandy soil. Sun or light shade is fine; bulbs planted in shady areas often grow taller and last a bit longer. Before planting, work the soil to a depth of a foot and a half—add compost, and peat or sand if the structure of the soil requires it. I add a bulb booster to improve the perennialization of the bulbs where possible, and I always mix in well-rotted manure, but this must be kept below the level of the bulbs, never touching. A fertilizer, such as bonemeal or those specially prepared for bulbs or even the all-purpose 10-10-10, is important. Since rodents are especially fond of tulip bulbs, it may be wise not to use bonemeal as it is also an attractant. Apply fall topdressings of fertilizer (I use well-rotted manure) on previous plantings. In spring, sprinkle bulb fertilizer or superphosphate as soon as shoots appear and immediately after flowering—to give the foliage, food for next year's flowers, a boost.

Bulbs look best clustered; keep smaller bulbs separated by 2 to 3 inches, and larger ones by 4 to 6. For a naturalized look, toss a handful on the ground and plant, separating any that fall too close together.

Planting depth varies with bulb type and size. Those from mail-order houses or garden centers usually come with planting instructions. A useful rule of thumb is to plant them twice as deep as their diameter in average or heavy soil, deeper in sandy soil; very large bulbs may require even deeper planting. Measure from the top of the bulb to soil surface.

Bulbs can be set individually in the ground with a long-handled bulb planter; use a spade to dig large areas for clusters. Cover, firming soil around bulbs; thoroughly water and continue throughout autumn and winter during dry periods. (If squirrels raid your tulip plantings, lay some chicken wire over soil surface.) After the ground is frozen hard, mulch with evergreen boughs to prevent heaving during extreme temperature fluctuations. Remove in spring before shoots are higher than an inch or so.

When buying bulbs, look for unblemished heavy bulbs with no soft spots—the larger the bulb, the larger the flower. Some have skins, called tunics, while others are protected by scales. Don't worry about loose tunics, but avoid bulbs that have sprouted. Purchase in fall and plant as soon as possible. If you must store bulbs, put them in an open paper bag in a cool, dry location.

ABOVE: *In the herb garden I planted early spring-flowering bulbs such as squill and iris. I find it helpful to transfer bulbs into shallow baskets, which are easier to reach into than a paper bag or cardboard box.*

ABOVE AND BELOW: *The dibber, a small hand tool, makes holes 6 inches deep in which I plant* Scilla Tubergeniana *about 5 to 6 inches apart. The flowers are light blue with darker petal stripes and bloom in my garden in April.*

Tulips. The top of the bulb should be about 6 inches below ground level, but some gardeners say planting tulips from 1o to 12 inches deep will lessen the number of new bulblets formed each year—thus delaying crowding and giving newly formed bulbs a chance to flower better. The center of tulip bulbs die after flowering and new bulblets are formed.

Overcrowding usually occurs in a few years, and when the vigor of flowers fades, rejuvenate the bulbs. After the foliage has yellowed in late spring or early summer, dig, separate bulblets and replant immediately. The larger bulbs may produce flowers the following year but the smaller ones require a couple of years before they reach blooming size. When planting mixed tulips, it is very important to consider height as well as color.

Narcissus. Unlike tulips, narcissus blooms are best their second year. The bulbs reproduce by forming smaller bulbs called "offsets" around the main "mother" bulb. If flower quality and quantity diminish, separate bulbs after the foliage has died back. Only remove the offsets that separate easily. Replant, taking care to keep bulbs out of direct sunlight.

Fritillaria. Plant in early autumn to maximize root development. Set bulbs 3 to 4 inches deep, about 4 inches apart. These bulbs prefer partial shade. Water thoroughly during the growing season—do not allow them to dry out in the hot summer. Separate every three years or so, if flower quality diminishes. Most fritillaria grow well with other flowering bulbs; the checkered lily, however, likes a damper, sandier soil.

ABOVE: *Against a backdrop of golden yellow foliage, the herb garden looks beautiful, even with the big beds bare in preparation for bulb planting. To make sure the bulbs are planted in straight lines, I draw strong cotton twine securely between two stakes.*
BELOW LEFT: *This is an inexpensive bulb planter that works in very well prepared soil. Some garden-supply catalogues now offer a sturdier version made from hand-forged steel.*
BELOW RIGHT: *Make sure you have the pointy side up and flat root side down; often one must look carefully at a bulb to realize which is the top. Hyacinth bulbs are especially beautiful; each color flower creates a different-hued protective skin on the bulb.*

Hydrangeas

HYDRANGEAS FLOWER IN SUMMER and early autumn, but I appreciate them most in late October, when my garden is almost bare of blooms, and the huge, subtly colored, naturally dried blossoms of the hydrangeas are invaluable in flower arrangements.

Very shade tolerant, most hydrangeas will do well on the shady side of a building, making them welcome additions to any garden. I prefer the old-fashioned types like *H. paniculata* 'Grandiflora', known as "pee-gee," a tree form that in the fall is covered with foot-long flower clusters which are at first white, changing later on to a subtle coppery pink. Oakleaf and Lacecap are two other choices for the old-fashioned garden or perennial border; *H.* 'Annabelle' produces gigantic white snowballs of blooms.

Very high acid content (or a dressing of aluminum sulfate) in the soil causes hydrangea to produce blue flowers ('All Summer Beauty', in acid soil, is covered with very grand, blue, globe-shaped flowers that can be dried easily). High alkalinity results in pinkish flowers.

The relatively unknown *H. anomala petiolaris,* a climbing hydrangea, is another favorite of mine. I've planted these along the divider fence that separates my property from the neighbors. In just four years they have grown full and bushy and produces shiny dark green foliage, showy exfoliating bark, and fragrant snowy white flowers. They can climb, unsupported, up trees and fences, to a height of 80 feet.

LEFT: *The lower vegetable garden near the chicken coop is very well protected and even in October is still full of leeks, winter spinach, sage, and kale.*

FAR LEFT: *I try to keep the vegetable gardens free of leaves until all the crops are harvested. Vegetables that are overripe but still edible are given to the chickens.*

LEFT: *Long after leaves fall from the golden crabapple tree, the fruits hang on, making a wonderful display in the fall garden. This high-pectin variety is very good for crabapple jelly, and can also be used as a natural thickener for jams and jellies like peach and strawberry.*

FAR LEFT: *Hickory trees are turning golden brown, and the old red Ford tractor, bought at auction in an enthusiastic moment but much too unwieldy for my confined gardens, sits in its usual place awaiting winter.*

ABOVE: *Plain brick stairs are a perfect place to set a row of jack-o'-lanterns. A pachysandra bed grows along one side, and a euonymus covers a wall on the other.*
LEFT: *When picking pumpkins from the garden, always leave a length of stem.*
RIGHT: *The shade garden is at its best in early spring, and again in autumn after the leaves fall and sunlight can penetrate.*
OPPOSITE: *Each year I pick armloads of hydrangeas and dry them, stripped of leaves, in containers.*

Pumpkins

OCTOBER ENDS WITH ONE OF MY favorite holidays, Halloween. Some years we have a Hallow's Eve party, with fresh doughnuts rolled in cinnamon sugar, apples from the orchard for dunking, white ghosts fabricated from old sheets hung high in the pine trees, black witches flying on wires under the eaves of the porch, great stands of giant corn husks, baskets of gourds, and, most important of all, scary, candle-lit pumpkins carved with originality and humor, some into traditional jack o' lanterns, others with designs inspired by the architectural de-

tails of the house, or with the features of birds and other animals. After many years of experimenting, I have found that the best pumpkins for carving are:

'BIG MAX': Often grows to 100 pounds or more. Plant 8 feet apart for pumpkins more than 70 inches in circumference.

'SPIRIT HYBRID': Grows 10 inches across, very symmetrical, almost perfectly round and uniform; bright yellowish orange in color.

'AUTUMN GOLD HYBRID': Nicely shaped, with hard exterior and dense, rich interior. Becomes golden earlier than other pumpkins.

'BIG MOON': Can grow to 200 pounds;

has fine textured flesh and great shapes for carving.

'JACK BE LITTLE': A true miniature pumpkin (just 3 inches in diameter) usually grown for decorative purposes, but excellent for baking whole, filled with savory or sweet fillings.

'SMALL SUGAR': Grows to about 7 inches across. I grow lots of these because they are superb for individual covered soup tureens.

For carving, pick the pumpkins while the skin is still hard and firm and the color a uniform yellow or orange. If the stem is left long, the pumpkin will remain fresh longer (the stem is also a use-

ful handle for the top when the pumpkin is carved into a lantern or tureen). I use fat votive candles inside my pumpkins (they burn for up to six hours and will not topple over), and place the jack-o'-lanterns on the front and back steps to welcome trick or treaters, and throughout the garden to guide my guests.

Of course, after all that carving, we have great mounds of pumpkin flesh, none of which goes to waste. Pumpkins are a wonderful source of vitamin A, and the flesh can be used for soups, breads, pies, and custards, or just pureed. I also cut it into strips, dot with butter, top with herbs, and roast it as a vegetable.

ABOVE: *Flowering cabbages, collards ('Hicrop Hybrid' or the larger 'Georgia'), kale ('Blue Surf F1' or 'Winterbor Hybrid'), and ornamental kale keep the vegetable garden looking pretty in the late fall. All of these vegetables are nutritious, easy to grow, and greatly prolong the life of the garden.*
LEFT: *Each year I experiment and grow a batch of gourds and mini-pumpkins, treasuring those with bumps and shapes that will make the children laugh.*
OPPOSITE: *The Brussels sprouts in October have matured beautifully; the stalks are filled from top to bottom with plump, well-sized sprouts that will remain tender all through December and January.*

ABOVE: *Even this late in the year, spring onions ('Early Yellow Globe' or 'White Welsh') are useful in the kitchen.*

RIGHT: *Two late cabbages ('Green Joy' and 'Spivoy Hybrid'), planted in August, will mature in October but will never grow quite as large as the spring-grown seedlings of the same type.*

BELOW RIGHT: *When I had my catering business, I found ornamental cabbages wonderfully useful for decorating large tables and for making interesting and subtle arrangements. I still grow many varieites, and always search for new types. Flowering cabbages grow on very strong stems. If I am going to use them as decorations or as ornaments in an arrangement, I cut them off the stem with a machetelike knife or garden clippers.*

BELOW: *A late seedling of leaf lettuce still provides a tender and flavorful salad.*

ABOVE: *I have not succeeded in growing a true fig "tree" in Westport, but my bushes have now reached a height of about 1o feet, and they produce if the shrubs are carefully wrapped in paper and burlap and insulated with leaves and wire surrounds to protect them during the winter months.*
LEFT: *More rows of late-sown lettuces. Because it is so late in the season, they would not transplant for heading up, so I just thin the leaves as I need them in the kitchen.*
BELOW LEFT: *These ornamental cabbages were planted from seed in August. As a result of the late planting, the cabbages did not have time to mature into sizeable specimens. But they are still quite lovely.*
BELOW: *By the middle of October, the figs have dropped all their leaves; only unripened, dessicated fruits remain on the branches.*

1. For a festive and special Halloween dinner table, I decided to gild pumpkins for the table. Working outdoors (good ventilation is essential), I filled a huge tub with cold water and sprayed the surface of the water with metallic spray paint (I used both copper and gold).

2. The oil-based paint will float on the surface of the water. Swirl the water to form patterns in the paint film, and immediately plunge the pumpkin down into the water, then quickly pull it up again. (Remember to wear rubber gloves to protect your hands.)

3. When you pull the pumpkin up through the water it will be glistening with streaky coats of the metallic paints. The process can then be repeated with various shades or colors of paints. Here the surface of the pumpkin is coated in gold.

4. An overlay of real copper and gold leaf, available in little books from art-supply stores, will further enhance the marbleized gilding. Still working outdoors, on a table protected with layers of newspaper, I coat the painted surface of the pumpkins with spray adhesive.

5. *The metallic tissues are incredibly fragile and should be handled carefully. I work in a quiet atmosphere; there must be absolutely no breeze to whisk away the precious leaves as they are gently lifted from their books onto the pumpkins.*

6. *The leaves can be patted down with a soft brush (professionals use sable or ermine), a soft cloth, or even the fingertips if necessary. Some real metallic leaf is edible (23 karat or better gold, for example), but some (like copper) is not and must be used with care in decorating for the table.*

7. *Three finished products. The larger potiron will be used as part of the centerpiece, and the smaller sugar pumpkins can be used hollowed out (cut very carefully with a sharp paring knife) as bowls for the piping-hot pumpkin-squash soup, which will be the first course at my dinner party.*

Menu

PUMPKIN SOUP

GRILLED DUCK BREASTS

CRANBERRY RELISH

MIXED GREENS WITH WILD
MUSHROOMS

THREE BERRY COBBLER

ABOVE AND OPPOSITE: *This dinner was held in honor of my friend Joe Antonini, the chairman of K mart. I wanted a harvest theme menu, and created this one with Sara Foster, who helped with the catering. I served the pumpkin soup in individual gilded pumpkins, and with a roaring fire in the background, the table was very inviting.*

Pumpkin Soup

SERVES 6

This soup uses pumpkin (butternut squash could be substituted), ripe pears (for sweetness), and fresh herbs.

  2 tablespoons unsalted butter
  1 large onion, finely chopped
  1 leek, trimmed, cleaned, and
    thinly sliced
  2 shallots, finely chopped
  2 pounds pumpkin, peeled,
    seeded, and cut into 2-inch
    pieces
  2 ripe pears, peeled, cored, and
    cut into chunks
  3 carrots, peeled and cut into
    small pieces
  1½ quarts chicken stock, preferably
    homemade
    Fresh thyme sprigs
  ½ cup half-and-half
    Salt and freshly ground pepper
  6 fresh sage leaves
  6 fresh thyme sprigs
  ½ cup sour cream

1. In a heavy-bottomed soup pot over medium heat, melt the butter. Add the onion, leek, and shallots. Sauté until tender but not brown, about 5 to 7 minutes.

2. Add pumpkin, pears, and carrots and sauté until pumpkin begins to soften. Add the stock and a few thyme sprigs. Cover; simmer for 30 minutes, until vegetables are tender.

3. Remove thyme sprigs and discard. Puree the soup in a food processor.

4. Return soup to pot and add half-and-half. Season to taste and heat for 5 minutes.

5. Ladle soup into individual bowls or gilded hollowed-out pumpkins. Garnish with sage leaves, thyme sprigs, and dollops of sour cream.

Grilled Duck Breasts

SERVES 6

Duck breasts should be trimmed of all excess fat before they are grilled.

- 1 cup extra-virgin olive oil
- ½ cup fresh rosemary sprigs
  Salt and freshly ground pepper
- 3 whole Moulard duck breasts, well trimmed of excess fat and skin

1. Whisk together the first 3 ingredients in a glass dish. Add the duck breasts and marinate for at least 3 hours, turning from time to time. If this is done the night before, cover the bowl with plastic wrap and refrigerate until ready to grill.
2. Prepare the grill.
3. Grill the duck over hot coals until rare, about 7 to 9 minutes on each side (they should be quite pink in the middle). Remove from the grill and set aside for 5 minutes.
4. Slice thinly and serve hot with Cranberry Relish.

ABOVE LEFT: *The duck breasts were marinated in a simple mixture and then grilled; the resulting flavor was marvelous. Tart cranberry relish offers a counterpoint.*
LEFT: *The berry cobbler, made from fruits frozen in July, is an easy yet elegant ending to this somewhat rich meal. I made a traditional lard-and-butter crust that bakes golden brown and flaky. For easier handling, I brought the cobbler to the table on an old round wooden bread board.*

Cranberry Relish

MAKES 2 CUPS

Fresh ginger, orange, and lime, including the peel, add unusual flavorings to this delectable relish. It can be made a week or two in advance.

2½ cups sugar
½ cup water
1 seedless orange, cut into ¼-inch dice, including peel
1 lime, cut into ¼-inch dice, including peel
1 tablespoon minced fresh ginger
1 cup raisins
2 3-inch long cinnamon sticks
1 vanilla bean
3 bags fresh cranberries

Place the sugar and water in a heavy saucepan. Dissolve over high heat and continue cooking until the liquid is slightly carmelized. Stir in the remaining ingredients and simmer for about 10 minutes or until the cranberries begin to pop. Transfer to a bowl and cool.

Mixed Greens with Wild Mushrooms

SERVES 6

Autumn leaf lettuce thinned while still small and tender makes this salad special. The dressing is made with balsamic vinegar, an aged red-wine vinegar from Italy. Use shiitake or any wild-type fall mushroom like porcini, chanterelle, or morel.

6 handfuls assorted greens (radicchio, arugula, mustard, frisée, mâche, baby spinach)
18 small shiitake mushrooms
2 tablespoons extra-virgin olive oil

Vinaigrette

3 tablespoons balsamic vinegar
½ cup extra-virgin olive oil
1 teaspoon Dijon mustard
Salt and freshly ground pepper

1. Wash and dry the greens and place them in a bowl.
2. Remove the mushroom stems and, using a small, sharp knife, score the tops of the mushroom caps in a cross-hatch pattern. Heat the olive oil in a large skillet over medium heat. Add the mushroom caps and carefully toss for 2 to 3 minutes. Remove from heat and set aside.
3. Whisk the vinagrette ingredients together. Pour desired amount over greens and toss. Arrange on salad plates and place 3 mushroom caps on each plate. Serve immediately.

Three Berry Cobbler

MAKES 1 9-INCH COBBLER

I freeze a great many berries dry, without sugar, and pack them in rigid containers for use in other seasons. This dinner was a great excuse to use up some of my blackberries, raspberries, and blueberries; the combination made an excellent cobbler. Serve with dollops of whipped crème fraîche, flavored with a bit of orange liqueur or brandy.

Pastry

2 cups all-purpose flour
½ teaspoon salt
½ cup cold lard
4 tablespoons (½ stick) unsalted butter
⅓ cup ice water
½ cup sugar
¼ cup milk

Filling

1¼ cups fresh or frozen blackberries
1¼ cups fresh or frozen raspberries
1¼ cups fresh or frozen blueberries
½ cup sugar
¼ cup freshly squeezed lemon juice
2 teaspoons cornstarch
2 tablespoons unsalted butter

1. To make the pastry, sift together the flour and salt into a bowl. Using a pastry cutter, cut in the lard and butter until the mixture resembles coarse meal. Sprinkle water over the pastry and gather it using your hands. Divide into 2 flat rounds. Wrap in plastic wrap and chill for at least 20 minutes.
2. Preheat the oven to 425°.
3. Sprinkle a pastry board with ¼ cup sugar. Roll out 1 piece of pastry to ⅛ inch. Place in the bottom of a pie tin. Sprinkle the remaining ¼ cup sugar and roll out the other piece of pastry to be used as the top.
4. Fill the pie shell with berries. Sprinkle with sugar, lemon juice, and cornstarch. Dot with butter. Brush the rim of the dough with milk. Place the top crust over the berries and seal the edges by crimping with your fingers.
5. Cut a few slits on the top crust to release steam during baking. Brush with remaining milk. Bake for 45 minutes or until golden brown.

NOVEMB

E R

I AM NOT SURE IF GLOBAL WARMING has already come to affect our weather, but I am yearly amazed at the number of warm days in the middle of the coldest months. There has not been a really good blizzard in Westport for more than twelve years, and that snow was just not like those we had when I was a child—when it was dry and crisp, and in the snow banks left by the plows one could construct igloos high enough to stand in. ❧ Snow is good for the garden, my dad always told me. The thicker the snow cover, the taller the delphiniums, he said when his specimen spikes of blue and purple were seven feet tall. Snow insulated the plants and protected their crowns from dry winds and cold. To compensate for this lack of soft, natural insulation, I wrap and mulch all of the gardens in an attempt to prolong the life of my perennials and bulbs and roses and berries. ❧ This task is but a small part of "garden keeping," the process of cleaning up the garden spaces and putting the beds to sleep for the winter—tasks that must be completed soon, before the holidays of Thanksgiving and Christmas take us indoors. ❧

ABOVE: *This tomato vine is completely dessicated, yet the last fruit is hanging on. I often use these very late tomatoes in green tomato mincemeat, or sliced, lightly breaded, and fried.* LEFT: *"Garden keeping," which occupies most of November, is relieved by the occasional harvest. I can still stop and pick some of the longer-lasting vegetables.*

JOURNAL

Dying plants pulled up and composted.

Garden raked clean of debris.

Soil lightly tilled for next spring.

Crowns of rhubarb mounded with compost.

Roses, berry bushes, and fragile perennials protected with compost.

Currants, gooseberries, and blackberries protected with an additional thick mulch of golden straw.

Outdoor water faucets turned off (except deep, frost-proof hydrants).

Cold frames covered with protective canvas.

Rose climbers checked for insecure ties.

Espaliered trees lightly pruned.

All leaves finally raked up (even the sycamore maple).

Heat lamps fixed over watering cans in Palais des Poulets.

Outdoor garden equipment cleaned and stored for winter.

Tractor serviced for use as snow plow.

Hardiest vegetables still harvested in garden.

RIGHT: *Early in November this portion of the vegetable garden needs a lot of work. The weather was warm enough to slow the clean-up and persuade me to allow the last cabbages and leaf lettuces to grow a little while longer.*

ABOVE: *Eggplants, okra, bush beans, peas, most tender herbs, squash, and melons die at first hard frost. The lettuce, past its prime, continues to grow so the chickens can get fresh vegetation every day.*

ABOVE: *Sweet pepper plants are among the first to perish as fall weather gets colder, but every now and then I find one or two last peppers, still alive and edible, protected by a comforter of dry foliage.*

ABOVE: *Curly kale, 'Blue Surf (F1)', heavily laden Brussels sprouts plants, and a bit of mâche will stay in the garden until harvested. The low hedge provides some protection from chilling winds.*

ABOVE: *Behind dead tomato vines still laden with unripened fruit, healthy Swiss chard and a few cabbages can be harvested until late in November if the weather does not turn bitter cold.*

ABOVE: *Even the frost-bitten tomatoes will not go to waste: all of the dead and dessicated vines and plants are chopped up and added to the compost bin.*

LEFT: *Autumn carrots taste superb—they are good in stews and purees.*

RIGHT: *The seeds for these leeks were purchased in Japan by my friend Yoichi. I put the seedlings in trenches 6 inches deep, and as the leeks grew the soil was gradually pulled around the white portion to act as support and to help whiten the bottoms. They were more than 20 inches long at maturity; I was so proud of my success I sent Yoichi a photograph, using an arm's length for scale.*

ABOVE: *Several varieties of red hot peppers, forgotten, have dried on the plants. If they've dried totally, the frost will not hurt them and they can still be used in the kitchen—or made into wreaths.*

ABOVE: *It is time to check soil condition. I always top-dress the perennial borders with the Bulpitts' compost, which itself is enriched with manure and plant foods.*

ABOVE: *The Easter Field border was quite barren the first year, but I am always happy to have extra spaces that can be filled with new plants or divisions of others.*

ABOVE: *There is still a thick covering of buckwheat-hull mulch evident, but most of it blew away or was washed away during two winter storms.*

Garden Keeping

"GARDEN KEEPING" IS MY PRIVATE euphemism for those tasks that, like housekeeping, are essential to happiness and good health. I spend much of the fall cleaning up the garden spaces and putting all the beds to sleep for the cold months of winter.

PERENNIAL BEDS. I cut most of my herbaceous perennials to 4 inches above the ground. Anything that is still green, such as sedum, I don't touch. My monkshood dries right on the stalk. Any diseased portions of plants are destroyed; the rest goes on the compost pile. I top-dress each bed with at least 1½ inches of rich compost and manure. In January, after the winter holidays, I take leftover evergreen boughs and layer the perennial bed to a height of 6 inches to lessen damage from freezing and thawing caused by fluctuating temperatures.

HERB GARDEN. I do not cut my perennial herbs until early spring. Rosemary is not winter hardy in Connecticut and comes into the house in fall. Before it goes through the doorway, I always thoroughly inspect it for insects to avoid contaminating my indoor plants. The ornamental ivy that adorns the containers in the herb garden is also dug up, cut back, and potted for indoors. Like all the perennial beds, the herbs are given a top-dressing of compost or manure. Once the ground is frozen, I also mulch the herbs with evergreen boughs.

VEGETABLE GARDEN. Only a few of the more hardy vegetables, such as kale, collards, and Brussels sprouts, produce through the cold months. The rest are cut down and all healthy debris is composted. The garden is plowed in fall with a supplemental feeding of compost, manure, and fertilizer, and again in spring for aeration right before seeds are sown.

SMALL FRUITS. After all the garden debris is removed from around the raspberries, blackberries, gooseberries, blueberries, and currants, I top-dress with well-rotted manure and compost, mounding extra amounts of compost on the crowns of the less hardy gooseberries and currants. Finally I mulch everything with a good, warm layer of golden straw.

ABOVE: *This crop of luxurious Nordic spinach was planted in high summer, seeds sown more thickly than usual since the germination rate suffers in the heat.*
OPPOSITE ABOVE: *A well-balanced utility garden cart with a wire insert holds much more than an ordinary wheelbarrow and does not tip over when fully loaded.*
OPPOSITE BELOW: *A couple of Thanksgiving turkeys forage in their yard for worms and corn.*

ABOVE: *Once the vegetable garden is thoroughly cleaned, I run the little Mantis cultivator over the soil to aerate and smooth it; in areas harder to reach, the soil is spaded and turned with a fork.*

LEFT: *Nutrient-rich compost is shoveled over the crowns of all the rhubarb plants. I use this same compost as a winter coat for berries, roses, and tender herbs.*

RIGHT: *Max, the black chow chow, observes as all trellising and supports are removed and taken to the shed, where they are stored until the following spring.*

ABOVE: *Golden straw (good quality straw with no seeds) is an excellent mulch for the large berry bushes and asparagus. I add a few pitchforks of well-rotted manure on top.*
LEFT: *The new chicken coop was a plain shingled structure. To dress it up a bit I built a geometric trellis around the doors and on a portion of the sides.*
RIGHT: *Blackberry bushes, well pruned, and fig trees not yet wrapped for the cold. Here I used buckwheat hulls as mulch, but found a white mold beneath the hulls. In the future I shall use compost instead.*

Forcing Bulbs

AFTER SPENDING OCTOBER PLANTING bulbs outside, I begin planting others indoors, timing them so that the house will be full of flowers for the holidays and the bleak first months of the new year.

The bulbs easiest to force are those of the paper-white narcissus. Garden centers and catalogues sell these ready to bloom; all you do is plant and, in four to five weeks, see results. Hardy bulbs, such as tulips and crocuses, require a cold treatment (anywhere from eight to sixteen weeks depending on the type of bulb) before they will flower.

When choosing hardy bulbs, take your cue from catalogues, which identify those best for forcing. Bulbs should be firm, unblemished, and good-sized. If they are not planted immediately, store them in marked paper bags in the vegetable bin of your refrigerator. When you begin forcing, use one of three basic media: soil, pebbles, and/or water.

SOIL. I use a mixture of compost and potting soil; if compost is not available, try equal parts of potting soil, coarse sand, and peat moss. A soil medium is important for many hardy bulbs, such as tulips, but any bulb will do well in it. Any container with drainage holes, tall enough to allow 2 inches below the bulbs for root development and space above the bulbs to just cover, will work well. Terra-cotta and porcelain pots are attractive; porous clay pots should be soaked overnight before use. Place a pot shard over the drainage hole and add about an inch of small pebbles, followed by a base of soil medium.

ABOVE: *Amaryllis bulbs need seven to ten weeks to bloom: I plant them early in November to decorate the house at Christmas and the New Year. Blooming can be staggered by keeping the planted bulbs at different temperatures; those at 50° will flower weeks later than those that are forced at 68° to 78°. Most top-size bulbs will produce two stems with four or five huge blooms each.*

ABOVE: *In shallow pottery or plastic saucers I grow groups of narcissus that bloom in four to five weeks; by staggering the planting I am able to have blooms all winter long. I grow 'Galilee' (an Israeli bulb producing up to four stems of pure white flowers), 'Soleil d'Or' (delicately scented yellow blooms), and 'Cragford' (white with orange cups).*

PEBBLES. This is a very attractive method for forcing bulbs; the bulb roots anchor among the pebbles submerged in water, and are visible in a clear glass container. Polished stones, washed marble chips, gravel, and glass marbles work equally well. Fill a bowl or shallow watertight container to a ½ inch below the rim with pebbles. Spring- and autumn-flowering crocuses, squill, hyacinths, grape hyacinths, narcissus, and paper-whites perform well in this environment.

WATER. Some bulbs—especially hyacinths, crocuses, and amaryllis—can be forced in water alone. Use a special glass forcing vase or a carafe with a wide cup-shaped top. The bulb fits in the cup and the pale, hairlike roots descend into the water.

PLANTING. Place bulbs, with the pointed side up, a bit below the container rim and cover with soil, or gently twist downward into pebbles. If you tip the flattish side of a tulip bulb toward the outside of the container, the lowest tulip leaf will grow on that side and drape gracefully over the edge. Plant groups of bulbs close, but not touching. Amaryllis look best one to a pot (set these with two-thirds of the bulb above the soil line). Water thoroughly; if using pebbles or if forcing in a glass forcing vase, water should just touch the base of the bulbs.

All hardy bulbs need a cold period to encourage root development. Unless they were sold precooled, bulbs must spend some time after potting at 35° to 40°. Place potted bulbs in a paper bag or box in the refrigerator, an unheated garage, or a cold frame outside. Check regularly to maintain moisture. (If the refrigerator is cramped and there is no access to a sheltered outdoor spot, bulbs can be buried in damp peat moss inside a shoebox, and stored in the refrigerator's bottom drawer.) After roots develop, the bulbs can be put in a forcing vase or even into pebbles; do not cool bulbs in this manner if you want them to grow in soil.

After the bulbs have cooled, check for root development. When a good network is visible, take the planting out of cold storage to a room with indirect light and a temperature of not more than 65°. Water regularly. When growth begins, move to a sunny window—light is crucial at this time for good flower color. When flowers open, you can prolong the blooming period by moving plants into a cooler room with indirect light.

AFTER FORCING. Some gardeners suggest reduced watering after hardy bulbs flower, allowing the foliage to die naturally, then planting outdoors when the weather warms. But don't expect flowers the following spring; bulbs need time to recoup their strength. I find paper-whites are so depleted by forcing that it is best to compost them.

RIGHT: *I keep my amaryllis bulbs from year to year, letting them lie dormant during the summer and forcing them again for the winter. Oftentimes the flower stem will not attain normal height before the flower blooms and I will get a stumpy, short plant with huge blossoms, like this 'Apple Blossom' amaryllis—really a nicer table height than the full-size plants. The silver lustre horn is full of wood hyacinths; I have not yet managed to force these.*

ABOVE: *Each November I make potpourri for Christmas presents, using all the dried flowers and herbs and seed pods that I've saved over the course of the summer, supplemented with other dried ingredients that I purchase from various sources. From a great array of bowls the dried ingredients are carefully mixed and then scented with fragrant combinations of oils.*

OPPOSITE: *Cellophane florist's bags are filled halfway with my special homegrown mixture of potpourri, and each bag is topped with dried roses and rosebuds that have been collected during blooming season and air dried in the attic. Tied with a pretty ribbon, they are perfect small gifts, bringing the scent of the garden indoors during barren winter months.*

COLD PERIOD FOR HARDY BULBS

Tulips (*Tulipa* sp.): 12 to 16 weeks.

Daffodils (*Narcissus* sp.): 12 to 14 weeks.

Grape hyacinths (*Muscari* sp.): 8 to 10 weeks.

Squill (*Scilla* sp.): 10 weeks.

Hyacinths (*Hyacinthus* sp.): 8 to 10 weeks.

Lily-of-the-valley (*Convallaria* sp.): 8 to 10 weeks.

Crocus (*Crocus* sp.—really a corm): 8 weeks.

Autumn-flowering crocus (*Colchicum autumnale*—really a corm): no cold required. Blooms in fall but produces its leaves in spring. Easily forced in late summer or fall. Afterward, if planted outdoors, will produce leaves in spring, and be ready to rebloom in the fall.

PERIOD REQUIRED FOR TENDER BULBS TO FLOWER

Paper-whites (*Narcissus Tazetta* varieties): 4 to 5 weeks.

Amaryllis (*Hippeastrum* hybrids): 7 to 10 weeks. Amaryllis, grown in soil, will continue on in a pot. Remove stalk when flowers are spent and fertilize monthly with a water-soluble fertilizer. Reduce watering by half in midsummer. Once leaves yellow, cut foliage to an inch above the bulb and store in a dark, cool location for a minimum of 6 weeks. Bring out to a sunny location and water well. The cycle begins again.

African blood lily (*Haemanthus multi-florus*): 6 to 8 weeks. Grow in a pot and treat like an amaryllis.

ABOVE LEFT: *Lavender blossoms, removed from the stems and thoroughly dried, form the scent "base" of my potpourri mixture.*
ABOVE RIGHT: *Dried gray poppy pods are not scented, but they do add an interesting dimension and some bulk to each little bag.*
LEFT: *A mixture of the tiny petals from my roses, stocks, and delphiniums gives the potpourri a beautiful pinkish apricot color.*
BELOW LEFT: *Silver gray lamb's ears (Stachys byzantina) and reddish cockscombs (Celosia 'Red Velvet') are soft and velvety additions to the mixture.*
BELOW RIGHT: *Globe amaranth flowers (Gomphrena globosa) resemble clover blossoms. When dried, these ball-shaped flowers are bright puffs.*

ABOVE LEFT: *Between the new rose borders and the trellised roses, we have plenty of rose petals, which are highly scented and very colorful, even when dried.*

ABOVE RIGHT: *Rosebuds can be air dried (like these), or individually dried in silica gel whereby they'll retain more color and perfect shape.*

RIGHT: *Lemon verbena leaves are sweetly scented and a good addition, even though they are very delicate and crumbly.*

BELOW LEFT: *Nigella damascena 'Persian Jewels' bears starry flowers that mature to puffy, gently spiked seed pods.*

BELOW RIGHT: *Blue mallow, an old wildflower related to the hollyhock, fades very little when dried and adds bright color.*

Menu

ROAST PORK LOIN

CARAMELIZED APPLE SLICES

MACERATED PRUNES

PEA PUREE

POACHED FRUIT

Roast Pork Loin

SERVES 6

Pork loin, boned and with all of the fat removed, becomes even more flavorful if the meat is marinated a couple of hours in a fragrant infusion of herbs and oil. Carmelized apples and macerated prunes go well with roast pork and are a pleasant change from the ubiquitous applesauce.

2 garlic cloves, minced
2 tablespoons olive oil
2 sprigs fresh rosemary, or ½ teaspoon crushed dried rosemary
1 whole boneless 3-pound pork loin, trimmed, with ⅛-inch layer of fat
2 tablespoons canola or peanut oil
Salt and freshly ground pepper

1. Combine the garlic, olive oil, and rosemary in a container roughly the size of the pork loin. Add the pork and rub with the marinade. Let it sit for 2 hours.
2. Preheat oven to 400°. In a heavy-bottomed skillet or ovenproof sauté pan over a high flame, heat the canola oil until smoking hot. Remove the fresh rosemary, if used, and season the pork with salt and pepper. Carefully place the pork in the oil, and cook on all sides until golden brown, about 5 minutes.
3. Pour off excess oil. Put the pan in the oven and cook until pork loin feels stiff to the touch, about 15 minutes. Let rest for 5 minutes and serve in ½-inch slices with Caramelized Apple Slices and Macerated Prunes.

Caramelized Apple Slices

SERVES 6

1 tablespoon freshly squeezed lemon juice
3 Golden Delicious apples
2 tablespoons unsalted butter
2 tablespoons sugar

1. Add the lemon juice to 1 quart of water. Peel, core, and halve the apples. Cut each half into 6 slices and keep in lemon water until ready to sauté.
2. In a heavy-bottomed pan over medium heat, heat the butter and sugar until sugar begins to melt. Drain the apple slices, reserving ½ cup lemon water, then add them to the pan. Lower heat to moderate and cook until slices are soft and golden, about 8 minutes.
NOTE: If apples seem to be sticking to the pan or caramelizing too quickly, add reserved lemon water as necessary.

Macerated Prunes

SERVES 6

½ cup water
2 tablespoons sugar
½ cup cognac or bourbon
30 pitted prunes

1. Bring water and sugar to a boil. Remove from heat and add the cognac or bourbon. Press the prunes down into the mix to cover, and let sit in a warm place for at least 2 hours.

OPPOSITE: *The earthy tones of the meal are set off by an old English silver lustre plate made by Johnson Bros. The crystal goblet sits atop a lace doily, and the napkin is oversized linen damask.*

Pea Puree

SERVES 6

Use the last peas from the garden or frozen baby peas if you don't have fresh. The crème fraîche can be eliminated, or heavy cream can be substituted, but the flavor will not be the same.

2 cups fresh peas, shelled
Salt and freshly ground pepper
¼ cup crème fraîche

1. Bring a pot of salted water to a boil.
2. Put the peas in the boiling water for 1½ minutes, then strain, reserving the water. Plunge the peas into ice water to stop the cooking process. Drain well, then puree in a food processor with 3 to 4 tablespoons of reserved water. Press the puree through a strainer into a large bowl with the back of a wooden spoon or rubber scraper. Season to taste, then mix in crème fraîche. Serve immediately.

ABOVE: *Santa Rosa plums poached in Chardonnay. The use of different wines is what makes these desserts special.*
OPPOSITE PAGE:
ABOVE LEFT: *Poached figs. One sees these old-fashioned glass cake pedestals at tag sales and flea markets everywhere.*
ABOVE RIGHT: *The poached cherries are served on one of my favorite glass pedestals—the whimsical dolphin stem always amuses me.*
BELOW LEFT: *Spices from the poaching liquid garnish the pears.*
BELOW RIGHT: *The cinnamon stick adds a very subtle flavor to the wine syrup of the poached peaches and apricots.*

Poached Pears

SERVES 8

8 firm, ripe pears
2 cups Merlot or other flavorful
  red wine
2 tablespoons lemon juice
1 cup sugar
1 cinnamon stick
  Zest of 1 lemon
1 vanilla bean

1. Peel the pears without removing the stems. Put them in a deep saucepan.
2. In another saucepan, bring to a boil the wine, lemon juice, sugar, cinnamon, lemon zest, vanilla bean, and enough water to cover the pears. Pour the liquid over the pears and simmer very slowly until just tender, about 10 minutes.
3. Remove the pears to a serving dish. Rapidly reduce the liquid to about 1 cup. Pour over the pears.
VARIATION: For a Cabernet Sauvignon syrup, use 2 cups of Cabernet Sauvignon, zest of 1 lemon, 2 cinnamon sticks, 1 vanilla bean, and ¾ cup sugar, and follow poaching directions above.

Poached Plums

SERVES 8

8 Santa Rosa or Italian prune
  plums, unpeeled
2 cups Chardonnay
2 star anise
¾ cup sugar

Follow directions for Poached Pears.

Poached Peaches and Apricots

SERVES 8

8 peaches, peeled
8 apricots, peeled
1 bottle Cabernet Blanc
1 cinnamon stick
12 black peppercorns
  Zest of 1 lemon
¾ cup sugar

Follow directions for Poached Pears.

Poached Cherries

SERVES 8

1 pound cherries (Queen Anne or
  Bing), stems left on
2 cups Sauvignon Blanc
1 vanilla bean
¾ cup sugar
1 cinnamon stick
6 cloves

Follow directions for Poached Pears.

Poached Figs

SERVES 8

8 fresh black or green figs,
  unpeeled
2 cups dry red wine, preferably
  Merlot
1 cup sugar
  Zest of 1 lemon
1 vanilla bean
  1-inch piece of peeled ginger
  root

Follow directions for Poached Pears.

DECEMB

THE GARDEN IS VERY FORLORN, swept by chill winds, plunged into the frigid temperatures of dead winter. Most color has left the landscape; in its place is a palette of grisaille tones. The last outdoor task, wrapping the roses and perennial borders in burlap, is accomplished. All at once I have time and reason to concentrate on beautifying my house, filling it with living plants and flowers. ❧ During the rest of the year each room is graced with cut blooms from the garden. Even in November I can find branches of crabapple, hydrangea, and bittersweet to fill the vases and baskets. But in December this is impossible in Connecticut; the frozen berries are shriveled, and the leaves are dessicated. We must turn to growing indoors. ❧ The bulbs we forced in November are coming into full bloom, filling the house with delicate scent. Decorative topiaries stand on either side of doorways; red cabbages in six-inch mossy pots (overfed to grow tall and spindly) look quite extraordinary on a formal table.

ABOVE: *A mass of roses just 3 months ago, the pool-shed trellis is bare.* OPPOSITE: *From left to right: Stephanotis grows around a cage of rabbit wire. Lavender cotton, or gray santolina, is perfect for a true standard. Lemon-scented geranium, 'Prince Rupert', becomes a pyramid. A very tall* Laurus nobilis, *or common bay standard, must be constantly pruned; I carefully prune a standard* Eugenia myrtifolia *right after it has bloomed. A shorter but equally delicate standard, the* Myrtus communis, *or Greek myrtle, is easily maintained with a monthly "haircut."*

E   R

JOURNAL

Burlap placed around all rose beds and perennial borders.

Fig trees wrapped.

Heavily trafficked walks tied off to protect grass.

Fallen branches picked up.

Yew and box tied up to prevent snow damage.

First catalogues of new season perused.

Indoor topiaries groomed daily.

Wreaths woven from garden vines and boughs.

Stones loosened from walls chinked back whence they came.

Garden searched for tiny pine cones and other decorations.

Tiny white lights strung in the apple trees and big beech.

Garden gifts of jams, jellies, pickles, preserves, and such wrapped and packed in baskets to be given away.

RIGHT: *My houseplants are not stereotypical; I tend to favor the unusual shapes of topiary and wire-trained plants. Though many interesting topiary wire forms are now commercially available, I prefer to make my own from chicken, rabbit, and hog wire, or simply to trim the plants by eye in a pleasing shape.*

Blood lilies forced for December bloom look like stunted *Allium Giganteum,* and are the most wonderful shade of Christmas red. Trellised on homemade wire mesh forms, giant pansies take on an entirely new character, and amaryllis, grown the second year with multiple feedings and less light than usual, produce huge blooms on short stems.

My eye is now trained to search shops and florists and flower shows for peculiar plants like yellow Clivia, with long shiny black-green leaves and a once-a-year profusion of multiple blooms. I have learned to plant containers with several types of plants, or many of the same plant. Agapanthus, which grows almost wild in California, is prized in the East when planted in huge jardinières for display in front of parlor windows or on balconies in warmer weather. Bearded iris, planted all one color in a giant pot, blooms beautifully; once the flowers fade, impatiens or pansies or annual herbs can be planted in and around the iris plants to conceal the browning foliage from view. And antique or "antiqued" urns look extraordinary when planted with five or six types of trailing miniature-leafed ivies around a centered topiary of rosemary, myrtle, or geranium.

All is not new in my house at Christmas, however; I am very fond of one old holiday standard, the Christmas Cactus (Schlumbergera Bridgesii). I have several that belonged years ago to my father and to his mother before that. One measures more than 30 inches in diameter and it always blooms during Christmas week, a fine and tangible reminder of my garden creed: To garden for the future.

Topiary

I AM NOT A HOUSEPLANT PERSON. Generally my home is devoid of the typical ficus, asparagus fern, Boston fern, and philodendron that seem to thrive in friends' living rooms. You will not find African violets or *Dracaena Marginata* or schefflera on my porch or in my house. This is not because I don't appreciate or admire these plants, but because after years of halfhearted effort, I realized that these plants require very special placement, correct light, and specific care. And I realized that I was not interested enough to provide it.

But four years ago I met two indoor gardeners who changed my attitude. Allen C. Haskell and J. Liddon Pennock, Jr., among America's greatest plantsmen, were kind enough to teach me about indoor topiary. Greatly encouraged by their ideas, I have had good success. The decorative topiary is a fine alternative to the ubiquitous ficus and the common spider plant. A tall pyramid of variegated 'Calico' ivy or a globe of 'Gold Heart' ivy is easy to create and quite simple to care for. A large-scale standard of scented geranium or dark green laurel is long-lived and hardy; all are much more imaginative and creative—and beautiful—than a pot of poinsettias.

The principle of topiary is simple: to train a plant to an unnatural—often formal—shape. The standard, my favorite, is a straight-stemmed plant topped with a round, lush, leafy mass, or sphere. A more complex version, sometimes called the "poodle" variation, usually has three round forms of diminishing size, some-

times more and often odd numbered. Herbs are some of the preferred choices for topiary, and with good reason. Their scents, leaf shapes, and colors are naturals for this art.

Training a standard for indoors is relatively easy but demands patience. Start with young plants that have strong, straight shoots, perhaps 4 or 5 inches high in a 4-inch pot. Before beginning, choose a size and form that is attractive to you.

Of course, your plant's environment is important. A sunny location with even light is ideal; if you have only one sunny window, be sure to turn the pot so the stem grows straight; otherwise it will lean toward the light. Use a balanced water-soluble fertilizer on a regular basis. It is handy to have a supply of pots and stakes of graduating size for repotting your plant as it grows.

Insert a narrow stake into the soil next to your tiny plant; a 10-inch bamboo stake is a good start. Eliminate side branches and tie the stem to the stake every 3 inches; use raffia or other material that will secure without binding. Check the ties as the plant grows and the main stem enlarges; if they are too tight, they can mar or even strangle the plant.

Retain at least an inch of the side branches at the top to allow the plant to manufacture food; pinch off others below. Leaves that grow directly from the stem can be left on temporarily; usually they fall off in time. Have patience; standards can take many years to accomplish. Fast growers like scented geraniums are gratifying for beginners. Once the plant reaches the desired height, usually after at

least two repottings, it is time to clip the main growing tip to stimulate multiple side branching. Set the plant's last stake a few inches shorter than the final height. Keep as many side branches for the standard top as you wish, pinching at a node when these are about an inch long. Frequent pinching is indispensable for creating dense top growth.

If you want a tiered look, with three spheres, employ the same method for standards. However, allow branches to remain where the first two spheres will form, pinching these back at the nodes for fuller growth. When your plant has reached the desired height, pinch off the tip to form the third sphere. Continue pinching the side branches. Once they are fully formed, trim the spheres to a slightly bottom-heavy circle and to diminishing size. Pruning in this manner allows sunlight to reach lower branches and keeps them green.

Other topiary can be created on wire forms, usually cone- or pyramid-shaped. Position the forms in pots before filling with soil. Vines, such as creeping ficus and ivy, are the easiest and fastest-growing plants for this topiary; set plants in a circle near the outside of the pot in strategic positions to grow on the frame. Use raffia to tie them to the wire near the soil line and continue tying as plants grow. If you do not use vines, look for plants with top-to-bottom branching habits for the best coverage of forms.

When choosing plants for any topiary, consider evergreen foliage, which is attractive year-round, and smaller-leafed plants for smaller-sized topiary and for denser leaf display.

SUGGESTED PLANTS FOR WIRE FORMS

Creeping fig *(Ficus pumila)*

Ivy *(Hedera helix* 'Glacier', 'Itsy-Bitsy', 'Ivalace', 'Shamrock', 'Telecurl', and other cultivars)

Baby's tears *(Soleirolia Soleirolii)*

Stephanotis *(Stephanotis floribunda)*

Thyme *(Thymus vulgaris)*

SUGGESTED PLANTS FOR BOTH STANDARD AND WIRE FORMS

Lemon verbena *(Aloysia triphylla)*

English lavender *(Lavandula angustifolia)*

French lavender *(Lavandula dentata)*

Lemon-scented geranium *(Pelargonium crispum)*

Pelargonium crispum 'Prince Rupert'

Lavender cotton *(Santolina Chamaecyparissus)*

Green santolina *(Santolina virens)*

SUGGESTED PLANTS FOR STANDARDS

Flowering maples *(Abutilon* hybrids)

Chrysanthemums *(Chrysanthemum)*

Eugenia myrtifolia (also called *Syzygium paniculatum)*

Licorice plant *(Helichrysum petiolatum)*

Weeping lantana *(Lantana montevidensis)*

Sweet or common bay *(Laurus nobilis)*

Australian tea rose *(Leptospermum scoparium)*

Dwarf myrtle *(Myrtus communis* 'Microphylla')

Australian Mintbush *(Prostanthera rotundifolia)*

Rosemary *(Rosmarinus officinalis)*

Marmalade bush or orange browallia *(Streptosolen Jamesonii)*

Victorian rosemary *(Westringia rosmariniformis)*

OPPOSITE: *Inspired by the topiaries, I created egg pyramids for the hall tables. On a twig or vine base, and around a polystyrene cone, blown or raw eggs are arranged in a cone shape. I used a combination of turkey, guinea fowl, quail, and chicken eggs. (The Auracana hens lay assorted blue, green, and khaki eggs.) Tufts of sheet moss, hyacinth blossoms, or baby's breath fill in any empty spaces.*

ABOVE: *Brussels sprouts, one of the vegetables that actually improves in flavor with a few frosts, wait for the kitchen. Always pick sprouts from the bottom up, and leave the top foliage intact.*

ABOVE: *A flurry of snow left the upper perennial garden looking bleak and deserted. Free-standing roses are surrounded with protective wrappings of burlap; fallen leaves are gathered from the lawns and piled within the burlap to offer even more protection from ground heaving and drying winds.*

Winter Wrapping

THE WINTERS IN CONNECTICUT ARE marked by strong, drying winds and dramatic fluctuations in temperature that can cause more damage than severe cold will. Plants that are only marginally hardy in this area require special protection.

MATERIALS. I buy both 1-by-2s and 2-by-2s, which I have cut into 4-foot lengths at the lumberyard. Some I paint green—those that will be used in highly visible areas. At a masonry supply house I purchase 100- and 200-foot rolls of 36-inch natural burlap; use only materials that breathe or you will smother the plants you are protecting. My staple gun is loaded, and my sledge hammer is at the ready.

ROSE GARDEN. In late fall, after all debris—fallen leaves and prunings—is removed from the garden, I mound compost around the crown of each rosebush and pile leaves, at least a foot high around tender roses to further insu-

ABOVE: *Always on the lookout against marauding deer, Zuzu patrols an alley of snowy sweet pea fencing.*
LEFT: *These cement urns are strong enough to withstand the rigors of winter; I like to keep them outside to enhance the barren landscape.*

late them. (The following spring the leaves are removed, but the compost stays to enrich the soil.) Next, burlap screening goes around the rose garden. To construct screening, sink 2-by-2s at least 1 foot deep at 6-foot intervals around the perimeter. Staple burlap onto each of the 2-by-2 posts, from top to bottom, pulling it taut between each one. BOXWOOD (BUXUS) AND YEW *(Taxus).* The delicate branches of these evergreens can snap under the weight of snow. In late fall before the first hard freeze, I take natural twine and secure gently, without binding, the branches of my yews. Attach the twine loosely to the trunk where it has been protected with a piece of burlap, and begin wrapping from bottom to top, round and round the heavy boughs. The branches, held close to the trunk, will not catch falling snow. For boxwood I construct tepees of 1-by-2s over each plant, driving the pointed ends into the soil at a safe distance from the roots. Burlap, stapled to the outside of the posts, completes the shelter. After heavy snowfalls I use a pole to knock snow off the burlap shelter and at the same time I dislodge any snow weighing down the branches of taller evergreens that are not wrapped.

FIG TREE (FICUS CARICA). My prized fig tree is not winter hardy in Zone 6. If left to the mercy of the elements, it would die by spring. But with a little extra care it has survived innumerable Connecticut winters and has flourished. After the leaves drop, I wrap each branch with strips of newspaper, tied with natural twine. Next I construct a cage around the tree with a wire mesh fencing—all the way to the top of the tree—and fill it with leaves. A layer of plastic wrap or a tarpaulin over the wire blocks the wind and snow; in this case, plastic insulation is necessary for this unusually tender tree. Finally, burlap covers everything, purely for cosmetic reasons.

ABOVE: *It takes a leap of faith to believe that in a few months' time, these climbing roses, snow-shrouded and wrapped in burlap, will be laden with fragrant blooms.* RIGHT: *An early December storm blanketed the garden with a soft cover of snow. Not thick enough to provide good insulation, the snow nevertheless gave moisture to the dry ground—and provided the appropriate background for Max, the black chow chow.*

Menu

BLINI WITH SALMON ROE
AND CRÈME FRAÎCHE

RACK OF LAMB

GALETTE OF POTATOES

PARSNIP PUREE

FENNEL PUREE

MÂCHE SALAD WITH
CHAMPAGNE VINAIGRETTE

PEAR TATIN

Blini with Salmon Roe and Crème Fraîche

MAKES ABOUT 35 BLINI

When serving blini as a first course, don't skimp on the amount of caviar used. Make the blini slightly larger than a silver dollar, a good size for passed hors d'oeuvres.

1 package active dry yeast
½ cup warm water
1 cup milk
1½ cups all-purpose flour
3 large eggs, separated
½ teaspoon salt
　Pinch of sugar
6 tablespoons (¾ stick) melted
　butter
1 cup crème fraîche (or thick sour
　cream)
1 3.5-ounce jar salmon roe
　Fresh dill, for garnish

1. Proof yeast in the water for 5 minutes.
2. Put the yeast, milk, flour, egg yolks, salt, sugar, and melted butter in a food processor. Blend for 40 seconds. Scrape down sides and process 10 more seconds.
3. Pour the batter into a large bowl. Cover with a cloth towel, and let rise in a warm, draft-free place for 1½ to 2 hours.
4. Beat the egg whites until stiff peaks form. Fold into risen batter.
5. Heat a heavy skillet or griddle and brush with melted butter. Drop a teaspoon of batter onto hot surface. Turn when the first side is lightly browned, and cook briefly on the other side.
6. Place blini on a warm platter until batter is used up. When ready to serve, place a small dollop of crème fraîche and several grains of roe in the middle of each blini, and garnish with a sprig of dill.

Rack of Lamb

SERVES 6

Our traditional Christmas feast is rack of lamb. Allow two chops per person.

½ cup dry white wine
½ cup olive oil
1 shallot, thinly sliced
3 small sprigs fresh thyme
3-4 fresh bay leaves
3 sprigs fresh marjoram
1½ pound rack of lamb (8 chops)

1. Mix together all ingredients except the lamb in a medium bowl. Add lamb, cover, and let sit for several hours.
2. Preheat the broiler. Remove lamb from the marinade and cover the ends of the bones with foil to prevent burning.
3. Line a shallow roasting pan with foil. Place the lamb in the pan, fat side down. Broil for about 4 minutes. Turn lamb over and continue broiling for another 4 to 5 minutes. The meat should be pink.
4. Let lamb sit for 5 minutes. Slice into individual chops and serve.

Parsnip Puree

SERVES 6

Big autumn parsnips taste even better cooked with a pear or two for sweetness.

4 parsnips (about 1 pound), cut
　into 1-inch pieces
3 tablespoons unsalted butter
½ cup water
1 very ripe pear
1 large sprig fresh rosemary

In a medium saucepan over low heat, combine ingredients and cook until very soft, about 25 to 30 minutes. Remove rosemary. Puree and serve immediately.

Galette of Potatoes

SERVES 6

This giant potato pancake can be made an hour or so in advance and reheated, but it must be cooked through or else the potatoes will darken while it stands.

5 large Idaho potatoes
8 tablespoons (1 stick) unsalted
　butter, clarified
　Salt and freshly ground pepper

1. Peel the potatoes and place in a bowl of cold water to prevent browning.
2. Coarsely grate the potatoes. Dry by rubbing them between two clean kitchen towels.
3. In a 12-inch nonstick skillet over medium-high heat, melt the butter until it sizzles. Add the potatoes in a flat, even layer. Sprinkle with salt and pepper. Shake the pan frequently to prevent the potatoes from sticking.
4. After about 3 minutes, invert the potatoes onto a plate and carefully slide them back into the pan to continue cooking on the other side. Reduce heat to low and continue to cook for another 20 to 30 minutes, shaking the pan from time to time.
5. Keep the galette warm until ready to serve. Cut into wedges.

OPPOSITE: *I set the table with my favorite holiday Wedgewood china, the Fallow Deer pattern in copper lustre. The centerpiece, candles, and soft hurricane lighting make the table appear to glow. The silver globes are huge witches' balls of mercury glass.*

Mâche Salad with Champagne Vinaigrette

SERVES 6

Mâche, also known as lamb's lettuce, has delicate, dark green leaves with a unique nutty flavor. Mâche never seems to get bitter, even after the tiny plants have gone to flower. Always serve this green with a delicate vinaigrette and a light oil.

Champagne Vinaigrette
1 tablespoon champagne vinegar
1 teaspoon red wine vinegar
2 tablespoons avocado or grapeseed oil
2 tablespoons extra-virgin olive oil
Salt and freshly ground pepper

30 heads mâche, root trimmed but left intact

Whisk together all dressing ingredients in a large bowl. Add the lettuce and toss; serve immediately.

Fennel Puree

SERVES 6

If you want the puree to be as delicate as those served by the best French chefs, press the puree through a fine sieve before reheating and serving.

2 medium fennel bulbs
8 tablespoons (1 stick) unsalted butter
$\frac{1}{4}$ cup long-grain rice
$\frac{1}{4}$ cup heavy cream
Salt and freshly ground pepper
2 sprigs fresh marjoram

1. Slice the fennel in half lengthwise. With a small sharp knife, remove the triangular core. Slice crosswise into strips $\frac{1}{4}$-inch thick.
2. In a large skillet over low heat, melt the butter. Add fennel, cover, and cook until tender, about 25 to 30 minutes.
3. Meanwhile, cook the rice in a small pot of boiling water until soft, about 15 to 20 minutes. Drain.
4. Combine the fennel and rice in the bowl of a food processor. While processor is running, add the cream through feed tube. Season to taste with salt and pepper. Garnish with marjoram sprigs.

Pear Tatin

SERVES 6

Pear Tatin is my favorite winter dessert, using the best fruit of the season. I find that Comice or Packham pears are wonderful if they are not too juicy; try Bosc pears if you have difficulty with the Comice.

1 cup sugar
$\frac{1}{4}$ cup water
4 tablespoons ($\frac{1}{2}$ stick) butter, cut into small pieces
6 Comice pears, peeled, cored, and halved
$\frac{1}{2}$ recipe Pâte Brisée

1. In a cast-iron skillet over medium heat, combine the sugar and water. Bring to a boil, lower the flame, and cook until the liquid begins to thicken and turn amber. Remove from heat and stir in the butter.
2. Arrange the pear halves on top of the caramelized sugar, cut sides up. Return skillet to the heat and cook over low heat for about 20 minutes, or until the syrup thickens and is reduced by half. Remove from the heat and let cool.
3. Preheat oven to 375°.
4. Roll out the Pâte Brisée to $\frac{1}{8}$ inch and place over the pear halves in the skillet. Trim the edges. Bake for 20 minutes or until the pastry is golden brown. Let cool for 10 to 15 minutes, then loosen the pastry from the pan using a sharp knife. Place a platter over the skillet and invert quickly. Serve immediately.

ABOVE: *I served the lamb, vegetable purees, and potato galette, "garnished" by the salad, on an antique silver platter.*

Pâte Brisée

MAKES 2 8- TO 10-INCH
SINGLE CRUSTS

2½ cups all-purpose flour
1 teaspoon salt
1 teaspoon sugar (optional)
1 cup (2 sticks) cold unsalted
   butter, cut into small pieces
¼–½ cup ice water

1. Put the flour, salt, and sugar, if desired, in the bowl of a food processor. Add the pieces of butter and process for about 10 seconds, or until mixture resembles a coarse meal.

2. Add the ice water, drop by drop, through the feed tube with the machine running, just until dough holds together without being wet or sticky; do not process more than 30 seconds.

3. Turn the dough out onto a large square of plastic wrap. Use the ends to help form the dough into a flat circle. Wrap the dough in the plastic and chill for at least an hour, or until ready to use. (You can also freeze the dough.)

ABOVE: *A rich, buttery pâte brisée makes a wonderful base for the Pear Tatin. Use the ripest, most beautiful pears you can find, and you won't be disappointed. I like to serve tatins in elegant silver dishes like the one shown here.*

SOURCES

Aitken's Salmon Creek Garden
608 NW 119th Street
Vancouver, WA 98685
206-573-4472
Irises, hybridizing, and quality plants.

Barnee's Gardens
Route 10, Box 2010
Nacogdoches, TX 75961
409-564-2920
Irises.

Breck's
U.S. Reservation Center
6523 North Galena Road
P.O. Box 1982
Peoria, IL 61656
800-221-0734

W. Atlee Burpee & Co.
300 Park Avenue
Warminster, PA 18991-0003
800-888-1447
Plants, supplies, and all garden materials.

Comanche Acres Iris Gardens
RR #1, Box 258
Gower, MO 64454
816-424-6436

The Cook's Garden
P.O. Box 65
Londonderry, VT 05148
802-824-3400
A fantastic assortment of European and American vegetables. All types of basil; dozens of lettuces.

Gurney's Seed Nursery
110 Capitol Street
Yankton, SD 57079
605-665-1930
A very interesting compilation of seeds, plants, trees (including fruit trees), berries, and shrubs.

Harris Seeds
60 Saginaw Avenue
Rochester, NY 14623
716-442-0410

Le Marche
P.O. Box 190
Dixon, CA 95620
Wholesale only; seeds from around the world; excellent catalogue descriptions.

Park Seed Co.
Cokesbury Road
Greenwood, SC 29647-0001
800-845-3369
Seeds, plants, and bulbs.

Nichols Garden Nurseries
1190 Pacific North Highway
Albany, OR 97321
503-928-9280
Mail order and shop specializing in herbs and rare seeds.

Reath's Nursery
P.O. Box 521
100 Central Boulevard
Vulcan, MI 49892
The most extensive and interesting collection of herbaceous and tree peonies.

Shepherd's Garden Seeds
616 Highway
Felton, CA 95018
408-335-5216
Specializing in European and unique seeds; emphasis on high germination rate.

Shemin Nurseries, Inc.
1081 King Street
P.O. Box 64, Glenville Station
Greenwich, CT 06830
203-531-7352
Horticultural distribution center.

Stokes Seeds, Inc.
P.O. Box 548
Buffalo, NY 14240
800-263-7233 (in NY and OH)
800-263-5733 (rest of US)
Vegetable and flower seeds of excellent quality and variety.

T & T Seeds Ltd.
Box 1710
Winnepeg, Manitoba
Canada R3C 3P6
204-943-8483
Only flower and vegetable seeds can be shipped into the U.S.

Thompson & Morgan
P.O. Box 1308
Jackson, NJ 08527
908-363-2225
800-274-7333 (outside NJ)
fax 908-363-9356
An English mail-order catalogue of immense scope, offering seeds for flowers, vegetables, succulents, etc.

Tranquil Lake Nursery
45 River Street
Rehoboth, MA 02769-1395
508-336-6491
Daylilies and Siberian and Japanese irises.

K. Van Bourgondien & Sons
P. O. Box A
245 Farmingdale Road
Babylon, NY 11702
516-669-3520
800-284-9333
Dahlias, lilies, peonies, gladiolas, and many other perennials and groundcovers. Large wholesale and mail-order business.

Van Engelen Inc.
Stillbrook Farm
313 Maple Street
Litchfield, CT 06759
203-567-8734
203-567-5662
Wholesale mail-order catalogues, fall planting flower bulbs.

Dan Walker
Flowerfield
210 Cutlers Farm Road
Monroe, CT 06468
203-268-3645
Ground cover plants.

Wayside Gardens
1 Garden Lane
Hodges, SC 29695-0001
800-845-1124
An amazing catalogue filled with the best shrubs, flowering trees, roses, peonies, bulbs, grasses, and tubers.

White Flower Farm
Litchfield, CT 06759-0050
203-496-9600
A most informative, erudite catalogue offering an interesting assortment of perennials and bulbs for planting. Shrubs of terrific quality.

OLD GARDEN ROSES

The Antique Rose Emporium
Route 5, Box 143
Brenham, TX 77833
409-836-9051

High Country Rosarium
1717 Downing Street
Denver, CO 80218
303-832-4026

Pickering Nurseries, Inc.
670 Kingston Road
Highway 2
Pickering, Ontario
Canada L1V 1A6
416-839-2111
Very small company, mail order and retail.

Roses of Yesterday and Today
802 Brown's Valley Road
Watsonville, CA 95076
408-724-3537
America's foremost source for old roses. Bareroot plants sent in excellent shape for spring planting. Gallica, damask, moss, rugosa, grandiflora, centifolia, musk, tea, and bourbon among roses offered.

ROSES

Jackson & Perkins
1 Rose Lane
Medford, OR 97501
800-292-GROW
Known for roses and spring bulbs.

Spring Hill Nurseries
110 West Elm Street
Tipp City, OH 45371
800-544-0294 for catalogue
513-667-4079 (garden center)

Wayside Gardens
1 Garden Lane
Hodges, SC 29695-0001
800-845-1124

HERBS

Catnip Acres Farm Herb Nursery
67-NG Christian Street
Oxford, CT 06483
203-888-5649
Top-quality herb seeds and plants for all purposes. Hard-to-find varieties: 19 types of artemesia; 19 kinds of sage! Also dried flowers.

The Cook's Garden
P.O. Box 535
Londonderry, VT 05148
802-824-3400
Seed catalogue, source for untreated seeds and organic gardening supplies.

Epicure Seed, Ltd.
P.O. Box 450
Brewster, NY 10509
914-279-8204
800-343-1059
800-833-2900 (outside NY)

Gilbertie's Herb Gardens
7 Sylvan Lane
Westport, CT 06880
203-227-4175
Garden center specializing in herbs. Open year round, no mail order.

FRUITS AND BERRIES

Adams County Nursery, Inc.
26 Nursery Road
Aspers, PA 17304
717-677-8105
Fruit trees.

Ahrens Strawberry Nursery
Route 1
Huntingburg, IN 47542
812-683-3055
Strawberries.

Allen Co.
P.O. Box 1577
Salisbury, MD 21801
301-742-7122
Strawberries.

Ames' Orchard & Nursery
Route 5, Box 194-F
Fayetteville, AR 72701
501-443-0282
Specializing in disease-resistant fruit varieties.

California Nursery Company
Niles District
Box 2278
Fremont, CA 94536
415-797-3311

Country Heritage Nurseries
P.O. Box 536
Hartford, MI 49057
616-621-2491
Plant nursery specializing in strawberries and raspberries.

Cumberland Valley Nurseries
P.O. Box 471
McMinnville, TN 37110
(615) 668-4153
800-492-0022 (outside TN)
Wholesale nursery specializing in fruit trees.

Dyke Bros. Nursery
Route 1, Box 251-S
Vincent, OH 45784
614-678-2192
Pick-your-own, nurseries for blueberries and blackberries.

Edible Landscaping
Route 2, Box 77
Afton, VA 22920
703-361-9134

Fruitwood Nursery
Box 303
Molena, GA 30258
404-495-5488
Apples adapted to the South.

Greenmantle Nursery
3010 Ettersburg Road
Garberville, CA 95440
707-986-7504
Specializes in old and unusual fruit varieties and classic roses (over 250 species and varieties); mail order.

Hartmann's Plantation, Inc.
310 60th Street, P.O. Box E
Grand Junction, MI 49056
616-253-4281
Specializes in blueberry plants.

Ison's Nursery & Vineyards
Box 191
Brooks, GA 30205
800-733-0324
Any kind of fruit and nut trees.

Lawson's Nursery
Route 1, Box 294
Ball Ground, GA 30107
404-893-2141
Specializes in fruit trees, especially old-fashioned and unusual apple trees.

Henry Leuthardt Nurseries, Inc.
Montauk Highway
Box 666
East Moriches, NY 11940
516-878-1387
A small family business devoted to the propagating and selling of old varieties of apples, pears, peaches, plums, grapes, and other fruits and berries. Dwarf, semi-dwarf, and espalier fruit trees.

Makielski Berry Nursery
7130 Platt Road
Ypsilanti, MI 48197
313-434-3673
Specializes in raspberry plants.

J. E. Miller Nurseries and Co.
5060 West Lake Road
Canandaigua, NY 14424
800-836-9630
fax 716-396-2154

Henry Morton
Old-Fashioned Apple Trees
Route 1, Box 203
Gatlinburg, TN 37738
615-436-4340

New York State Fruit Testing
Cooperative Association, Inc.
Geneva, NY 14456
315-787-2205

Nourse Farms, Inc.
New England Strawberry
Nursery
Box 485 RFD
South Deerfield, MA 01373
413-665-2658
Strawberry, raspberry, and blackberry plants.

Oikos Tree Crops
721 Fletcher
Kalamazoo, MI 49007-3077
616-342-6504
Fruit, nut, and native trees.

Raintree Nursery
391 Butts Road
Morton, WA 98356
206-496-6400
Mail order for organic fruits, berries, and nuts

Rayner Bros. Inc.
P.O. Box 1617
Salisbury, MD 21802
301-742-1594
Mail-order nursery specializing in strawberry and blueberry plants and asparagus roots.

Savage Farms Nurseries
P.O. Box 125 PL1234
McMinnville, TN 37110
615-688-8902
Over 250 kinds of plants.

Sonoma Antique Apple Nursery
4395 Westside Road
Healdsburg, CA 95448
707-433-6420
Antique apple and other fruit trees.

South Meadow Fruit Gardens
and Grootendorst Nurseries
15310 Red Arrow Highway
Lakeside, MI 49116
616-469-2865
Mail order, specializing in antique fruit trees.

Stark Bros.
Highway 54
Louisiana, MO 63353
314-754-4525
800-843-5091 (outside MO)
Fruit trees.

Sunny Rows Plant Farm
Route 1, Box 189C
Currie, NC 28435
919-283-5605
Strawberries of all types.

Waynesboro Nurseries
P.O. Box 987
Waynesboro, VA 22980
800-868-8676
Wholesale nursery.

EQUIPMENT AND TOOLS

Charley's Greenhouse Supplies
1569 Memorial Highway
Mount Vernon, WA 98273
800-322-4707
Mail order.

Gardener's Eden
P.O. Box 7307
San Francisco, CA 94120-7307
415-421-4242
Mail-order garden products, catalogue.

Gardener's Supply Co.
128 Intervale Road
Burlington, VT 05401
800-5448-4784
Mail order; general composing, seed starting, organic lawn-care products

A. M. Leonard, Inc.
P.O. Box 816
Piqua, OH 45356-0816
513-773-2694
Mail order and walk-in; horticultural tools and supplies.

Mantis Manufacturing Co.
1458 County Line Road
Huntingdon Valley, PA 19006
800-344-4030
Mail-order garden products.

Al Saffer & Co., Inc.
Pearl and William Streets
Port Chester, NY 10573
914-937-6565
Store, no catalogue. Greenhouses.

Skagit Valley Gardens
1695 Johnson Road
Mount Vernon, WA 98273
206-424-6760
Professional horticultural tools and supplies; retail nursery and wholesale growers.

Smith & Hawken
25 Corte Madera
Mill Valley, CA 94941
415-383-2000
Gardening supplies and clothing.

GARDEN ORNAMENTATION

Garden Stoneware
Seahorse Trading Co., Inc
P.O. Box 677
Berryville, VA 22611
703-955-1677
Specializing in Victorian wire furniture and sundials imported from England.

Haskell's
Allen C. Haskell
787 Shawmut Avenue
New Medford, MA 02749
508-993-9047
Topiaries, etc. No catalogue.

Redwood Stone
46 North Road
Wells, Somerset BA5 2TL
England
0749-73601
Urns.

White Flower Farm
Litchfield, CT 06759-0050
203-567-0801
800-888-7756 for catalogue
Open April through October; interesting and unusual items.

BEES

A. I. Root Co.
P.O. Box 706
623 West Liberty Street
Medina, OH 44256-0706
216-725-6677
Manufactures and distributes candles and bee supplies.

Rossman Apiaries, Inc.
P.O. Box 905
Moultrie, GA 31768
800-333-7677
Packages bees, queens, and bee supplies.

Edward Weiss
3 Whipstick Road
Wilton, CT 06897
203-762-3538
Bee supplies, beekeeping equipment, all kinds of honey.

POULTRY

Crow Poultry and Supply Co.
Box 106
Windsor, MO 65360-0106
816-647-2614
Mail order for poultry and poultry equipment.

Marti Poultry Farm
P.O. Box 27
Windsor, MO 65360-0027
816-647-3156
Mail-order poultry farm.

Murray McMurray Hatchery
P.O. Box 458
609 Ohio Street
Webster City, IA 50595
800-798-3280
fax 515-832-2213
Mail order, rare and unusual poultry. Largest source of rare-breed poultry in the country.

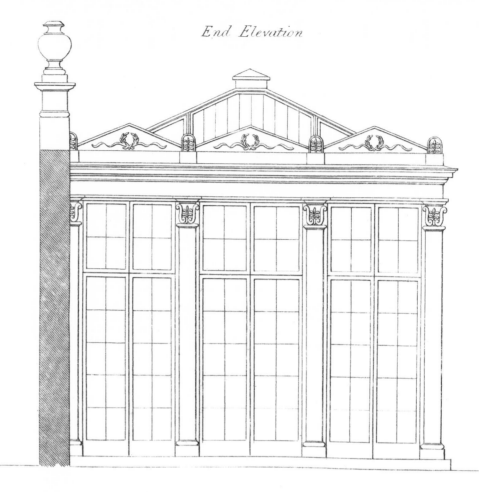

End Elevation

FLOWER AND PLANT SOCIETIES

The American Daffodil Society,
Mary Lou Gripshover
1686 Grey Fox Trails
Milford, OH 45150

American Horticultural Society
Joseph M. Keyser
7931 East Boulevard Drive
Alexandria, VA 22308

The American Iris Society
Jeane Stayer
7414 East 60th Street
Tulsa, OK 74145

American Peony Society
Greta M. Kessenich
250 Interlachen Road
Hopkins, MN 55343

American Rose Society
Membership Secretary
P.O. Box 30000
Shreveport, LA 71130

The Garden Club of America
Mrs. E. Murphy
598 Madison Avenue
New York, NY 10022

Herb Society of America, Inc.
Leslie Rascan
9019 Kirland Chardon Road
Mentor, OH 44060

Heritage Rose Group
Miriam Wilkins
925 Galvin Drive
El Cerrito, CA 94530

The National Sweet Pea Society
J.R.F. Bishop
3 Chalk Farm Road
Stokenchurch, Bucks
England HP14 3TB

BIBLIOGRAPHY

GARDEN BOOKS

Anonymous, *The Language of Flowers,* Frederick Warner and Co., Ltd., London, 1979.

Antique Collectors' Club, *Gardens in Edwardian England,* repr., Newnes Books, 1985.

Armitage, Allan, *Herbaceous Perennial Plants,* Varsity Press, Inc., 1989.

Staff of the L. H. Bailey Hortorium, Cornell University, *Hortus Third, A Concise Dictionary of Plants Cultivated in the United States and Canada,* Macmillan, 1976.

Bailey, Lee, *Country Flowers,* Clarkson Potter, 1985.

Balantyne, Janet, *Joy of Gardening Cookbook,* Garden Way, Inc., 1984.

Baron, Leonard, *Lawns and How to Make Them,* Doubleday, Page and Co., 1910.

Beales, Peter, *Classic Roses,* Henry Holt and Co., 1985.

Benenson, Sharon, *The New York Botanical Garden Cookbook,* The Council of the New York Botanical Garden, 1982

Bennoit, I. D., and Adolph Kruhm, ed., *The Vegetable Garden,* repr., Doubleday, Doran and Co., 1928.

Besler, Bisilius, *The Besler Floriegium,* repr., Abrams, 1989.

Best, Clare, and Caroline Boisset, eds., *Leaves from the Garden: Two Centuries of Garden Writing,* W. W. Norton and Co., 1987.

Betts, Edward M., ed., *Thomas Jefferson's Garden Book,* American Philosophical Society, 1914.

Biandrini, F., and F. Corbetta, *The Complete Book of Fruits and Vegetables,* Crown, 1976.

Bittman, Sam, *Seeds,* Bantam, 1989.

Blair, Edna and Laurence, *The Food Garden,* Macmillan, 1942.

Blake, Clair L., *Greenhouse Gardening for Fun,* William Morrow and Co., 1972.

Blanchan, Neltje, *Nature's Garden,* Doubleday, Page and Co., 1907.

Brookes, John, *The Indoor Garden Book,* Crown, 1986.

Brooks, Barbara, *Fine Flowers by Phone,* Atlantic Monthly Press, 1989.

Brown, Vinson, *The Amateur Naturalist's Book,* Little, Brown and Co., 1951.

Bush-Brown, Louise and James, *America's Garden Book,* Charles Scribner's Sons, 1953.

Clarke, Ethne, and George Wright, *English Topiary Gardens,* Clarkson Potter, 1988.

Clausen, Ruth R., and Nicolas H. Ekstrom, *Perennials for American Gardens,* Random House, 1989.

Clevely, A. M., *The Total Garden,* Harmony Books, 1988.

Clifford, Derek, *A History of Garden Design,* Frederick A. Praeger Publishers, 1963.

Connolly, Sybil, and Helen Dillon, *In an Irish Garden* Harmony Books, 1986.

Cook, E. T., *Gardens of England* A & C Black, Ltd., 1911.

Cox, Jeff, *How to Grow Vegetables Organically,* Rodale Press, 1988.

Cox, Madison, *Private Gardens of Paris,* Harmony Books, 1989.

Creasy, Rosalind, *The Complete Book of Edible Landscaping,* Sierra Club Books, 1982.

Creasy, Rosalind, *Cooking from the Garden,* Sierra Club Books, 1988.

Creasy, Rosalind, *Earthly Delights,* Sierra Club Books, 1985.

Douglas, William L., and others, *Garden Design: History, Principles, Elements, Practice,* Simon and Schuster, 1984.

Dunhill, Priscilla, and Sue Freedman, *Glorious Gardens to Visit,* Clarkson Potter, 1989.

Ellacombe, *In a Gloucestershire Garden,* repr., Century, 1982.

Elliott, Brent, *Victorian Gardens* B. T. Batsford Ltd., 1986.

Ely, Helena R., *The Practical Flower Garden,* The Macmillan Co., 1911.

Ely, Helena R., *A Woman's Hardy Garden,* The Macmillan Co., 1903.

Everett, Thomas, *The Illustrated Encyclopedia of Horticulture,* Garland, 1982.

Fagan, Gwen, *Roses at the Cape of Good Hope,* Breestrat Publikasies, 1988.

Fairbrother, Nan, *Men and Gardens,* Knopf, 1956.

Faust, Joan Lee, *The New York Times Book of Vegetable Gardening,* Quadrangle/The New York Times Book Co., 1975.

Ferguson, J. Barry, and Tom Cowan, *Living with Flowers,* Rizzoli International, 1990.

Findlay, Hugh, *Garden Making and Keeping,* Doubleday, Doran and Co., 1932.

Foster, H. Lincoln, *Rock Gardening,* Timber Press, 1982.

Frieze, Charlotte M., *Social Gardens: Outdoor Spaces for Living and Entertaining,* Stewart, Tabori and Chang, 1988.

Galle, Fred C., *Azaleas,* Timber Press, 1985.

Gallup, Barbara, and Deborah Reich, *The Complete Book of Topiary,* Workman Publishers, 1987.

Garden Center of Greater Cleveland, *Flowering Plant Index of Illustration and Information,* G. K. Hall, 2 volumes, 1979 (2 vol. supplement, 1982).

George, Michael, and Patrick Bowe, *The Gardens of Ireland,* New York Graphic Society Books, 1987.

Gibbons, Euell, *Stalking the Wild Asparagus,* David McKay Company, Inc., 1962.

Gilbertie, Sal, and Larry Sheehan, *Home Gardening at Its Best,* Atheneum, 1977.

Gottleib, Jane, *Garden Tales,* Viking Penguin, 1990.

Green, Samuel B., *Vegetable Gardening,* Webb Publishing, 1909.

Grey, Wilson Christopher, *The Kew Five-Year Gardener's Diary,* Collingridge Books, 1984.

Grissell, Eric, *Thyme on My Hands,* Timber Press, 1987.

Hadfield, Miles, *Topiary and Ornamental Hedges,* A & C Black, Ltd., 1971.

Hamilton, Geoff, *The Organic Garden Book,* Crown Publishers, 1987.

Hardie, Dee, *Hollyhocks, Lambs and Other Passions,* Atheneum, 1985.

Harkness, Mabel G., *The Seedlist Handbook,* 4th edition, Timber Press, 1986.

Harpur, Jerry, *The Gardener's Garden,* David R. Godine, Publisher, 1985.

Hatton, Richard G., *Handbook of Plant and Floral Ornament from Early Herbals,* repr., Dover Publications, 1960.

Henderson, John, *Henderson's Handbook of the Grasses of Great Britain and America,* Journal Publishing Co., 1875.

Henslow, T. Geoffrey W., *Garden Development,* Dean and Son, Ltd., 1923.

Hill, Lewis, *Fruits and Berries for the Home Garden,* Storey Communications, 1977.

Hobhouse, Penelope, *Borders,* Harper and Row, 1989.

Hobhouse, Penelope, *Private Gardens of England,* Harmony Books, 1987.

Holt, Geraldene, *Recipes from a French Herb Garden,* Simon and Schuster, 1989.

Hudson, W. H., *Afoot in England,* Knopf, 1922.

Hunt, John D., and Peter Willis, eds., *The Genius of the Place: The English Landscape Garden 1620-1820,* Harper and Row, 1975.

Hunt, William L., *Southern Gardening,* Duke University Press, 1982.

Hyams, Edward, *The English Garden,* Abrams, 1964.

Ingram, Vicki L., *Elegance in Flowers,* Oxmoor House, 1985.

Jabs, Carolyn, *The Heirloom Gardener,* Sierra Club Books, 1984.

James River Garden Club, Edith T. Sale, ed., *Historic Gardens of Virginia,* William Byrd Press, Inc., 1930.

Jefferson, Thomas, and Robert C. Baron, ed., *The Garden and Farm Books of Thomas Jefferson,* Fulcrum Publishing, 1988.

Jekyll, Gertrude, *Colour Schemes for the Flower Garden,* repr., The Antique Collectors' Club, 1982.

Jekyll, Gertrude, *Garden Ornament,* repr., The Antique Collectors' Club, 1982.

Jekyll, Gertrude, *Lilies for English Gardens,* repr., The Antique Collectors' Club, 1982.

Jekyll, Gertrude, *Roses for English Gardens,* repr., The Antique Collectors' Club, 1982.

Jekyll, Gertrude, *Wood and Garden,* repr., The Ayer Company, 1984.

Jekyll, Gertrude, Penelope Hobhouse, ed., *Gertrude On Gardening;* , David Godine Publisher, 1984.

Jekyll, Gertrude, and Lawrence Weaver, *Gardens for Small Country Houses,* repr., The Antique Collectors' Club, Ltd., 1981.

Jenkins, Dorothy H., *The Complete Book of Roses,* Bantam, 1956.

Johnson, Hugh, *Principles of Gardening,* Simon and Schuster, 1984.

Keen, Mary, *The Garden Border Book,* Capability's Books, 1987.

King, Francis, *Variety in the Little Garden,* Atlantic Monthly Press, 1923.

Kowaldchik, C., and William H. Hylton, *Rodale's Illustrated Encyclopedia of Herbs,* Rodale, 1987.

Kramer, Jack, *Gardens for All Seasons,* Abrams, 1981.

Kramer, Jack, *Orchids: Flowers of Romance and Mystery,* Abrams, 1975.

Kriegel, John, ed., *The Houston Garden Book,* Shearer, 1983.

Kruhm, Adolph, *Home Vegetable Gardening From A to Z,* Doubleday, Page and Co., 1918.

Lacy, Allen, *The American Gardener: A Sampler,* Collins, 1988.

Lacy, Allen, and Christopher Baker, *The Glory of Roses,* Stewart, Tabori and Chang, 1990.

Lawrence, Elizabeth, *Gardening for Love,* Duke University Press, 1987.

Lawrence, Elizabeth, *The Little Bulbs: A Tale of Two Gardens,* Duke University Press, 1986.

Leighton, Ann, *Early American Gardens,* Houghton Mifflin, 1970.

Lequenne, Fernand, *My Friend the Garden,* trans., Doubleday and Co., 1965.

Lisle, Clifford, *Pastures New: Hill Farm in the Making,* Farrar, Straus, and Cudahy, 1955.

Lloyd, Christopher, *The Adventurous Gardener,* Vintage Books, 1985.

Lloyd, Christopher, *The Well-Tempered Garden,* Random House, 1985.

Mabey, Richard, *The Frampton Flora,* Prentice Hall, 1986.

MacQueen, Sheila, *Complete Flower Arranging,* Hyperion, 1979.

Madderlake, *Flowers Rediscovered,* Stewart, Tabori and Chang, 1985.

Maier, Mathilde, *All the Gardens of My Life,* Vintage, 1983.

Marranca, Bonnie, ed., *American Garden Writing,* PAJ Publications, 1988.

Masson, Georgina, *Italian Gardens,* Abrams, 1961.

McDonald, Elvin, *Handbook for Greenhouse Gardeners,* Lord and Burnham, 1971.

McGourty, Frederick, *The Perennial Gardener,* Houghton Mifflin, 1989.

Melady, John Hayes, *Better Vegetables for Your Home Garden,* Grossett and Dunlap, 1952.

Midda, Sara, *In and Out of the Garden,* Workman, 1981.

Milland, Scott, *Gardening in Dry Climates,* Ortho, 1989.

National Gardens Scheme, The, *Gardens of England and Wales Open to the Public,* 1986.

Nearing, Helen and Scott, *Living the Good Life,* Schocken Books, 1987.

Nearing, Helen and Scott, *The Maple Sugar Book,* Schocken Books, 1970.

Nichols, Beverly, *Down the Garden Path,* Cape, Ltd., 1932.

Nichols, Beverly, *How Does Your Garden Grow?,* Doubleday, Doran and Co., 1935.

Nichols, Beverly, *A Village in a Valley,* Jonathan Cape, Ltd., 1934.

Nisbet, Fred J., ed., *American Rose Annual: 1954,* The American Rose Society, 1954.

Nuese, Josephine, *The Country Garden,* Charles Scribner's Sons, 1907.

Ohrbach, Barbara Milo, *The Scented Room: Cherchez's Book of Dried Flowers, Fragrance, and Potpourri,* Clarkson Potter, 1986.

Otis, Denise, and Ronaldo Maia, *Decorating with Flowers,* Abrams, 1978.

Ottewill, David, *The Edwardian Garden,* Yale University Press, 1989.

Packer, Jane, *Flowers for All Seasons: Summer,* Fawcett Columbia, 1989.

Page, Russell, *The Education of a Gardener,* Vintage Books, 1985.

Pearson, Robert, ed., *The Wisley Book of Gardening,* Collingridge Books, 1981.

Penn, Irving, *Flowers,* Harmony Books, 1980.

Pereire, Anita, and Gabrielle Van Zuylen, *Gardens of France,* Harmony Books, 1983.

Perenyi, Eleanor, *Green Thoughts: A Writer in the Garden,* Random House, 1981.

Pettingill, Amos, *The White-Flower Farm Garden Book,* Knopf, 1971.

Phillips, Roger, *Wild Flowers of Britain,* Pan Books, 1977.

Phillips, Roger, and Martyn Rix, *The Bulb Book: A Photographic Guide to Over 800 Hardy Bulbs,* Pan Books, 1981.

Phillips, Roger, and Martyn Rix, *Random House Guide to Roses,* Random House, 1988.

Phillpotts, Eden, *My Garden,* Charles Scribner's Sons, 1906.

Pistorius, Alan, *Cutting Hill: A Chronicle of a Family Farm,* Knopf, 1990.

Pizzetti, Ippolito, and Henry Cockes, *Flowers: A Guide for Your Garden,* Vol. 1 and 2, Abrams, 1975.

Pond, Barbara, *A Sampler of Wayside Herbs,* Chatham Press, 1974.

Powell, E. P., *The Orchard and Fruit Garden,* Doubleday, Page and Co., 1916.

Prenis, John, *Herb Grower's Guide,* Running Press, 1974.

Prentice, Helaine K., and Melba Levick, *The Gardens of Southern California,* Chronicle Books, 1990.

Pyle, Robert, *How to Grow Roses,* The Conard and Jones Co., 1923.

Raphael, Sandra, *An Oak Spring Pomona: A Selection of the Rare Books on Fruit in the Oak Spring Garden Library,* Oak Spring Garden Library, 1990.

Raphael, Sandra, *An Oak Spring Sylva,* Oak Spring Garden Library, 1989.

Reader's Digest Encyclopedia of Garden Plants and Flowers, Reader's Digest Assn., 1975.

Reader's Digest Illustrated Guide to Gardening, Reader's Digest Assn., 1981.

Riker, Tom, et. al, *The Gardener's Catalogue,* William Morrow and Co., 1974

Robinson, William, *The English Flower Garden,* repr., Amaryllis Books, 1984.

Rodale, Robert, ed., *The Basic Book of Organic Gardening,* Ballantine Books, 1987.

Rogers, Julia E., *Trees,* Doubleday, Page and Co., 1926.

Rokach, Allen, and Anne Millman, *Focus on Flowers: Discovering and Photographing Beauty in Gardens and Wild Places,* Abbeville Press, 1990.

Rose, Graham, *The Traditional Garden Book,* Dorling Kindersley, Ltd., 1989.

Royal Horticulture Society, The, *The Vegetable Garden Displayed,* 1981.

Sackville-West, Vita, *The Illustrated Garden Book,* Atheneum, 1986.

Salisbury, Marchioness of, *The Gardens of Queen Elizabeth the Queen Mother,* Viking Penguin, 1988.

Schinz, Marina, *Visions of Paradise,* Stewart, Tabori and Chang, 1985.

Schreiner, Olive, *The Story of an African Farm,* repr., Crown, 1987

Scott-James, Anne, *Sissinghurst: The Making of a Garden,* Michael Joseph Ltd., 1974.

Sedgwick, Mabel C., *The Garden Month by Month,* Frederick A. Stokes Co., 1907.

Seebohm, Caroline, and Christopher Simon Sykes, *Private Landscapes,* Clarkson Potter, 1989.

Seymour, John, *The Complete Book of Self Sufficiency,* Faber and Faber, 1976.

Simonds, John O., *Landscape Architecture,* McGraw-Hill, 1983.

Sperry, Neil, *Complete Guide to Texas Gardening,* Taylor Publishing, 1982.

Steffek, Edwin F., *The Pruning Manual,* Van Nostrand Reinhold, 1969.

Stern, William T., *Botanical Latin,* New Edition, Redwood Burn Ltd., 1989.

Stoner, Carol, H., ed., *Stocking Up: How to Preserve the Foods You Grow Naturally,* Rodale Press, 1977.

Strong, Roy, *The Renaissance Garden in England,* Thames and Hudson, Ltd., 1979.

Sturtevant, E. L., and U. P. Hedrick, ed., *Sturtevant's Edible Plants of the World,* repr., Dover Publications, 1972.

Sunset Magazine and Book Editors, *Western Garden Book,* 5th edition, Lane Publishing Co., 1988.

Taft, L. R., *Greenhouse Management,* Orange Judd Co., 1910.

Tankard, Judith B., and Michael R. Van Valkenburgh, *Gertrude Jekyll: A Vision of Garden and Wood,* Abrams, 1989.

Tanner, Dyden, *Gardening America,* Viking Penguin, 1990.

Taylor, Patrick, *Planting in Patterns, The Classic English Gardening Guides,* Harper and Row, 1989.

Taylor, Sir George, *Meconopsis,* repr., Waterstone, 1985.

Tharp, Leonard, *An American Style of Flower Arrangement,* Taylor Publishing, 1986.

Thomas, Graham, *The Art of Planting,* J. M. Dent and Sons, Ltd., 1984.

Thorpe, Patricia, *The American Weekend Garden,* Random House, 1988.

Time-Life Encyclopedia of Gardening, Vegetables and Fruits, Time Inc. 1972.

Tolley, Emelie, and Chris Mead, *Herbs: Gardens, Decorations, and Recipes,* Clarkson Potter, 1985.

Turner, Kenneth, *Flower Style,* Weidenfeld and Nicolson, 1989.

Verey, Rosemary, *Classic Garden Design,* Congdon & Weed, 1984.

Verey, Rosemary, *The Scented Garden,* Random House, 1987.

Walters, S. M., and others, *The European Garden Flora,* 2 volumes, Cambridge University Press, 1984.

Warner, Charles D., *My Summer in a Garden,* James R. Osgood and Co., 1870

White, Katherine, *Onward and Upward in the Garden,* Farrar, Straus, Giroux, 1979.

Whiteside, Katherine, *Antique Flowers,* Villard Books, 1988.

Wilder, Louise Beebe, *Color in My Garden,* repr., Atlantic Monthly Press, 1990.

Wilder, Louise Beebe, *The Garden in Color,* The Macmillan Company, 1937.

Wilson, Helen Van Pelt, *Own Garden and Landscape Book,* Doubleday, 1973.

Winkler, A. J., *General Viticulture,* University of California Press, 1965.

Wood, Denis, and Kate Crosby, *Grow It and Cook It,* Faber and Faber, 1975.

Wood, Louisa F., *Behind Those Garden Walls in Historic Savannah,* Historic Savannah Foundation, 1982.

Wright, Richardson, *The Gardener's Bed-Book,* Garden City Publishing, 1939.

Zabar, Abbie, *The Potted Herb,* Stewart, Tabori and Chang, 1988.